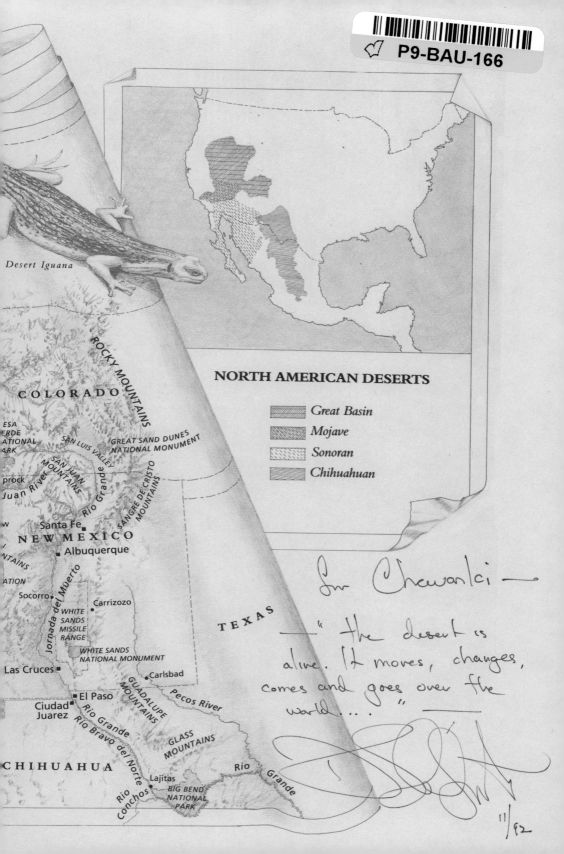

Desert Iguana

NORTH AMERICAN DESERTS

Great Basin
Mojave
Sonoran
Chihuahuan

ROCKY MOUNTAINS

COLORADO

MESA
VERDE
NATIONAL
PARK

SAN LUIS VALLEY

GREAT SAND DUNES
NATIONAL MONUMENT

SAN JUAN MOUNTAINS

prock

Juan River

Rio Grande

SANGRE DE CRISTO MOUNTAINS

Santa Fe

NEW MEXICO

Albuquerque

NTAINS

ATION

Socorro

Carrizozo

Jornada del Muerto

WHITE
SANDS
MISSILE
RANGE

WHITE SANDS
NATIONAL MONUMENT

Las Cruces

TEXAS

Carlsbad

GUADALUPE MOUNTAINS

Pecos River

El Paso

Ciudad
Juarez

Rio Grande

Rio Bravo del Norte

GLASS
MOUNTAINS

CHIHUAHUA

Lajitas

Rio
Conchos

BIG BEND
NATIONAL
PARK

Rio Grande

for Chewonki —

*— "The desert is
alive. It moves, changes,
comes and goes over the
world . . . " —*

11/92

Clarence E. Allen
Natural History Center

This book
was donated to the
Roger Tory Peterson Library
IN HONOR OF

_____

by *Caroline Carroll*

on *March 1993*

Also by Diana Kappel-Smith

Wintering
Night Life: Nature from Dusk to Dawn

Desert Time

Chewonki Foundation
RR 2 Box 1200
Wiscasset, Maine 04578

Puma and Petroglyphs

What one notices is the size of the paws and the strength of
the forearms, and the length and fluency of the round tail.
The maker of the petroglyph in the Painted Desert of Arizona
noticed these things, too. When the puma leaps the tail lashes
for balance, but it's always an accurate indicator of mood,
curling and licking the air even when the animal is asleep.

Desert Time

A Journey Through the American Southwest

DIANA KAPPEL-SMITH

LITTLE, BROWN AND COMPANY
BOSTON   TORONTO   LONDON

First Edition

Library of Congress Cataloging-in-Publication Data

Kappel-Smith, Diana.
  Desert time : a journey through the American Southwest / Diana
Kappel-Smith. — 1st ed.
      p.   cm.
  ISBN 0-316-48298-6
  1. Natural history — Southwest, New.   2. Desert Fauna — Southwest,
New.   I. Title.
QH104.5.S6K37   1992
508.79 — dc20
                                                            92-25040

10 9 8 7 6 5 4 3 2 1

BP

*Published simultaneously in Canada
by Little, Brown & Company (Canada) Limited*

Printed in the United States of America

For Oscar
for bringing me chocolates in the Ajo Range
for being here when I left and when I came back

and for Christine
who survived dust devils
and the Why Wash
and monster chimichangas
and laughed

and for Coulter
my companion

contents

acknowledgments

Without these people and institutions this book could not have been made. Some of them appear live in here and others don't; others appear in disguise. There are also many people whose books (and pamphlets and papers and reports) I've read and made use of.

You made this with me, you gave me your time, your knowledge, and yourselves. I am profoundly grateful.

Orin (OJ) Anderson; Dan Baldwin, Jackson Baldwin; Jenny Barnett; Kristin Berry; Christine Bolin; Patricia Brown-Berry; Robert Burton; Tom Cade; Calvin (Cobby) and Carol Cobb; Nancy Dumas; Julie Fallowfield; Mike Gregg; Mike Hess; Scott Huber; Ed Jagels; Rosita Jones; Amos Johnson; Philip Leitner; Barbara Malloch-Leitner; Chico and Lynne Livingston; Paul Martin; William (Bill) McGibbon; Sandra McFarland; Dennis Miller; Norman Nunley; Phil Ogden; Ken Peterson; Bill Pyle; Ray Roberts; Dick Sandlin; Ed Schultz; Coulter Smith; Craig Stevenson; the Reverend Paul Stone; Douglas L. Threloff; Adam Truran; Raymond M. Turner; Oscar Turner; Helga White; Fred and Rita Wood.

Plus: the Hopi Tribal Government; the Navajo Tribal Government; the Tohono O'odham Tribal Government; the Ganado United Presbyterian Church; the Chihuahuan Desert Research Institute; the Boyce Thompson Southwestern Arboretum; the State of Nevada Department of Wildlife; the Arizona–Sonora Desert Museum; the

Living Desert Zoological and Botanical State Park; the New Mexico Bureau of Mines and Mineral Resources. From the United States Department of the Interior: the United States Bureau of Land Management, the National Park Service, the Bureau of Indian Affairs, the National Forest Service, the Division of Refuge Management, the United States Fish and Wildlife Service.

desert time

an introduction

Presently you will meet a carver of kachina dolls, a family of Navajo women, and an uncle who will offer you mutton stew. There will be a missionary whose mission is clear, a cattleman whose future is not clear, a trapper and tracker who can read language on the ground, and a couple of bearded men hiding from the sun in a desert saloon, some Indian children who like oranges, and a prospector who found what he was looking for, and some scientists who have fallen in love with a bird and with each other. There will be other people, too, some of whom have vanished, and some animals that have vanished, and some stones that you will have to turn over and over in your hands in order to understand what they mean.

You will meet a piece of a river, strange trees, coyotes, bees, birds, bighorn sheep, and more cacti than you may care to think about. You will meet a tortoise that is passionate and methodical. You will go to a place where wars have been fought and where they are being prevented, or exacerbated, depending on your point of view. You will meet a man who is crazy about snakes. You will meet other men who are crazy about the past. You will meet the author's eleven-year-old son, Coulter, who asks very good questions.

This book is an attempt to write landscapes with people in them, and animals and plants, too. The landscapes of the American Southwest are so immense that one can hope for no more than a scraped acquaintance anywhere. One can come away with a few sketches, verbal and visual, as I've done here. In a very real sense this whole book is an introduction. It is an introduction to particulars. It does not attempt generalities.

In any case, this book was written backward. It had no outline in the usual sense. Outlines are often made by going to libraries and taking notes on other people's books, and in the beginning I did not do that. The outline was this: a rim that contains a large part of the deserts of North America. The outline was a map that was pasted together and slid for safekeeping behind a bookcase at home. I've made a copy of it to put in here, because I think that you may need it, too.

I spent a week crawling around on this map before I bought a ticket to Albuquerque. Afterward I spent more time on it, until it was tattered and smudged and much bescribbled, until it was largely contained between my ears. As the seasons passed I bought tickets to Vegas, Salt Lake City, Phoenix, though I spent little time in cities; within hours of arrival I'd left town. Over a year and a half I marked the track of my travels on the map with a green felt pen whenever I came home, until the scrawls traced a journey of more than twenty-five thousand miles. This was the sum total of mileage on Rent-A-Wrecks and their equivalents and didn't take into account the mileages on foot, horseback, river rafts, or other people's pickups.

Every time I came home, after having scribed the latest green lines, pack and duffels still in my hallway, I'd sit cross-legged on the map with my hand over my mouth and look at the gaps.

I'm looking at them now: the spaces that are never empty or twice the same. I collected stories with plenty of white space around them. Space, and time.

Time is strangely transparent in the desert in a way that is never true where there are trees and numbers of people. What I mean by this is that huge passages of time are visible in the present.

Anglo culture — meaning the influence of white northern Europeans — is a veneer of only a century and a half. This is so thin in places that it isn't very important.

Much of that country was a Spanish colony since 1540, when Francisco de Coronado's first expedition rode (and walked) through

Arizona, New Mexico, and Texas. Spaniards controlled the place —
or maintained the illusion of control, on paper anyway — until the
Treaty of Guadalupe Hidalgo in 1848. They named mountains,
towns, rivers; they left their people, religion, and food; much of the
rural Southwest is more closely related to the culture of Mexico than
to that of either coast.

Then there are Native American people that were there when the
Europeans first came. Most of these are still around. They are coherent peoples with their own languages, beliefs, territories, and trou-
bles, and to understand them one has to make a spiritual crossing as
profound as the voyages of Columbus.

Behind these (behind is a relative term; I mean before these in
time though as nakedly *there* as anything else) is the evidence of
native people who built towns and cities in the Southwest almost a
millennium ago, people who had trade routes as far as Central
America. There is hardly a canyon unmarked by their work. In
their time, most of these deserts were more thickly settled than they
are now.

Then there are places where one can find the tools and encamp-
ments of the first human beings to discover this continent, more than
ten thousand years in the past.

There are also places where one can find all that is left of uncount-
able thousands of enormous animals that lived in the time of the
glaciers. These places look like stables where animals sheltered from
the midday sun just a month ago, though the creatures have been
gone for thousands of years. The dry climate has preserved these
things as though they were in amber.

Behind all these is a planet stripped so naked that you have no
choice but to see the stories of the land itself. This is written in stone,
and the books it is written in are mountains, but you are never far
from mountains.

And everywhere but thinly spread, as if to make each individual
that much more important, is desert wildlife.

Among other things I am a naturalist, which means that I tend to
approach plants, animals, and rocks in the same way that I approach
people. I like to know their names and where they live and what
they do. I like to find out what is important to them. I like to discover
their relationships to the land and to each other.

It was in this egalitarian spirit that this book was made. I asked: what is in that country? Why?

In here you will find a few odd answers, set down by an outsider, an interloper with a notebook. It's a personal collection, a kind of map, an armful of wide-eyed stories, an introduction, a love affair. It is finished, but incomplete. My hope is that you will add to it yourself, slipping your own notes, photographs, portraits, sketches between the pages, shocking people with your own peculiar tales, amusing them with absurd notions, tilting them toward magnificence.

Partial, elusive, fragmentary answers. It is the nature of life that it cannot be grasped. It can, however, be experienced.

DKS
Connecticut, 1992

PART ONE

Autumn

Star Dune
Great Sand Dunes National Monument, Colorado

1

sand

Great Sand Dunes National Monument, Colorado

Along the eastern slopes of the San Juan Mountains are a few foothill
farms trailing into the San Luis valley in a tinny smatter of irrigation
works. There's a gas pump and a great little dive where you can get
oversized buffalo burgers; the buildings there look new and old,
both, hastily thrown up and already peeling. They are overpowered
by the sky.

The rest of the San Luis has been left to itself. I crossed it at noon,
moving east. The sand dunes loomed ahead, bleached like a ghost of
hills, and the Sangre de Cristos rose behind them. In the afternoon
there was a skitter of pronghorns around the dune fringe, copper and
white, delicate, with ebony sculpts of horns.

I parked in the Great Sand Dunes National Monument parking
lot and went in and filled out a ticket at the desk. It was like a desk
at a museum except that the staff wore uniforms, and they were there
to be helpful — they wear the worn smiles of professionally helpful
folk — and one of the ways they're helpful is that they make sure
the ticket is filled out. You need to fill out a ticket if you're going
to pack into the country. They take your data — name address license
plate number number in party number of nights — and they give
you a copy. The copy is made of white cloth, like the cloth tags on
mattresses. This comes with a piece of wire so you can attach it to
yourself. It's the National Monument and Park version of a dog tag.
Afterward, I hiked some miles in along Medano Creek where it

comes down off the Sangre de Cristos and skirts the dune field and then I set up camp and ate some jerky and walked into the sand.

A mile in, I lay down on a dune and breathed. That's all. There was sky, sun, sand, mountain wall, air: that's all. The cloth tag flapped from my pack zipper a mile away, and I could bleach to unidentifiable bones and be buried in a morning's breeze. So simple. No fuss. The sky achingly blue and the sun an absolutely round fire. All around me nothing but sand.

The sand is a quirk; a conspiracy of river, wind, ancient rain, and the Sangre de Cristo Mountains.

The Sangre de Cristos are still rising. Their rock is pressing up an inch a year like the arc of a spine. The peaks rise six thousand feet from the valley floor and the long vanishing line of them is curved like the blade of a saw pushed against a wall. They give a twist to the sky as if they could spring anytime and throw a hefty chunk of central Colorado — the Wet Mountains on which they brace their backs — clear to the Appalachians like a hockey puck.

The Sangre de Cristos start their run north and then curve northwest, here, where the sand is, at the angle of tension. Held in their serrated curve is the flat valley of San Luis, a hundred miles long — almost half the length of the state — and nearly fifty miles wide and eight thousand feet high. With less than ten inches of rain a year and day after day of strong wind and high-altitude sun, the San Luis is parched like the surface of a stove, if one can imagine a stove top larger than the state of Connecticut paved with grit and rabbitbrush.

At the far edge of the valley the San Juan Mountains rise, a bulk of volcanoes that shoved into old seafloor some thirty-five million years ago. From here, from the sand, the San Juans are a curved wall the color of shadow. Down them runs the continental spine and in them are the source waters of the San Juan River — a major tributary of the Colorado — and the headwaters of the Rio Grande.

The Rio Grande comes down this way into the San Luis, flowing east off the Great Divide as it did all during the last ice age, and when the ice began to melt some twelve thousand years ago there was a lot more water there and the Rio Grande was a lot more river. It carried the outwash of the San Juan glaciers and the runoff of the rains that rimmed the glaciers and all that water clawed the San Juans as it came. This river (truly Grande then) came through the San Luis and on south through a slot in the Rockies into New Mexico, where it still runs, more or less; only it ran big then and chaotic and rumbling with glacial debris. It braided itself across the whole of this valley, dropping levees of sorted stuff at high water and puncturing these or looping around them at low, leaving a valley full of silty oxbows and bars and beds of grit and cobbles. The Rio Grande then bore little relation to the modest countrified body that it is now, tucked in the lee of the San Juans, wreathed in cottonwoods; in those days it rolled glacial rubble off naked rock and ground it to powder and spread it, generously, south.

The wind — never a small thing either — has since brought some of this north again.

Picture this: twelve thousand years ago a spring southwesterly came up here, as up a flight of stairs, into the San Luis. It met a dried-up oxbow, picked up what it could, and went on as a kind of fog. This wind had a long fetch and was urged to greater speed by the first north-trending wall of the Sangre de Cristos. Funneled up the valley the faster the higher it came it swept like a howling broom over a flat floor that had nothing much on it then but glacial and riverine grit. The prevailing wind here still runs from the southwest and still blows strongest in spring and early summer, and still picks up what naked grit it can, as a matter of course, and has been doing this now for quite some time, naked grit being plentiful.

What I've heard at the buffalo-burger dive is: "the gol-darned dusters up here'll blow yer hat clear to South Dakoty some days an' blow you after it too if y'ain't got a horse t' hold you down . . ."

Which is the size of it, I imagine. Then, right here, the thickened wind meets the barrier of the mountains' curve. Pushed into updraft, eddied, its energy lost to friction and turbulence, the duster drops some of what it carries. The wind doesn't stop exactly but it does drop the heavier part of its load, which happens to be from two to three tenths of a millimeter in diameter. It keeps its finest dust and carries that up through Mosca Pass and Medano Pass and Music Pass (in order from south to north) and so on, over the top. In June here there are days on end when the whole rise of the Sangre de Cristos is veiled in a brownish cloud.

So nowadays there are trillions of tons of grit here, a hundred and fifty square miles of wind-dropped sand, some of it piled in dunes a thousand feet deep.

I came out of the dune field an hour ago and now the last red light has faded from the mountain wall, a red brighter than burgundy and deeper than raspberry, the reason maybe for the name: Blood of Christ Mountains. Sangre de Cristo has an echo of Coronado or Oñate and their ragtag troops coming a-horseback down Medano Pass long ago and camping, maybe, close to here, on Medano Creek. In Spanish, *medano* means dune.

Now the dunes have gone mauve behind the cottonwoods that line the creek. The dunes rise there like a wall.

The sand has the texture of coarse flour or fine-ground cornmeal. There are grains of russet sandstones, white quartz, and black magnetite from the volcanic San Juans. The cumulative color has the sensuality of sunbaked flesh. The black magnetite grains are heavier than others; they tend to lie on the dune faces after other lighter bits have blown away. These ripples of darkness give some slopes the double color of coyote fur.

Once it's here the sand is combed into lines of transverse dunes — from the air these look like monster ripples — or, at the fringes, *barchans:* rams' horns in Arabic. When the sand is blown out of some loosely vegetated pile, it takes on the shape of a reversed croissant, a U-shaped or "parabolic" dune, arms facing the wind this time and held there by roots. Where winds swirl and back and fill, the sands pile up and up, creating their own stable currents in the air, building star dunes: single high peaks rooted in a series of trailing arms. Here the winds do turn in summer, coming back down the Sangre de Cristos, herding the sand into itself, building up some of the most monumental star dunes to be found anywhere. Some are a thousand feet high and more. Plumes of blown grit sift from their crests.

I climbed one of these this afternoon, no easy thing. I straddled the crest of an arm and went up slowly, heavy going, leaving dents. The wind moved in sighs, throwing sand under me in spurts of gold; the slopes glittered with moving grains tossed from ripple to ripple in a movement called *saltation* — meaning leaping — but these are little leaps, the sand never moving up higher than inches, grains bouncing and streaming across the dune face and leaving the crest itself sharp and serrated like a tomato knife. When these leaping grains come to the creek they fall in and are washed away. They don't jump high enough to cross the water. The creek — six feet wide — is the eastern edge of all this.

The wind has been northerly here for a while now, you can tell; the steeper dune slope is always the one downwind. The shallow slope guides the air up and over the edge, cutting its force into space, sending it into turmoil, and at the leeward side the sand drops out. It happens that sand won't lie at a steeper angle than 34 degrees so that once it does pile that high it begins to slip — as it does under-foot — shifting downward in long cascades, taking one partly with it, so it takes a while to get up top.

From there, from the star's high center point, the dunes stretch immense and endlessly varying into the mountains' rise. Their perfect curves go gold and black in the late light. Perfect is the word I wrote down, up there, again and again, meaning shape — curves and rip-ples — and light, which lies in these shapes.

The wind moves steadily past one's ears. Up there the sand con-forms to the body, warm, steady, sifting into every pant leg and sweatshirt wrinkle, burying one's boots; smoothing one into perfec-tion, too. Down between dune peaks are scant furrings of blowout grass, curved like hairs in a body hollow. Out in the heart of the dunes nothing lives at all except three species of insects: a circus beetle, a tiger beetle, and a giant sand treader camel cricket. All of them are nocturnal, all make their livings on whatever the wind blows in for them to scavenge. None of them lives anywhere but here. No one knows much about them. Trillions of tons of sand and one hundred and fifty square miles of country are all theirs.

The night is too long to sleep through. When it gets too dark I light a candle lantern and write home, watching the stars against the dunes' smooth curve. It gets cold fast here. Dry land does that, and dry air. We're already eight thousand feet up and the mountains loom six thousand feet farther, starfields scattering between peaks.

In the morning there are still stars over the sand's flanks, different ones. The creek is still making its small creek song in the darkness. Sometimes in late summer the creek disappears into its bed, goes underground, and then the sand crosses the creek's hollow and dunes march this way. They've done this again and again. When the creek fills up with autumn rain it washes through what barriers have blown in, leaving new raw dunes stranded on this side. These grow over, grasses coming in, then brush, trees. This place between creek and mountain wall is filled with the rumpled curves of forest and high prairie; the land shape under them is dune. In dawn light I walk down the crest of one of these, down a trail worn there by mule deer and everything else. High ground is where you travel when what you want is to keep an eye out for everything else.

Grasses, low junipers, red-leaved currant bushes. Trails of rabbits and kangaroo rats, burrows like a warren. A single nuthatch spirals up a cottonwood. Dawn sunlight comes in one spreading ray through Medano Pass; the predawn light leaking evenly from the sky gives red and yellow leaves the brilliance of a dream. A single mule deer grazes on the rise of the first dune. Sunlight creeps down the flank of naked sand at her back until she is silhouetted on her ridge.

Crossing the creek where it bends, I hear her cough and thump off. The sand is damp with dew and wears the perfect imprints of everything that moved in the night. A printed page.

The ricegrass is seeding, heads bent and heavy. Here and there is a bright head of a sunflower in bloom, black seeds half quarried away, foursquare tracks of white-footed mice coming and going; it's high autumn stash-building time. Their foraging trails are woven and crossed by tracks of the Ord's kangaroo rat (must be Ord's, no other K-rat lives this far north), only its hind toes touching and eight- to nine-inch leaps between these, single trails branching from packed trails . . . to a burrow, trampled; a single arc of entrance in damp sand. Tracks of insects: beetles, crickets. Here and there holes the width of pencils, the foci of insect scrawls. Now, everything is underground. I quarry down among the snarls of grass stems coiled like pale wire. Less than two inches down the sand is cool, dark, the texture of milk chocolate. This is where they've gone. Roots, animals, this is where they are. In summer the sand surface can heat to 140 degrees F and that's no place to be.

There are bird tracks in the ricegrass, too. The deep pokes of deer. The days-old trail of a coyote on the ridge. The sun is full on the dune face and I strip off vest, sweatshirt. After another mile I start back toward the creek. It's still in shadow there. There's something too Saharan on the dunes at nine A.M.; a hot bright drumming in the ears.

Down the last tilt of naked sand and down a slope of ricegrass, scurf pea, through clumps of yellow-blooming rabbitbrush. By the creek are clusters of young cottonwoods, slim trunks blue-gray, leaves deep gold over creek water running brown dark with slashes of sky blue. The green-silver slope of grass, the sand pale as sugar in the light. Tiny paths everywhere. The grasses filled with birds: chirps, pips, nasal chatter. The ground alive with the rising falling of birds jumping to peck at ricegrass heads that hang like green drops.

Lying in the cottonwood shade, belly to slope, I watch the birds come all around. Up there the shoulder of a star dune is as sterile as the Mare Tranquillitatis of the moon, as baked as the scarps of Mars; the sand shifts itself too fast for anything to keep a foothold. Here the grasses have wired themselves down and hold the desert fringe. Then . . . huff of breath, rip of grass torn, and four mule deer come, slowly, two does and two half-grown fawns, moving the slow grazing way like cattle toward water or shade this time of day, still breakfasting.

They come within ten feet. Then one doe lifts her head, fast, black nostrils wide, she's got wind, and with a snorting whistle — loud barking wheeze of alarm — they're all four off across the slope running heads up and tails up, leaping zig and zag on all four feet at once *thump thump* like deer-shaped superballs dropped from the blue. The last doe pauses on a sand brink against blue sky, on the ridge of raw sand, then she's gone over.

She won't go far. Nothing does, except the crickets and beetles that live in the heart of the dunes. That's the unchanging place that's changing always. Desert core, quirk and masterwork of elemental things.

Kangaroo Rat Tracks and Scurf Pea
Great Sand Dunes National Monument, Colorado

2

point of no return

Mesa Verde National Park, Colorado

When you come west out of the foothills of the San Juans the land rises like a prow and then like many prows, like stone aircraft carriers rafted together. The Spaniards named all this like shooting from the hip: Mesa Verde, the green table, which isn't an unlikely name, if you can imagine yourself looking up at a dining table from the perspective of an ant — or, in this case, a man on horseback (same thing in this country). It does look as if it had been spread with a green cloth. No one bothered to get to the table's top for a long time after the name had stuck, and when they did the greenery proved to be a tapestry of pinyon, juniper, and oak.

From the perspective of the air, or on a topographical map, the mesa takes on again the image of clustered boats; a twelve-by-fifteen mile clutch of flat decks rising from the sea of the Montezuma valley. Back from those northern prows the whole business slopes steadily to the Mancos River; it's all a little down at the stern, so to speak. This canted land is clawed all the way by deepening canyons whose walls are as sheer as the sides of ships. In these walls are caverns, arcing caves, like portholes half opened.

The canyons drain cold air away and rainwater, too, when there is such a thing. The south-tilting surfaces absorb extra warmth like the tilted panes of a cold frame, so the growing season on the table's top is longer than you'd think; as long as it would be on flat-lying land that happened to lie two hundred and fifty miles farther south (near Socorro, New Mexico, say; breadbasket country of the Rio Grande, home of the chili pepper). This is like that.

More rain falls up on top than you'd think, too, from down below. Eighteen inches a year is what the mesa gets now, twice as much rainfall as the surrounding desert; and more than enough for dry-ground farming. Fourteen inches of rain a year is the threshold of farming possibility, as long as at least four inches of that falls in the summer monsoon. If the pattern and amount of rainfall are just right then corn can tassel, beans can fruit, squashes can fill out like ribbed balloons. You could farm on Mesa Verde now just fine, but no one does, though for eight hundred years or more, people did.

Then, suddenly, they didn't. What they did was up and leave.

It isn't hard to picture them leaving. Their leaving is as tangible as anything they've left, and they've left a lot.

There are more than a thousand of their dwellings in the caves of Mesa Verde's canyon walls. Many of these have houses that are three or four stories high; turrets and towers and squared rooms cluster in there like pueblo condos. There are over five thousand rooms altogether, tucked in the vertical sandstone. This is what's there in the half-open portholes of the mesa: houses, villages, towns, all of them deserted intact.

Most of them consist of rectangular rooms made of found or shaped sandstone, chinked and mortared. Roof beams are round — whole tree trunks peeled — and beam-ends jut from the walls a foot or so before the walls end. It's a familiar Southwestern style: everyone has copied it since.

Strewn among these houses are round sunken rooms called *kivas*. These are older still: developed from ancient pit houses built back when the people were seminomadic. Of all house forms these are the best adapted to the landscape, with its seasons of extremes of heat and cold. Underground, the earth kept kivas warmer and cooler than any surface dwelling could be. The kivas were solidly roofed and the roofs made handy outdoor living space, like plazas. They could be entered through a hole in the plaza center from which a wooden ladder went down. A ventilation shaft went down as well, along one wall, the air moving in through a square hole at kiva floor level. In front of this hole was a stone baffle and in front of the baffle was a fire pit, and beyond this pit there was — still is — a tiny round hole called a *sipapu:* the people's place of entry from their previous world. Air could come down the shaft, hit the baffle, and circulate around the room, exiting with woodsmoke through the central hole.

The central hole let in light, people came in and out there. The entrance hole echoed the tiny sipapu beneath.

Whether the kivas were cozy living space for all comers, or for extended families, or for clans, or clan elders only, no one knows. In other words, whether kivas had spiritual significance or whether they were secular, no one is sure. But I do know that our own culture is fairly unique in having separated one from the other, and that other people don't often try to keep secular and sacred as far apart as we do, and that this seems to be worth keeping in mind when one looks at a thing that another culture made. The question — sacred or secular? — may have no significance outside the here and now.

Most of the houses and kivas have mud grouting between stones and white or rose plaster smoothed over that. Many rooms have been replastered many times; you can see this, it's like looking at flaking paint; now and again the smoke-darkened walls were freshened up. The round wood rafters between house stories were layered with smaller poles and fibrous juniper bark, then slathered with damp adobe to make flat roofs, kiva plazas, balconies on jutting beam ends, floors for the rooms above. The living rooms have fireplaces and small windowlike doors that you have to cock a leg over to get through. These half doors kept warm air in and cold air out. Winters here are cold. Stone doors fit in a groove in the doorsill and were held in place by a stick poked through wooden loops embedded in the outer wall. Smaller unplastered storerooms have plenty of pegs in the walls, handy for hanging baskets, lengths of twine, bunches of drying corn. Stone turkey hutches fill spaces in the caves that are too low-ceilinged for living in or storing goods.

Some of the dwellings are only a room or two or three (hut, homestead, what they call nowadays a starter-house?). Others had more than two hundred rooms: these were towns. In the cliffs these huts, villages, towns didn't interfere with farmland, were protected by rock roofs from sun and rain, were kept more temperate by rock walls, and were easy to defend, since there were only so many ways

to get down to them from the mesa above or up from the canyons
below. Eight hundred years ago there were six thousand people,
more or less, farming the mesa tops and living in those rooms.

When they went they left whatever they couldn't carry: bowls,
mugs, baskets, blankets, belts, medicines, jewelry, bedding, clothes.
They left eight hundred years' worth of trash: outmoded houses,
worn-out sandals, corncobs, potsherds, shit, ash, bodies buried in
fetal curls, used stone cores, chipped arrowheads, turkey bones,
beads and baubles, axheads dulled beyond regrinding, broken grid-
dles, pieces of hemp rope, bean pods, manos and metates for grinding
corn.

There they go, over the rim. They are as small as I am and smaller,
the same size as Europeans were too, back then. The men are about
five feet four and the women mostly under five feet, the size of
modern ten- or twelve-year-olds. The women carry baskets or ribbed
pots bound with willow handles and filled with shelled corn and
beans, pinyon nuts, yucca pods. A pair of half-made yucca sandals
dangles from a bundle, wrapped in a hank of fiber. The men carry
bows, coils of fiber snares, stone axes, sheaves of arrows tipped with
arrowheads of flint, chert, jasper, obsidian, chalcedony, quartzite. A
girl bends double under the weight of a rolled turkey-feather blanket
that is bound to her forehead by a tumpline. A small boy carries a
digging stick and is being softly rebuked for banging it on stones.
He is being rebuked softly, because nobody is saying very much. An
old woman, lean and arthritic, forty perhaps, walks in front of the
others, dressed in worn buckskin, carrying a basket of herbs tied
together and another basket holding medicine stuffs bound in buckskin tatters: shell and stone beads, turquoise, willow splints, quartz
and galena crystals, loops of sinew, doghair yarn.

There are no babies with this bunch, and only a handful — two,
three — old folks, which here and now means people over thirty-five.
The boy with the digging stick has a barrel belly and limbs not much
wider than the stick he carries. So one sees that the winter has been
hard, and that it has not been the first hard winter, but the last.

The eyes of the young men — fourteen, fifteen years old — glitter
and never stop moving from one thing to the next, maybe because
they have seen too much of old men quarreling and women wailing

over corpses of children, and their own mothers going grim and toothless, and their sisters and uncles coughing until they cough up blood and die. And this: raids and robbings by neighbors and even family until they've learned that no one can trust anyone else. They've grown into men without enough food in their bellies or peace anywhere and now the clan is going and they, anyway, are more than ready to go. They are the only ones here with any spring in their step. Oh, yes, and the two girls, there, thirteen-year-olds with the eyes of women.

Well, I see this very clearly.

The desert is alive. It moves, changes, comes and goes over the world, and is uninhabitable, unless you make it your profession. It wasn't their profession. They farmed.

Dry-ground farming depends on topography as much as rain. The higher one goes into the hills the more moisture there is, but the higher one goes the colder it gets, too; one climbs from shrubs and succulents of desert flats through sagebrush upland meadows into open groves of pinyon and juniper, and into Gambel oak, ponderosa pine, mountain mahoganies, up into firs, aspens; finally into spruce-fir forest and so on to tree line. To some extent this parade of vegetation is as much a function of moisture as it is of altitude, but neither moisture nor altitude can be divided from the fact of cold: that the higher one goes the shorter the growing season is.

Confusions abound, naturally, and Mesa Verde standing where it does and slanting as it does abounds in organic confusions; the canyons there hold spruce trees and shrubberies that belong, by rights, to the high scarps of the San Juans, perhaps because these canyons are shady and relatively moist; but one is likely to stumble out of a patch of mountain myrtle into a prickly pear or the knifelike spokes of a yucca. And the glories of this biotic tangle are a great distraction from the broad raw facts of life. Which are roughly these: farming here is possible only in a narrow band. The bottom border of this band is defined by moisture, by that fourteen inches a year coming at the proper times, and moisture increases as you go uphill. The band's top border is defined by length of growing season; by the number of frost-free days it takes for corn to tassel and squash to

ripen; and the growing season increases as you go *downhill*. So there
is this band, where you can farm. The farming band is the edge of
the desert, where there is enough moisture and it isn't too cold.

This band wriggles and loops through landscape like any biological parameter. Now, here, it ranges from sixty-six hundred feet to
about seventy-seven hundred feet in elevation. Look west to Ute
Mountain and south to Shiprock and the Lukachukai range at the
near rim of Arizona, and to the Manti-La Sals rising out there in
Utah, and the San Juans bulking to the northeast (you can see all this
from the high point in the bows of the mesa, where dry air puffs
upward from the Montezuma valley and strokes against one's chin
like blown spume) and take a mental paintbrush and color it in: the
band. The strips and hollows of farming possibility.

Between A.D. 600 and 750 the band was much the same as it is
now, but it didn't stay that way, any more than it will now, in spite
of the thousands of acres of pinto beans growing on the flanks of the
valley. The smell of ripening beans comes up with the wind as it
must have done years ago, but won't always. The lesson being, here,
on the desert fringe: trust nothing.

The climates of the past can be read in the record of the past —
pollens layered in montane bogs, fossil packrat middens, tree rings
in old trees — they are the bioequivalent of archaeology. And this is
what happened. Beginning in A.D. 750 or so the rains thinned,
drought squeezed the band from the bottom up. So in those days
people moved their fields onto higher ground.

The drought went on for two hundred years. Then, slowly, it
broke. By A.D. 1000 the winters were rainier, the summer monsoons
more predictable (predictability in rain increases with amount of rain;
a basic law of desert anywhere), and at the same time the weather
warmed. The band swelled upward and downward like a happy
balloon. Farms and villages with them grew as low on the slopes as
fifty-two hundred feet. This was the Native American golden age,
when cultural networks stretched from the Rockies to the great cities
of Mexico and Central America; there was a flowering of population,
technology, art. Then the drought came back.

In less than half a century, the drought came back. Summer rains
thinned. Canals, dams, reservoirs were built among the corn, but

less and less rain fell into them. Again the farmers moved to higher ground.

Then, in A.D. 1200 or so, it began to get cold. Families and clans moved into the cliff caves in a big way, building houses, villages, towns, to defend against the cold and against each other (one presumes; since there were too many people and too little food, and these were citadels, or could be), and the move to the cliffs left more earth on the mesa tops to grow what little grew; which wasn't enough, enough of the time, in the end.

In the end there is no defying climate, even with monumental architecture, even with farming techniques perfected over centuries, even with the pieties of dancing and prayer perfected too. And one can fairly assume that pieties came into it as they do anywhere when times are hard. And the cold continued to deepen and the rains continued to fade, crops froze in bloom, desert cobbles and dust invaded cornfields, the farmable band was squeezed in a vise of drought and cold that tightened more with every passing cycle of the seasons. In the late 1200s, the vise snapped shut.

By the end of that century the people were gone.

Just over a hundred years ago a rancher rode up on the mesa in winter looking for stray cows, and through the blowing snow he saw the ruins of a city in a canyon wall. That was the beginning of the mystery which is still a mystery: who were these people, where did they go, and why?

One evening, a park ranger took me down a cliff on an old trail. It was after work hours and the ranger had taken off his Smokey hat and wore jeans, normal boots, a flannel shirt. He was interested in the Anasazi — the name we give these vanished people — and in anything and everything to do with them. He kept a lot of data in his head, including the shapes and colors of things he may have seen only once: the sennet braid of a sandal sole, fingerprints in a smear of millennium-old plaster, the black-and-white zigzag patterning of a plate. We took a pack with rope and flashlights and water. We struck off through the junipers and pinyons, on no trail, but through the thick stand of solid trees. There were crushes of dry vegetation underfoot and tindery rustles of shed leaves, sliding gravel and slab, the crackle of boots over prickly pear, then the rounded shoulders of clean peach-colored stone at the lip of a canyon. At last, dodging trees, we found the trail. It went into the canyon down vertical rock and was made of spaced indentations — toe and finger holds — each the size of the top of a coffee cup. Below, like a whitecapped sea seen from the top of a mast, were treetops and stones of the canyon bottom. I lowered myself on faith. The trail was seven hundred years old at least and must have gone somewhere, then.

It led down fifteen feet to a ledge that sloped across the cliff. The ledge was half plugged with fallen stones and with boles and branches of junipers, and was slippery with fallen needles; then it opened. It was like sidling along a wall and then coming to the door of a cathedral: a high arc, like a bandshell, one quarter of a sphere.

At first this seemed filled with nothing but dust, pocked here and there with water drips. Then: the jut of hewn stone, the right-angle corner of a wall, the curve of a kiva. We saw things in the dust: clots of old mortar, a corncob the color of dark honey and the size of my finger, a pinkish core from which projectile points — arrow or spear heads — had been chipped. The stones of the wall were marked with spaced dints: stones that had been carefully shaped, by someone. The ceiling of the arc was blackened by years of smoke.

Dusk came, stars sprayed and glittered. The dry air filled with the quiet that had settled in eight centuries before. This house — three rooms and a kiva — was preserved in the dryness and dust and in this windless place like a thing boxed on a shelf. The stars came out in sprays, in thoroughness, more stars than not stars; the Milky Way like a band of smoke, a stellar beam, a light source. Looking out from the arc was like being in an eye.

The next evening the ranger took me to the biggest town of all. It's called Cliff Palace. You get down to it by stairs now and not by those cup-sized finger and toe paths they used, carrying corn and firewood down those trails in baskets on their backs.

This town has been freed from its rubble, its walls have been shored up, there are pathways and interpretive signs so people can go through it all day long, but as soon as the gates are locked on those stairs the quiet settles in again as if it had been waiting to come back.

It's a real town, and silence is oppressive in it. I conjure back the smells of smoke, sewage, bodies, roasting corn, the dusty-feather smell of turkeys; the rhythmic crush of grinding stones, voices, the grate of ax heads being sharpened in these hollows in this rock, the snarl of dogs, the pad of barefoot steps up this alley, the quarrel behind the wall, the clink of shards as the potter — the roof here is so blackened it has to be a potter — lays her kiln fire of juniper wood and dung chips.

The conjuring is incomplete. The silence is too large. We go on looking into every room we can. Some rooms are tiny, space enough for one or two to sit or lie curled. Other rooms are larger, their windows framed in decorative pale plaster, their fire pits rimmed by copings. Finger marks are plain where pasty adobe was smeared around a lintel. There are crude walls, dry-laid walls, mortared walls, and chinked walls, walls blackened by smoke and walls freshly plastered. The town is on four stepped levels that climb back under the cave roof in a maze of corridors, family precincts, storerooms, spaces for trash. In the end the size of the place defeats us, dusk comes, and we are only halfway through; there are two hundred and seventeen rooms. There are twenty-three kivas. One of these, near the outer brink, has plaster the color of a Peace rose.

I found myself looking at that kiva with a kind of longing. At last I asked the ranger if I could go in, and he said why not. He said he never had himself but that Pueblo people had come, Hopis he was pretty sure they were, and they had gone in there like it was a church. He'd brought them in here as he'd brought me, after hours. They'd entered in single file and had sat down in the kiva and maybe said some things or made some motions, he said he hadn't watched, he'd turned his back, but he saw afterward that they had left a thing: a scroll of paper with a feather. There it was. The size and shape of a hand-rolled cigarette, but not a cigarette, on the dry stone floor. Unless some National Park functionary came and cleaned it up, there it would be in ten thousand years.

So I went down in single file with myself and sat by the sipapu, in front of the stone baffle that protected the fire and deflected the draft from the ventilator. Near the cigarette thing but not too near.

The kiva roof was long gone, much of the far wall was broken away. The place was round and a soft warm pink, and it had been underground, to be entered from the center, so I'd come in all wrong; from nowhere, through the vanished roof. The top of the roof had been the plaza for this part of town, the place where work went on and people lived most of the time, the communal living room. Anyway, once in I sat, and I began to see things right away.

There were a lot of faces in semidarkness, looking at me; they were curious, of course, and so was I. I stared right back. I hadn't seen them from the front before, only from the back as they were leaving: the thin legs, the bowed heads, the bobbing bundles. Now I could see that their skin was smooth and that their eyes were dark. Their skin was like polished chestnut wood. A few old faces were wrinkled: chestnut wood carved to look like riverbeds. Their hair was black and as straight as fresh wire with an almost white shine, like a black picture under glass. They were curious about where I'd come from, and I was happy to see that they had not left.

After a while I looked up over the ruined wall and there was the rim of mesa, the far rim over the canyon, a tabletop covered with its green — now black with dusk — forest. Perched on this rim was the thread of a new moon, curved like a silver bow. To one side was a single star. The star was right there as if it had just been shot due south from that still bent bow. There was nothing else in the sky.

So, you went south.

It was all very clear.

That's enough, I thought. What more can I ask?

I went south, myself, next morning, but not before I noticed that the stars had changed. I'm not sure I should tell you this. It makes me seem scatty or peculiar, but I'm no more peculiar than anyone, I have a reputation among my friends of being too level-headed for my own good; but the stars did change. I wasn't looking for anything like it, that's all I can say in my own defense. I came to this place with nothing but ignorance. I didn't expect much, I wasn't even sure it would be interesting. I'd never even heard of Mesa Verde till I saw it on my map. The word *Anasazi* meant nothing to me. It meant nothing to the people it refers to. Anasazi is a Navajo word meaning ancient foreigners, and Navajo weren't around when they were here, not as far as anyone knows; it's the Navajo who were foreigners, Athapascan nomads who filtered into the country later on. The Navajo were here when white men discovered the ruins and needed a name for the people who'd left them. Whatever name we give does not in the end matter much. Sitting in their kiva at dusk had done something to me, as if I were a compass needle loose enough to swing, toward some new center of planetary magnetism.

I didn't know that this had happened until we'd climbed onto the mesa again. I looked up then and noticed that the stars had changed. I thought this was nonsense at first; stellar format shouldn't obey the vortices of prayer.

Half an hour later it was still there, when I bedded down in my tent, oak leaves having joined the dune sand in there with me. The new pattern in the stars was still there. The center of the sky held a stellar bow from which hung streamers of stars: rays, tassels, feathers, pathways, fickle rain.

Anasazi Pot and Pattern

This pot is in Keet Seel, an Anasazi village in Navajo National Monument in the Navajo Reservation in Arizona. The pot is a plain utility design without colored glazes and is much blackened by fire. It sits on a wall as if a woman had put it there after cooking breakfast eight hundred years ago. The black-on-white pattern framing it is taken from a potsherd found in the same place.

Wind and Ravens

The designs of the border are adapted from black-on-white Anasazi pots and bowls that are now in museums. The ravens are at every camp you make, they keep an eye on you; they always see you before you see them. The landscape is disappearing in the wind.

3

wind

Navajo Reservation, Arizona

I pulled off on the side of a dirt road to write that there was red sand blowing. I had come down through Four Corners south into Navajo country. It was just past dawn; the plains of rabbitbrush were silver in the light. Here and there a mesa or stone column stood, lone and red, the sedimentary layers stacked like blocks from a ruin. Vast eroded skirts poured from stone rims on which there were dark flecks of junipers.

When the sun rose higher the wind grew, and as I went south the wind kept me company all the way.

There are no periods in the pages I wrote in that day. There were no periods and no stopping places in the wind. One thing blew into another too fast. The country was too huge and too colored and too empty of habitation and of anything man-changed or made to be finalized in any way. I seemed to be blowing myself, rolling, bouncing in the ruts, sliding and plowing through growing drifts of sand.

I was lost when I wrote that I had come to a landscape of blood-red mesas veined with silvery sandstone. Los Gigantes Buttes; tailbones of the Chuska Mountains. The land around the buttes was the color of metal and bone. Later I pulled over and wrote that there were low houses with sheds, sheep camps, very far apart so that whenever I came on one — toylike in the great space — it was a surprise, the last one having vanished so long before. There were some sheep, a few red cattle, otherwise rolling arid ground with the high red buttes marching closer and past and then more appearing; the wind so strong that even the clouds were pink.

Then a sudden cemetery bristling with plastic flowers, the flowers vibrating in the gusts, and a low white building with white gates and a small white cross on the peak of the roof. This was the only building of more than one story anywhere, the only one painted any color. It must have put an idea in my head.

Before the morning was gone I understood that roads in Navajo country are not like roads elsewhere. Traveling into the land on them is like following the tributaries of rivers uphill. The tracks branch and narrow until they come to a single sheep or cattle camp at which they end. Then there's nothing to do but turn around. By noon I didn't think that I could find my way back to any road that was on a map. Buttes and roads made a labyrinth and since that day I've had a kind of labyrinth-dream again and again; a dream of being in red butte country still, in the wind that lived there, and that I can't stop thinking of as living there all the time, the only thing big enough for the place. By midday there was grit everywhere; on my paper, my lips, my eyelids, the dashboard. The air was thick, red dunes riffled in the lee of every stone and clump of rabbitbrush.

All the time the wind grew. When I found blacktop at last and drove on south the whole landscape seemed to have blown away. Here and there were knobs of rock so raw they looked as if they'd poured down and congealed like wax. Ahead, a roll of waxy hills. Dry plants jerked in the wind, perched on heaps of red soil held by their roots; this was the only stuff held down anywhere that wasn't stone.

Something hit the window with a slap and went over, dark like a dead bird. Russian thistle: tumbleweed. Russian thistles grow out nearly flat like starfish on roadsides and dirt lots and eroded banks. They're an alien species, symptom of disturbed and overgrazed — desertifying — land, and are so spiny they draw blood at the lightest stroke. They're held to the ground by a wee small stem like the narrow bit of a brandy glass, and when their seeds mature they dry out and curl up and catch the wind and the stem snaps and off they go, springing away like wads of barbed wire.

More of these went by in front and behind and over, I don't know how many.

The roll of gray waxy hills lay ahead with the road going through them like a scratch made with a pin. The air was vibrating and pale, all distances grayed out as if by mist. An odd phenomenon — nasal hallucinations: a strong smell of excrement, then of cooking meat. Cars had their lights on. There were not many cars, maybe six in an hour.

"Rock Point Arizona Pop. 400 elev. 5000" said the sign. Then cattle, red and white; a herd of mohair goats like dirty rugs. A shed-like building that said POST OFFICE with pickups parked in its lee, people walking bent with papers over their faces. A tumbleweed bounced up the post office roof and sailed down among the pickups. I heard someone yell. Perhaps a dozen buildings was all there was. The rest of the pop. was out in the country.

The land lay flat between stone monoliths. Layers of ancient dune and seabed sediments lie flat here on the Colorado Plateau, the high land that takes up most of northeastern Arizona and beyond. Up here the soft layers are eroding fast. Past Rock Point the coppery buttes were sandblasted smooth like enormous pots. I didn't know if I was hot or cold, if it was too bright or too dark, everything lost distinction, edges, shape, as if it were night, but there were glares and distortions everywhere, so I drove with my car lights on and my shades on, too.

The wind began to wail and shriek and grit rattled against the car. A dry creekbed was a river of white smoke. The light was wrong. Darkness seemed to come from overhead, from a mantle of reddish cloud with rents of sky that were smoke dark, rosy, green.

"Many Farms Arizona" said the sign, I didn't catch the pop. or elev., noting only that once again the second was larger than the first. There were no farms or any other buildings in sight and none appeared for a long time.

I had realized by then that this was foreign country. There was no way I could just camp beside the road. No tent would survive that wind. There were certainly no motels. I had nowhere to go. I'd just got here, I didn't want to leave.

Then a scattering of trailers, hogans, a trading post with a gas pump. I stopped at the trading post and used the pay phone. I'd noticed a red dot on the map some fifty miles south and red writing (very small) beside it: *Ganado Presbyterian Mission*. I'm Presbyterian

if I'm anything; this seemed identity enough in a world where anything else I could lay claim to seemed to have blown away. I talked
to Pastor Paul Stone and told him who I was and what I was doing,
said I'd work if I could stay. I was a wayfarer asking refuge of a
church.

"We've got work and we've got beds," he said. "Is that infernal
racket the wind or the Navajo telephone?"

"Both," I said. He laughed.

"Yeah. You can stay," he said. "Come along."

Outside two young men rounded up three ponies beside the road,
one man threw a lasso, manes and tails blew. A boy rode home from
school with his book bag over his face. The pony's head was tight to
its chest. Scattered hogans, stick paddocks and sheds, boxy prefabs,
trailers; these ended in flat darkening country through which the
wind went on.

Coyote and Two Gray Hills

The coyote is adaptable, always studying and learning, and her senses are doors to a mind always aware and at work. Here she listens behind and sideways while she looks forward, all the while reading the air with her nose.

The border around her is from a Two Gray Hills Navajo rug made in the first decade of this century. At that time a man named J. B. Moore owned a trading post in the Navajo Reservation, and to boost his trade he published catalogues of local rugs that could be made to order. He influenced local weavers' designs and materials, limiting colors to black, white, gray, red, and blue, and introducing Oriental patterns, among other things. The idea of a bordered rug is Oriental, and became Navajo. The Navajo are adaptable people; much of what we think of as their native culture is a rich pastiche of other cultures selected and changed by them to suit themselves. Two Gray Hills rugs are distinctive in design and color to this day, and no two are ever exactly alike.

4

mission

Ganado, Navajo Reservation, Arizona

When she was a little girl, Kerita and her sisters used to take the pouch of corn pollen from their mother's purse. They would dip their fingers into it and nibble the pollen, which was as sweet as candy. They lived in a sheep camp in the desert and their mother would be out with the flock all day, so the pouch was easy to borrow, and they would try not to eat so much that their mother would notice. In the bottom of the pouch were pieces of the Spirit Rock *hadahonye'*, and some of the pieces were carved into animals.

Once, they ate all the pollen. One of Kerita's sisters was red in the face from allergy, having eaten so much, and that time their mother was angry.

Whenever her mother prayed she'd take a bit of pollen from the pouch and touch it to her tongue and head — the top of the head, two inches or so back from the hairline. Kerita does this swift double-touch with an automatic grace when she shows how it is done. Medicine men will put corn pollen on the shoulders, palms, and soles of the person they're healing.

Kerita's mother told her that if she wore jewelry she would never be poor. In the camp they lived in a hogan, but later on her mother insisted on building a real house so the girls would grow up in the modern world. Their father was more traditional, very traditional, she says, but this is a society where women run things, so Kerita's mother got her way. She took the girls to a Christian church because that was the modern way. Kerita went to school, too — a boarding school because there was no other kind, and still is not, for children who live in sheep camps. She got her name "Kerita" there. She has another name, a Navajo name. She never told me that, and I never asked.

Two years ago her mother's sheep were sold. Kerita and her brothers and sisters sold them because the camp was falling into ruin, their mother was too old to manage the sheep alone, and none of the children wanted to live out there or shepherd the flock. Their mother had supported the family and had put the children through school by weaving her sheep's wool into rugs. She was a famous weaver of Ganado Reds in her time. Tears ran down her face when the sheep were sold, silent tears. Then she began to fall into ruin, too. Now she lives with Kerita. She hardly speaks. She half-lies, half-sits in a corner of Kerita's double-wide trailer like a collapsed sack with a mask for a face; her eyes never move, there is no expression in her mouth, she wears her silver and turquoise jewelry: bracelets, rings, necklaces, collar points, a concha belt. Her skirt is long and the toes of her black shoes poke out from the skirt like shoes that have been placed on the floor.

Kerita is not married and she has no children of her own, but three of her sister's daughters live with her, too. They run in and out and hug the dogs and hug your knees and look up at you, and when you sit down they climb in your lap. One of them is a fetal alcohol syndrome child. She is vague, a little slow. Happy natured, but with a smile that is delayed in coming or fading.

The girls go to a local public school that is an easy walk from the trailer. English is their first language; they understand Navajo but do not speak it. They wear jeans, sweatshirts, and sneakers, and have plastic barrettes in their hair. For sweets they buy candy from the store. On Sundays they go with Kerita to the Presbyterian Church of Ganado, the stone church of what was once the Ganado Mission.

The mission was established in 1901, the first Protestant mission on the Navajo Reservation. This is the largest Indian reservation in the world, nearly half the size of New England, taking in parts of northwestern New Mexico and southeastern Utah and most of northeastern Arizona. Nowadays it has a population of one hundred and eighty thousand Navajo plus forty thousand non-Navajo. The girls are Christians, as Kerita is, as Kerita's mother is, and they will tell you this to your face without being asked. The world of the spirit here — whatever its identity or denomination — is like a river open to the air, no subterranean current, but a substance in constant use, a source of vital utility, exactly like a river. Fifteen percent of the people on the reservation are Christian. The rest are Navajo. *Navajo* means both religion and race at once, something like the meaning of *Jew* — which also means both — and no one is sure what happens when you leave off half that meaning. On Sunday in Ganado half of the hymns are sung in Navajo, half the prayers are said in Navajo, and half the Bible readings are from the Navajo Bible.

Pastor Paul Stone of the Ganado Presbyterian Church is below middle height, white-haired, and walks with a limp like the Greek traveler Odysseus. He travels fifty to sixty thousand miles a year as a representative of the church, visiting his scattered flock on the reservation, going outside the borders to give lectures on the Navajo and gather funds for his mission (the Ganado Presbyterian Church is no longer an official mission church, Presbyterians having decided that missions are for foreign countries and that the Navajo Reservation is not a foreign country; a decision that Pastor Paul takes exception to). His car has 130,000 miles on its odometer, the truck 170,000, the jeep has 180,000. The reservation has fewer paved roads per square mile than Death Valley. The jeep has been towed out of the mud by a horse at three A.M.

Pastor Paul always wears his white pastoral collar and his black suit and the large silver and turquoise cross that was given him as a New Year's present by his congregation. He stands out in a crowd, and means to. He is proud of the fact that he is named for both the great Apostles: Paul, and *the rock of the church,* Simon Peter, the stone. He reserves his rage for the notion of Manifest Destiny ("The single most destructive philosophy man ever came up with!") and the BIA, the Bureau of Indian Affairs; he can rattle off chapter and verse of their systematic exploitation of Native Americans in general and of the Navajo in particular. He has no love for what are known as the Five Oil Sisters ("They've been cheating the Navajo out of sixty-five percent of their royalties for nineteen years!") and he does not love the border towns:

"You been there? They've got one K–Mart and fifty-six bars, and they call every Navajo they see a 'drunken Injun' just for coming into town to buy their jeans. Heck, one guy did that to a kid right in front of me, then looked me in the eye!"

He has no respect for Arizona's universities:

"One girl from here, a brilliant kid, was the only Indian in her class at ASU. She had one professor who was into high-pressure tactics, firing questions, playing academic hardball. English was a second language for this girl, remember, so maybe she was slow to respond. Anyway, day one, mind you, this professor said: 'I don't know why you Indians don't get back to the reservation and let some intelligent white kid come in here.' The girl was back here in five *hours*. She was in tears for weeks. The professor's still there. I know. I checked. And the girl never went back to college."

It pleases Pastor Paul that biblical imagery is so apt; it fits the people and landscape here so well. The desert, the shepherds, the sheep, even the "begats" — ancestry being serious business to the Navajo as it was to the Israelites. Other things, too. The slavery to Pharaoh, the enemy Philistines, the occupying force of Romans. The Navajo have been an occupied people for more than three hundred years. First held by the Spanish military, then by the Anglo military, they have generations of practice in being a subject people. A slave trade in Navajo children went on for fifteen years after the Civil War, New Mexican slave raiders carrying them off through Mexico for export to the aristocracy of Central America and Spain, but always baptizing them first; one reason for the general Navajo distrust of Roman Catholics. As for Philistines, enemy tribes have never been far away, though nowadays the border wars with the Hopi are mostly carried on in law courts and newspapers. Once in a while an intertribal fistfight does break out, between teenagers, mostly, but no one takes that very seriously now.

Miracles are familiar, too. In 1920, with the mission little more than a series of adobe huts, it was time to drill a well. The village gathered on a gravel plain against a soaring butte of naked rock; the well went down and was dry. The Reverend Fred G. Mitchell called a prayer meeting every night from seven to ten. Three more holes went down and were dry. The prayer meetings continued and were

well attended, and the fifth hole hit the aquifer, and in minutes the
well was filled with water. This is called the Presbyterian Miracle.

With plentiful water and in time, the mission became a campus of
stone buildings housing a boarding school, a modern hospital, a stone
church with a belfry, all lying in a sward of lawn with lines of trees,
like a New England college. Through the scrim of the cottonwoods
you can still see the ruddy wall of the butte and the silvery plains of
the desert, but here the desert has been beaten back.

"Here, Satan is not as disguised as he is in suburbia," Pastor Paul
says one day, when we are driving to Window Rock on an errand,
and he says it out of sequence as if he'd got to what he was about,
behind the daily struggles with human need: alcoholism, shattered
families, orphans, dropouts, hopeful college applicants bracing themselves for a foreign world, all the debris of culture shock. And the
rituals: the funerals and christenings and marriages, the Navajo cere-
monies that he's taken into the church, like the Ceremony of the
First Laugh; the first laugh being the third and final test for a child's
humanity. He says:

"Here, Satan doesn't need to be disguised. He appears frequently
in undisguised form."

There's a pause.

"And you see him undermine the church. As soon as he sees the
goodness and kindness and gentleness of Christian people, that's
what he tries to destroy or bring down.

"When I bring new Christians into the church I *warn* them. That
they will be sorely tempted, and soon. That they are still infants in
their faith . . .

"You learn not to underestimate the power of evil. Evil is the
sense that one has the *right* to hurt, kill . . . the *blindness* of evil . . .

"Here you see it unguarded. The malevolent side of medicine men
is what is called the skinwalker. You can hire one to put a hex on
someone you want to get back at. They can enter a body, animal or
human, and control it from the inside. It goes covered in animal
skins. Every Navajo has a skinwalker story they tell quietly among
themselves."

★   ★   ★

We drive on; the upland landscape outside has gone cold, the rolling sagebrush like blue-gray wool, like smoke and charcoal, the dark junipers like pointed flames.

"What difference does the desert make, to what you're doing?" I ask, and for a while he says nothing. This is out of character. Then:

"Everything. Everything. It makes every difference."

Another pause.

"Everything is separated and isolated. If you're afraid of wide-open spaces, this country can be terrifying. One girl came on a work camp from a church in the East and would not get out of the bus."

Then he goes silent again. At last he clears his throat. He says:

"So much of their life revolves around the sacredness of the land. The Navajo believe that *soul* comes from the land. If you leave the land, you leave your soul behind. You have to come back to the land, this land, to regain your soul."

After I've finished my mission work of stuffing envelopes or cleaning dormitory rooms, Kerita and I eat Navajo tacos at Ramon's Café — fry bread loaded up with beans, meat, salsa. The girls eat burgers. My rented car is useful; I've discovered that offering my service as chauffeur is the ticket I need to have company. We go shopping; she buys me a cloth calendar rolled on a stick with all the months written both in misspelled English and in Navajo. The Navajo language is all around, spoken softly, a punctuated murmur, thick with glottal stops and nasal vowels and oddly slurred consonants. Within days my own face — suddenly pinkly naked and too brightly colored, like my pale hair — looks strange to me in a mirror. One day we go to the Shiprock Fair, the Northern Navajo Nation Fair, and the two Anglos I see among the thousands of Navajo faces look so peculiar I have to stop myself from staring. We watch a two-hour parade of marching bands, rodeo champions, chiefs and counselors on horse-back, hoop-dancing Apaches, elaborate floats made and manned by schools, churches, veterans' groups, Boy Scouts, Navajo police, Army divisions, traditional chanters, gospel singers. We eat grilled mutton and grilled peppers with fry bread and salt. She teaches me Navajo words, but the only one I ever can remember is *tee'*, with the two *e* syllables, the second one nasal and ending in a glottal stop, meaning: let's go. Let's go: I've had enough to eat, enough parade, enough jewelry sellers and rug merchants and herbalists, the kids are sleepy, enough juniper smoke from ceremonial fires, enough dust.

On other days we drive for miles through the desert looking for her family's camps or sheep ranges, or the churches where she has gone for the fellowship times of gospel "sings" or services or retreats; more often than not we get lost. It doesn't seem to matter. Kerita laughs, she has an attitude of patience that is catching, a kind of waiting, an impassivity behind which is a foreign species of awareness; at those times I believe that she is thinking in Navajo. We're the same age, we get along with ease, she's a teacher of "special children" in the local school and is still studying for a college degree; she talks of autism and fetal alcohol syndrome, and wonders whether her mother has Parkinson's disease or acute depression, or some other malady peculiar to the sale of her sheep that no hospital doctor — no Anglo doctor — could be expected to diagnose or treat. There is collapse and confusion all around, and in spite of the steadiness in her, and her good humor and humorousness, I sometimes sense a pain so tidal and overwhelming that I gasp; I can feel it lapping at my own knees.

On the last night before I leave to go into Hopi country, we visit her uncle Amos. We drive up to the house — the children are in the back of the car, very quiet, with mischievous smiles; they are always very quiet — and we stop the car right there and keep the windows rolled up. Dogs boil out from under the porch, growl, howl, bark, race around the car, one yellow dog leaps at the windows with fangs bared; we wait until Amos appears on the porch and peers to see who it is. Then Kerita waves, I wave, the children wave. One by one Amos ties the dogs. The noise they make is, if anything, worse. The yellow one is lashed to the far corner of the porch with a length of rope as thick as my wrist. It leaps, twists, howls, its lips drawn back from its teeth, and we sit until we see that the knots hold. Then we get out and go into the house.

Amos's wife is feeding mutton stew to children in the kitchen; she nods, the children look up and nod before bending to their stew. Amos's daughter-in-law has run off with another man and nowadays the grandchildren are eating here.

"Would you like some stew? There is plenty," Amos says. "Plenty! You want some stew?"

I remember what Pastor Paul has said about the number four being the number of power. Anything really meant is to be said four times, and gathers meaning as it goes. We've already eaten; we thank him and say no. We sit in the living room.

"There is plenty of stew, you want some?" he asks.

"Thank you, we've already eaten," we say.

"We've already eaten," Kerita says again.

"We had dinner already, Uncle Amos," says one of the girls, then covers her mouth and laughs with her eyes.

Gourd rattles hang on the wall, the tables are covered with small rugs, the chairs with quilts and knitted throws. Amos is gray-haired, heavy. His face moves even less than Kerita's, he speaks in a slow orderly purposive way as if stacking the words like blocks, and keeps slipping off into Navajo, which is more expressive and watery, though still spoken with an almost ceremonial order. This is what I hear: a ceremonial order that is a kind of watchfulness. A protection, a virtue. Later, when I meet other Navajo who live off the reservation, I notice first of all the briskness of their speech, the mobility of their expression, most of all the informality of their bodies — the guarded quality gone — and they talk about *the Navajo way,* but it seems to have left them or they have left it; I know they've crossed the boundary. Whatever that boundary is. Of place, culture, spirit — how can they be separate? I only know that in Amos's house the watchfulness was there.

He shows us a piece of *hadahonye'* that he is carving in the shape of a bighorn ram. He brings out his box of silver-working tools; he's a silversmith of long experience, though he doesn't do much now. The box is full of delicate pliers, soldering wire and flux, pinked silver for settings, fine and coarse files, buffer wax, molds for drawing wire. He has an acetylene torch. In the old days, he says, they used a forge with bellows; the bellows had a "beak" and a "tail," so it was, in its own way, alive. Animate. That's it: things are animate, they have personality. Motive. Things may not be what they seem.

I ask him again about desert plants. At first he says nothing, talks about other things. I ask him again; specific questions, general questions.

After church on Sunday he sat on the wall and he talked about the desert for a long time, and all the time he kept reaching down and picking up handfuls of fallen cottonwood leaves, picking them apart and crushing them in his hands.

"The plants are alive. Even when dead they are alive. These" — he held out a palmful of crushed leaves — "these make good mulch. Very good mulch."

He said that what is frayed and scattered and dried and blown away can be brought to fruitfulness. He talked back and forth between the Bible and the leaves. He made jokes, in the Navajo way, dry and without a change of expression. He was talking about apparent emptiness, about the desert, where the only emptiness is in your eyes. He was talking about life. Tonight he says:

"Some plants are poison. Very bad. Other plants kill pain, are very good. The medicine men are the ones who know about plants."

Then:

"Many plants go away. They stay awhile, and are gone. They come back."

And:

"This drought is terrible. Two years. This rain is too late, will do no good. What will happen to cattle? Cattle eat long grass, with their tongues —" He makes a curling motion with his hands exactly like the tongue of a cow. "This grass is all gone."

They slip off again into Navajo.

"My uncle is talking about the Native American church," says Kerita. He nods.

"Peyote treated as divine," he says, shakes his head, gets up and takes his Bible from a shelf, a heavy silver-bound Bible, and opens and reads from Matthew: "And then shall many be offended, and shall betray one another, and shall hate one another. And many false prophets shall rise, and shall deceive many . . ." He shakes his head. "These people grow peyote in pots! In pots!"

He sits down again and spreads his hands, spreads all his fingers.

He waits. We wait. His fingers are spread very wide, he is conjuring the desert, the silvery plains and the red buttes, waiting, impassive and wide.

"The mist comes down to earth and sows the seed," he says. "We are very high here, the mist is just clouds, and when it comes down it sows the seed. It does. And when it goes away," he lifts his hands, "then you see plants coming up." He puts his thumbs and forefingers together to show tiny seedlings, and I do see them, pinches of green. "That is the traditional belief. But the mist does come down here. To sow the seed. It does. It does."

Navajo Children Dancing in Traditional Costume
Northern Navajo Nation Fair, Shiprock, New Mexico

5

mesa

Shongopovi and Oraibi, Hopi Reservation, Arizona

At the edge of the mesa the corn is spread to dry on racks made of juniper wood. The racks are held off the ground by stones, cement blocks, an old chair, a truck tire, a broken pail. Far away are the dun outlines of mountains.

The air up here is like a copper-gold lens colored as if it were filled with pollen, but as dry and as light as the out-breath of a kiln.

I stare at the corn, every kernel is an amazing thing; streaked, bright, glossy. Alex Kasknuna waits for me to tell him what I'm doing with my nose six inches from a cob of corn.

"I've never seen blue corn before," I say.

"No?" and then he laughs, and it's a pleased laugh.

When we go on he walks a little ahead, though sometimes we go side by side. The houses are arranged in no pattern; they press together and stack on top of one another so that ways between and to them angle and curve and then open suddenly to plazas. The kivas in the plazas are square, not round, but are easy to recognize because of the ladders poking up. The ladders are made of whole trees tapering to gray points in the air.

The houses are as rectangular as blocks. Beam ends jut from their tops and these are layered with brush and then adobe. The squared stone of the walls has been chinked and then plastered. Some houses are abandoned, their windows boarded, their walls unrepaired. Here and there new houses are being built of cement block.

This is higher, paler country than the Navajo Reservation that surrounds it. There is sand and dust and monumental rock with sometimes a juniper, or a pinyon, or a high hollow filled with the blue-green-gray pelt of sage. On the mesas, the houses are the same color and substance as the land.

All the time we are here I'm aware of seeing through two sets of eyes at once.

"I am . . . Hopi," Alex says. "Once, I considered myself a Baptist. Now I have found myself, my identity, my place on this earth."

In the dust streets time is of no consequence, the present has shifted; it's as if the present is of no consequence. The air is in continual shushing motion like air over mountaintops, and smells don't stay, but in whiffs they're here, the human smells: shit, roasting corn, soap, wetted dust.

Juniper smoke streaks the air. The juniper has been cut somewhere else and hauled in; whole tree lengths are piled against house walls, the thick boles torn and twisted and the bark fibrous. It looks like something once animal: dried baleen, chunks of mammoth jerky.

Sometimes there are coal-like heaps of dried sheep dung against the houses, too. The dung is in flattish gray slabs. To fire raw pottery in the traditional Hopi way you make a pile of juniper kindling and layer dried sheep dung over that. Broken shards are lapped on the dung like shingles, the raw pots are propped on there; more shards are layered on that and more dung on that until you have a dome of dung with pots at the heart. This burns slow and hot, for days. The shards protect the pots from most direct heat, but fumes do get in, unevenly, so pots come out streaked and clouded with oranges or creams as if they'd been airbrushed. Firebrushed is what they are.

Later we climb to Oraibi, on another mesa. Oraibi was established by the Hopi in A.D. 1150. It is the oldest continually inhabited village in North America. Here the streets are narrower, the houses smaller. From one comes the sound of a televised baseball game: high inside ball one. From another house comes the sound of chanting: hey . . . hey . . . ya ya ya.

Outside every house here is a stone bread oven. Neatly laid on the ovens are household things — bowls, knives, cobs of corn, yucca

leaves, bunches of herbs. Hanging on one adobe wall is a newly made
yucca sifter-basket. Alex tells me that when he was a kid he used to
watch his grandmother sift corn with a basket like that. She would
toss the corn up and the chaff would blow away and the corn would
fall exactly back. Alex smiles and shakes his head; it seemed like
magic, he says, that the corn always fell exactly back.

There is more blue corn, newly harvested, drying on a rooftop.
Again the colors: every shade of red and blue from blood to robin's
egg, indigo through purple, French blues, lavenders, carmines, blue-
blacks. No two cobs are the same. No two *kernels* are the same. The
light gives the corn a white gloss as if it were made of material as
durable as glass. Some cobs are as long as my forearm; the smaller
cobs, twisted, lie still in their husks in the dust.

We've come to a spur of rock, the village having petered out. The
most traditional of the Hopi still live on these mesas, Alex says. He
says it quietly. Until a month ago Alex's friend Jerry had a girlfriend,
a fiancée, up here — not in this village, but over there on Second
Mesa — and her family called Jerry (not always in jest) *pahana:* meaning white man, meaning One from across the Water, the lost white
brother; a word almost purely insulting, nowadays. Unlike Alex,
Jerry speaks English as a first language and Hopi only haltingly, and
he has what he calls "good manners," meaning *pahana* manners; but
these were foreign manners to his fiancée's family and they teased
him about that, so he was made to feel like a foreigner. Also, he
would not move in with her family in the traditional way. Jerry
insisted that he had his own life to live, that so did the girl, and that
these own lives could not be lived under the traditional matriarchal
roof; they needed a home of their own. The girl disagreed. So she
broke off their engagement.

"What did Jerry do?" I ask.

Alex lifts his chin toward the distance, the land below, the scattered settlements of trailers and prefabs and government developments that lie between the mesas.

"He's been visiting the bootleggers. I've tried to help him. To tell
him that is not the way. But he does not listen to me."

★   ★   ★

Sometimes Alex carves kachina dolls out of cottonwood roots, roots collected along the washes when rains have gullied earth away. The roots are seasoned for a time and then carved and painted and sold to traders or collectors, though he does give some as gifts; this is their original intent. The making of dolls is a traditional craft. For centuries Hopi have carved them for their children — for girls for the most part, for a young niece or daughter or sister. The kachinas themselves are spirits of the invisible forces of life (*china* means spirit, *ka* means respect) and there are hundreds of them — more than three hundred by an anthropologist's recent count — representing animals, plants, birds, people, clowns, clouds, stars, rocks, and other things of the past and present and future. Some fall out of use; others arrive. They come to the villages in the winter solstice and leave after Niman Kachina, the Home Dance, at the summer solstice. Then they go back to their ancestral home in the San Francisco Mountains near Flagstaff. During the six months that they are with the Hopi many cycles of their dances are held in the villages, dances at which anyone is welcome; kachinas dance for the good of all mankind. The dolls are given as gifts during the Home Dance especially. The dolls are not sacred, they are dolls, which is why they are allowed to be sold at all — but they are treasures.

Each one Alex makes is unique. Each piece of root that he takes up has its own character. He says that each doll is a form that he releases from the wood.

When he is not carving, or working with his family, Alex walks, on his own, for miles, at any hour, whenever the need strikes. He's been doing this all his life, since he can remember.

Last night he appeared in my camp in the canyon. One minute he was not there, then he was. He made no sound in the fallen leaves and he moved with that fast continuous glide which makes anyone nearly invisible in a mix of tree shadows, or anywhere, daylight or dark. Come now, I thought to myself then, wary of someone — of anyone — showing up in my camp in the dark; so, silent moccasins. Only these are workboots. The man in them is only a little taller than I, tough as wire, the color of cherry heartwood with a faint smell around him of wool and woodsmoke, beardless but with a grown man's lines in his face. The fact is that most people are clumsy and noisy when they move and that Alex is not, and when he appeared four feet off last night, I thought: not many people can move like that. Or, I still think now, like this.

He goes from stone to stone with a smooth gliding walk as if this were level land. The mesa out here is strewn with rubble; houses fallen long ago.

"Look." He bends down, picks and searches for a minute in the dust, then stands up again and pours a handful of things into mine: two pottery shards, feathers, yucca fiber, a piece of dried corncob. "Didn't you say that you found these things in Mesa Verde, too?"

Later Alex asks me:
"Can you read signs?"
We are sitting on rocks at the brink of the mesa.
"Signs?"
"I know some," he says, "oh, like birds, two birds just balancing and dancing together, you know, in the air, enjoying their life; that's a good sign. A hawk is a good sign. A hawk overhead even better. A hawk circling over your head, man, you are in harmony then! Foxes. Seeing a fox, especially if it has a mate, that's a very good sign."

We dangle our feet over the rim.

"I think I am close to the land," he says. "When I'm away from the land, I feel unhappy."

The village is half-hidden behind us, windowed blocks the color of mesa stone. Dust-colored valleys range below, dun-colored ground, eroded bones of farther mesas, arroyos striking into the plain like lightning bolts.

Below the mesas there are farm fields where desert scrub has been cleared away. There are plantings of apricot and peach and apple trees. The fields look like fields of dust, now, in the autumn, though the squash vines and tomato plants in them are richly green. The Navajo are the Hopi's best customers. The Navajo come right to the farms every summer and fall, in their pickup trucks, just as nomadic Navajo came to the farming Hopi a thousand years ago.

"You going to New Mexico tomorrow, huh?" he asks.
"Yes."
"What are you looking for there?"
"I'm not sure. I'm going to the malpais, the lava flows."

"Something interesting there?"

"I don't know. I've never been. That country is full of volcanoes. I've never been to one."

There's silence for a while. Then:

"You got country of your own? Your own land?" he asks.

I think about that.

"I have some land I own, where I had a farm once," I say, "but it's not my land. In the way that this is your land."

"Do you ever pray?" he asks.

"Sometimes."

Alex raises his chin and I follow his eyes: beside the path we came on is a polished barkless stick the length of my finger, one end wrapped with threadlike stuff. I didn't see it before.

"A prayer stick," Alex says. "Hopi always prays. Hopi believes in life," he says, and he laughs the same open laugh that has been with him all day long.

So, you went south, I think. It's as if time had folded on itself, centuries of pale stone and corncobs and pots not much changed, and here you are, not much changed, I think. Next to Alex I feel frail and loose, tenuous. I feel shaken, an odd unrooted stranger with a frail hold on life. Though by the time the sun sets I will learn that this is not true.

Later we walk up a canyon to the trickle of a spring. We sit with our backs against pinyons. We have bought a sixpack of Coke at the store and now we each drink the first one rapidly, the second more slowly, and nurse the third. The fizzed sweetness is blessedly cold, it washes the dust from my throat, from behind my eyes. We talk and fall silent, then talk again, starting anywhere about anything. The silences are filled with ease. The sun drops and the colors of things come back from the bleached day dust; the green of pinyon needles, the yellows of wildflowers, the blue of sky, the warm layers of the rock. The air clears like a washed window.

"Hey. Look," Alex whispers, pointing up.

"What?"

"Look!"

A pair of prairie falcons circles overhead. They dive, flip, circle, playing in the canyon air.

"Good God!" I whisper back.

"Yes," he says, "that is true."

We watch the birds dive, tease, dance, return overhead to begin the dance again.

"The falcons are good," Alex says, "they are dancing our harmony, see?"

"How do you know?"

"I know so." He grins. "You know so, too."

Rain over Hopi Mesas
Hopi Reservation, Arizona

6

water canyon

Cibola National Forest, New Mexico

This was marked as a campground on the map and I needed to get out of the desert for a while and "Water Canyon, Cibola National Forest" didn't sound like desert so I came up. I got here at sundown, a little late, but I've got so I can pitch a tent and set up camp in ten minutes even in the dark. It's a nice campground but I'm the only one here. There's just the canyon rising in a forested slice of ravine toward Mount Baldy, and there's a moon out, and I've lit my candle lantern and am writing home.

Not home, exactly. I found a nice note card back in Ganado and I'm writing to a man I've wanted for a long time and whom I spent a night with before I left home. I'm pretty sure I spent the night with him because I was just about to leave.

I'm fine on my own, see. Even so, it's only natural that when there are these little chinks in my time I find myself thinking of him. And I figure I'd be rude — not to mention downright transparently insecure — if I didn't send him some kind of note letting him know that I'm fine on my own, but that I think of him sometimes, even though I'm fine on my own.

Leaving Hopi country, I got into Holbrook by eight A.M. and spent two hours in a truckstop café eating the most monstrous breakfast I could hold, letting that ease the pang of reentry. I brushed my teeth and put some makeup on in the rest room along with a couple of lady truckers, we kidded around a little in there about a hell of a

this and the damned desert that, and that helped, too. It wasn't easy
coming out of the reservations. I'd been wearing the same pair of
jeans for a week. I'd lost about ten pounds. My eyes looked bleached.

After three fried eggs, tortillas and cheese and chilies, bacon,
homefries, two orders of toast, jam, juice, and uncounted refills of
coffee, I spread out a couple of maps and got out my field guides. I
spent the next two days crossing part of Arizona and half of New
Mexico looking at plants, birds, and rocks.

I was laying a kind of baseline. Coming to an understanding with
the natural history of the place, or the part of it that I could figure
out on my own. In order to get to the malpais, the lava flows, I
would have to come down off the Colorado Plateau down into the
Rio Grande rift, into another hotter and lower species of desert: the
northern fingering of the Chihuahuan desert that runs clear through
West Texas into the heart of Mexico. That would be something else,
something different again. I was going to miss this place. So I filled
up the dashboard with clippings of sagebrush and wildflowers and
pinyon cones and the back of the car with samples of sedimentary
and volcanic rocks. I made my lists of species, and made notes in my
field guides, but I had the nagging notion that some of this intensive
busyness was an escape from the heart of the matter. My soul had
been stirred back on those reservations. My heart had been touched,
I'd been frightened, awed; most of all I'd been *aware* in a new way,
as though I'd grown a new set of senses. Now the stars reverted to
their old Western mythical shapes — Perseus and the Big Dipper and
all that — and I spent some time at night learning the names of more
stars with my *Field Guide to the Heavens.*

I spent three hours in Magdalena talking with an old miner who
had two teeth left in his head and who knew his way around inside
the now defunct Kelly Mine, on the other side of Mount Baldy. He
showed me some pieces of smithsonite and chrysocolla and chunks
of turquoise big enough to choke a bear. Afterward, all I could think
of was the story that Pastor Paul told me about the origin of turquoise. It went something like this:

"In the beginning, the sky was made, and many spirits lived in the
sky. And there was a minor spirit called Turquoise who had made
nothing. And he liked the color of the sky a lot. So he stole a little

corner of it, down at the edge where he figured the other spirits wouldn't notice, and he carried it away to keep for himself. Anyway the other spirits did notice, of course they did, they notice everything, always have and always will, and so they shouted out as loud as they could: 'Who has stolen this piece of the sky!' and poor Turquoise got scared, naturally, and he did what anyone would do who was scared of being caught red-handed, he stuffed those bits of sky right into the mountains where no one could see them. And then he walked right out in the open with his hands out and empty and said, 'Well, heck, I didn't do it! Wonder who did?' just like some people I know. Like some people we all know. And he got away with it, too. And that's where it is, right in the mountains. It's sacred because it is pieces of the sky. And if you look closely, you can see the clouds in the sky. And that's why we call it turquoise.''

The rocks were getting interesting. Not the semiprecious ones so much but the regular ones, the bones of the landscape; in the desert you see these all the time. After I left the miner at Magdalena I drove to the edge of the rift. Down below was an enormous pale tan space, like blowing sand seen from an airplane. Way down there. The descent was pocked with cinder cones.

For a while, I'd been noticing that the layers of the landscape were not lying flat anymore. Coming across the dry highlands of New Mexico and the Mogollon Rim, you couldn't miss the disruption. The Mogollon field of extinct volcanoes, deep layers of colored ash, collapsed calderas, dark cones, black layers of basalt — old hardened lava flows — and whole hill-ranges of welded tuff: volcanic ash congealed at white heat to something that resembles, from a distance, bogus fun-park rocks made out of papier-mâché. Though volcanic action here began maybe sixty million years ago, most of it right here at the rift edge is only five to twenty-four million years old. Not old, as things go. Many semiprecious stones, and uranium, silver, and gold, were veined into the mountains by volcanic action. Turquoise itself comes from the weathering of alumina-rich rock in arid environments. It's a desert rock, in other words. Not a volcanic one. I was glad to hear this. As far as I could tell, it pretty much confirmed the Navajo story.

I went down into the rift in the early afternoon, through the fields

of cinder cones. It got hot, and hotter. I understood some pieces —
those rocks in the back of the car — but I didn't understand how
they went together. And I'd seen some little red writing on the map
that said "New Mexico Bureau of Mines and Mineral Resources"
right next to Socorro, which was down there in the rift, so that's
where I was going.

On the campus of the University of New Mexico in Socorro it
was 97 degrees in the street, the watered gardens were tropical. I
walked into the Bureau of Mines and etc. and started asking questions. I wound up in the office of Orin J. (OJ) Anderson, a grizzled
senior geologist, who was busy.

"What exactly is it that you want?" he asked.

"I want to understand one piece of it. Just one piece," I said. "Can
I go out there with you?"

"Are you a geologist?"

"No."

"Well . . ."

"My car is full of rocks!" I said, and there was a little pause, and
he nodded and climbed down off his chair, and then we got down
to business and wrote down each other's name and address. And I
knew it would happen.

After I got back to my ovening car I saw the words "Water Canyon" on the map and came back up here.

There's no water in the canyon right now. There's a coyote, though.
I saw his tracks in the dust when I came and now there's a scoot and
flicker of coyote-shaped shadow in and out of the junipers and the
stones. I've learned that every camp has what I call camp goons;
animals that make it their business to patrol human camps and scavenge. Coyotes are not unusual as goons go, but I've never seen one so
close up. Maybe it's late in the season. No one's here. Slim pickings.
Getting cold, and he's getting desperate, maybe. My campfire is
fifteen feet off and what's left of my chili beans are in the pot there,
and the spoon is lying next to the pot, and the fire is going out.

Hell with it. That chili was sure-nuff fiery and he's welcome to
it. Here he comes . . . there he goes again. I tuck my feet up on
my picnic table bench and alternate between writing in my notebook

and — once in a while, when an elegant cool little turn of phrase comes to mind — writing on that card from Ganado.

A barred owl calls from up-canyon, hoots and *hhars*.

The coyote-shadow scoots, flits, there's a clink, and the shadow vanishes.

I look down and see what I've written:

"Shit! The coyote just ran off with my spoon — ! I wish you were here. I really wish you were here."

Petroglyphs on Chinle Sandstone
The Painted Desert, Arizona

7

inferno

The Malpais, Carrizozo, New Mexico

At one in the afternoon something is wrong. The grasses and the clumps of tree cholla, and the hollylike Fremont barberry and the nolinas like sword bunches, the white surfs of flat-topped buckwheat, the black broken rocks, everything that's been in close focus for hours, even the hands in front of my face fade, blur, whiten; this is more than the midday light of the Tularosa valley. I've been out on the lava beds (the malpais, pronounced "mahl pie," meaning bad country in Spanish) since dawn; now something is wrong. Perhaps I didn't take the Spaniards seriously enough. The air is suddenly too thin to breathe and my vision narrows as if I were looking down the wrong end of a telescope, I'm losing touch with the ground. Sit down quick before you fall, I say to myself, into one of those black chasms, into the cholla, God forbid, too much to trip on here, don't move. Sit now, I say, and I do.

Dizzy, I'm dizzy, the world has faded like a photograph grossly overexposed. Heatstroke, honey, this is it for you, they'll find you here next month curled on this black volcanic griddle like yesterday's tortilla. Drink something, please. I fumble in my pack and field guides and binocs clatter to the stones, ahhh, canteen. Unscrew the thing. The water is tepid, like musty soup, it slides down anyhow.

No shade for miles. What is it you need, what do you need? Think. And I do, and one idea emerges full-blown and all-at-once: beer.

Color of amber with little bubbles popping and a white froth that chills the upper lip. Bitter, clean, cold, wet. Beer.

A vision, that's all you need to survive: an unattainable vision.

All else follows. I finish the contents of my canteen like a child taking milk of magnesia from a loving hand. I wait ten minutes. I haul myself upright and put one foot in front of the other foot all the way, talking myself back through this lava flow that came through the place less than a thousand years ago with the texture of lumpy cake batter. Right, up a little, whoa there, to the left now, woopsie do, right, left, easy now, good girl, not far now.

The lava flow is like cake batter. Was. When you pour it down, it flows tonguelike with a wrinkled surface and the plops and ploops only half sink in, it's full of air bubbles, just like this.

The lava cooled, a pour as broad as six miles wide and forty-eight miles long and black as your hat. It's two pours, actually, two batches, both belched from the same diminutive almost invisible pimplelike object some miles to the north. Can't see it now, it's unimportant anyway, doesn't merit the name volcano in any case, they call it a cone.

The lava rock poured thick and fast when it came. Fresh olivine porphyritic basalt is what it is; deep mantle material made up of metallic oxides, mostly silica but alumina too, iron and manganese, magnesia, a little lime, soda, potash, titanium. Recipe for inferno. Mix and pour. Let cool for a millennium. Here we are.

The distant *rurk* of a raven. There is always a raven. What you think of their comments depends on your mood.

When I worked on my farm, I used to think he said: "Work! Work!"

Now I think he says: "Weak! Weak!"

I'm weak; my legs are too flexible, as if I had too many knees. There are rhythmic creaks passing my ear; a grasshopper coming up with a yellow flash, going down. Five creaks: a pallid-winged grasshopper, then. The lava is black-gray with rusty stains where it has broken, the old surface almost glossy, wrinkly, the old fluid body of it shattered, caved in, cracked. Here in a crevice a spider has made a web with its "bedroom" in the round hole of an old gas bubble. Everything is used in the world. Some tube caves have fallen in, there's sharp rubble everywhere and ravines and ragged holes. No place to stumble around.

What brought me here and what has kept me here past good sense is this: it is a rich place. All those ingredients, those oxides! How do I know?

Look out there now, even in this bleaching light of one in the afternoon; beyond the lava there's nothing but pale flatness and then low hills all the color of bone, all bony land tufted with groundsel and snakeweed and prickly fetid marigold, all the clumpy hangers-on to arid nothing much. Beyond the Tularosa valley, beyond the low range that borders it to the west, is another wider valley: the Jornada del Muerto, the journey of death. Those Spaniards again naming things as they saw them in the raw, and this is raw all right, one of those deserts you don't want to be in. The dry empty heart of New Mexico. The odd stunted mesquite, the odd spot of a juniper dark on a slope. Otherwise only sandstone and limestone, the soil crusted with chalky white caliche: calcium carbonate capping the soil like whitewash. Desert ground whatever way you cut it. Then look at this lava bed, this malpais . . . all these things growing in here!

Here the grama grasses are high and gold. Here are rich thickets of yucca, squawbush, barberry. Clumps of flowers are in yellow bloom, and little red-flowered clammyweeds. There are tree cholla and prickly pear and hedgehog cactus and desert Christmas cactus, and clumps of feather peabush. The bare lava is lichened with soft green, yellow, orange, ochre. Every crevice is stuffed with herbs, mints. Painted-lady butterflies bat the air, the creakers rise and creak and fall. Now a white tumulus rises out of the black basalt: destination one. Camp. My car. It's not far now.

A thousand years ago the lava flowed around this outcrop of sandstone leaving it like an island. Steep-sided. I lean my way up its pale round rocks, through the uninteresting vegetation, avoiding the thorns of the mesquite. My car is like an oven but it starts. I still don't dare take off my hat. Drive, I tell myself, you can do it now, drive, honey, till you find that beer.

New Mexico Afternoon
Soaptree yucca in the Tularosa valley

8

outpost

Carrizozo, New Mexico

The Outpost Bar & Grill is on the outskirts of Carrizozo. Like a lot of towns out here, outskirts is mostly what there is. Main street's not long and it's the only street, and the desert is there, you can see it between buildings, alleyways guide the eye back into white-gray plains joined at the horizon by whitish air.

I take off my hat while I'm driving, suddenly aware that I'm going in among my own kind, aware that it's been three days now since I've been in any public place, since I've talked to anyone, since I've looked in a mirror. I brush the sweatband dent out of my hair with my fingers. Then there's a Bar & Grill sign hanging above the street and the red neon sign in the window that says OPEN, and I have this sudden vision of date palms poised around a pool: this is an oasis and no mistake.

I'm not far wrong; going in is like going into water, cool and blessedly dark, a submergence.

Two pool tables, orange leatherette chairs, dark red Indian-blanket-patterned rug, TV on, video games in their cubicle booths: Ms. Pac Man and so on, and the lit slanted surface of a jukebox. A sign by the pool tables: "Absolutely No Wagering!" Two gumball machines, the kind you put a dime in and turn the toggle, and a pay phone next to them and a calling-card-covered bulletin board next to that. For sale behind the bar: cigarettes, Mars and Hershey bars, peanuts, Alka-Seltzer, Wrigley's Spearmint gum, beef jerky.

I've been living out of my pack awhile so I hardly know where to begin; it's like Christmas morning in here, such a heap of goodies, but what is clamoring at me is thirst; so when the barmaid comes, which she does right away, placing my order is easy. Then I wait. It's the happiest waiting I think I've ever done. Between the drawn curtains come slits and wriggles of light as bright as an arc welder's torch: New Mexico afternoon. You can have it.

The beer comes in a dark brown bottle. It's as brown as lake water back East, I think, dark as lake water that's been filtered through the cakey duff of leaves and into streams chattering between stones, sweet clean water rich with dissolved organic acids and cold always. (Later I discover that this is part of heatstroke, this being overwhelmed by sudden nostalgia, and there it was: that bottle was beautiful.) With the beer is a bowl of tortilla chips and another of salsa. I get busy chilling my upper lip with foam and heating my mouth with chilies, which is a good excuse for another pull, not that I need excuses with the thirst I have, my first genuine desert thirst, that I do know won't be the last or the worst of these.

After a while I look around. The rest of the decor is a natural history collection if there ever was one. Two diamondback rattlesnake skins are stretched and mounted on polished boards, rattles and all and six feet long and as broad as my hips. Around the walls are mounted trophies of bighorn sheep, pronghorn antelopes, a peccary, two mule deer bucks — an eight-pointer and a ten. The eight is the larger of the two, a chunky fellow once well fed on someone's irrigated corn. He has a wide-beamed fawn-colored face and a gray forehead. These deer are as individual in coloring, bulk, expression, character, as any men. The men involved are named on the tiny brass plaques below the animals' chins.

There are a few men at the bar, too, behind a carved partition, and two more wandering around the pool tables, both in T-shirts, overalls, and beards. They're playing pool badly. It comes to me that the real reason they're in here is the reason I'm in here.

When the waitress comes with my second beer, one of them pipes up:

"I'm buyin' this round, with the lady's blessing, o'course," he says, and we go on from there.

"My name's Carl."

"My name's Sam."

I introduce myself. "How come I knew your name was Sam?" I say, because I did.

"Yosemite Sam, that's why, they copied him off me," Sam says, "they got the colorin' right and the height right and the crazy right 'cept they added a little weight and got his beard to do this, per-manent" — he grasps his coppery beard in both hands and divides it, like drawing curtains aside, so that the bib of his overalls is vis-ible — "like this here, like mine does, see, when I'm runnin' from a rattler, see. Don't run too good otherwise."

They've both been cutting firewood up on the mountain where Carl has gold mines.

"We're in here 'cause we're too hot to work and too broke to eat," Carl says.

"Is it always this hot?" I ask.

"Two weeks in summer it gets up over hundred de-grees. Seventy-five on Christmas day."

"You've got gold mines?" I ask.

"Yeah. Got twelve of 'em up there. Want to see 'em? Come on, I'll show you."

"Why are you cutting wood then?"

"Took ten years for me to figure out it takes fifty dollars in to get forty dollars out of gold. Only way to make money owning mines is to get some big company in to rent 'em and pay you royalties, then you can sit back an' smoke your see-gars an' let them take the dee-duction, or the gold. Same to you, either way."

They get down to telling stories, I'm a bona fide ignoramus, fair game, notebook open.

"Interested in animals, huh?" Carl says. "Well, heck, you're settin' with a couple."

"Want to hear about rattlers?" Sam asks. "I can't tell y' too much," he says, "mostly when I hear that ts-ts-ts-ts I get myself a-goin', though of course you know you can't never tell where they are, an' so, half the time, I run right over the things an' goin' so fast they can't tell where they are theirselves."

"We ain't neither of us ever been bit," Carl says, "but that ain't sayin' we couldn't step out of here right now and meet a six-footer the middle of Main Street."

"I'll tell you the worst that happened to me," Sam says, "I was hitchhikin' up in Oregon and camped by an overpass. It got dark so I got into my sleepin' bag there an' went to sleep. Anyhow the middle of the night the sprinkler system there come on . . . ts-ts-ts-ts-ts right in my ear! An' I didn't stop to think 'bout my boots or nothin', I just run across that overpass right in my sleepin' bag, yeah, takin' long hops in my sleepin' bag. Never lookin' left nor right. Rather be hit by a car than a snake any day. You OK, honey?"

"I'm OK," I say, wiping my eyes with the beer coaster.

"Y' think that's bad," Sam adds, "I had to change my di'pers too."

"The wild West ain't changed that much," Carl says, later, leaning over, talking low. "You see them four characters at the bar? I bet you anything five out of the four of 'em are packin' a loaded gun. Right now. Maybe two. A rifle they got in their pickup truck."

"Carl here ain't puttin' you on, neither," Sam says. "In Arizona they still have it on the books if a man steals your horse you can hang him from the nearest tree. In New Mexico you can shoot him. We don't have too many trees 'round here."

"But that's what you're cutting, right?" I ask. "Trees?"

"Heck, they ain't high enough but to hang a man's boots! I'm talkin' *trees!*" Sam exclaims.

"Here in New Mexico," Carl says, voice still low, "someone threatens you even with *words* you got a right to shoot him in self-de-fense."

Sam: "Better give me a loaded shotgun."

Carl: "Double barrel."

Sam: "Got a wide scatter on them things. Don't have to aim to hit."

Me: "Won't that blow you over backwards?"

Sam: "Not if I wedge my back good against a tree."

Me: "Thought New Mexico was short on trees."

Sam: "A rock then. Got plenty of rocks."

★　　　★　　　★

The conversation goes on decaying like this, in a pleasant way, for quite a while. The slits in the curtains fade to the rose of dusk and then to darkness and it's time to go. On the way out I buy gum and a chocolate bar, no, three chocolate bars, can't help myself; who knows when I'll see one of those again? Sam and Carl nod and say I'm acting like an honest to God natural native, that I must have got a bit of desert rat in me, that they figure I'll know to eat all that chocolate before sunup or it'll melt in my britches and then I'll be sorry. I promise them I will. They walk me to my car and open the door for me, touching their fingers to the line between tan and white where their hatbrims should be.

I drive back through outskirts and then down the desert descent, black spikes of yucca silhouettes against starry sky, to the black lava rocks, and within them to the paler rocks of camp.

Sandstone, home, bleached bone in its flow of volcanic batter, white and jumbled in starlight. I unlace my boots and crawl into my sleeping bag, my tent, my pale chrysalis with its arc of a door open to starlight. To stars. To trillions of nuclear fusion reactors out in the vacuum of space and coming to me now distorted by atmospheric gas. The lovely violence of sky.

I eat my chocolate bars, obedient as a child. I'm safe here. Gas and rock are here. I lie between, the one my bone and the other my breath, and the heat of me is solar heat pumped again, and the slight lovely spiraling of the world is the gift of beer, not heatstroke; and I am here. On the earth, here.

Side-Blotched Lizard on Limestone Rock

This is the most common lizard in the Southwest, but is
variable in color and pattern. This one is hiding his diagnostic
underarm black blot with his elbow.

9

reef

The Guadalupe Mountains, New Mexico and Texas

We're coming to the reef down the Pecos River valley and two hundred and fifty million years and the rim of the sky is the dusty blue of bleached jeans. The valley is a flat bowl of a place so wide one can't see edge; land and sky meet in sulfurous air. It's really sulfurous, with the dead-egg stink of gas wells. There are oil wells here, too, and artesian water wells. This is country where people drill down.

I orient myself via maps rustling over the other seat — geological maps, highway maps, ecologic zone maps, maps of Texas, maps of New Mexico. Over there, where the land rises at the other side of the Pecos, is the edge of the high plains and the end of the desert. The reef is up ahead.

We're east of the Rio Grande rift here and the soil is white. Caliche is what it is: calcium carbonate dissolved in groundwater, moved to the surface as water soaks upward, then left as the water dries away. If you turn a rock over here its underside will be layered with caliche like whitewash painted on again and again. In some places the caliche is thick enough to be mined for road pavings. Wherever you see it you know it came from below. You know that underneath is limestone, oceanic deposit, the bone minerals of vanished sea.

Plants have problems with caliche. The crust is in the way of roots and water — it's a physical barrier — and the chemistry is generally unfriendly, basic, bitter with salts and gypsum. This side of the valley is thinly furred by a slope of dun grass — gyp-grama mostly, so named because it tolerates gypsum and is an indicator of its presence. In this thin grass are bony shapes of cholla and low domes of mesquite. The mesquites are as transparent as greenish ghosts. Here and there are the hedgehog profiles of soaptree yuccas, typical of the Chihuahuan desert, which this is; I'd know them anywhere by their fireplace-poker fruiting branches and slim bristling anatomy. They lurk in the dried grama grass like imps, prickly and durable, as if they were made of spikes and tire rubber. This uncomfortable landscape is the legacy of what was wet long ago and is now too thoroughly dried away.

Midday: to the east the tops of floodplain cottonwoods shiver in the heat, taproots sucking Pecos water. The road is dissolved in watery mirage. There could be anything ahead, even time crinkles here like cellophane.

Two hundred and fifty million years ago we would be in a shallow sea. Just back there we'd have entered the lapping wavelets of lagoon. It's the end of the great Age of the Fishes, reptiles haven't hoisted themselves yet into dinosaurean ferocity, and between the lagoon and the warm seas that stretch between the continents of North and South America lies a massive reef. Someday in the future it will be called the Capitan Reef. It lies in a bulging U-shaped curve, nearly four hundred and fifty miles long and up to ten miles broad, through most of what will be West Texas. It's been growing there since the sinking of the Delaware Basin — the shallow seafloor — thirty million years past. It will grow for twenty million years more. Shaley organic limestones and fine-grained sandstones build in deep layers in the sea itself, out where the Rio Grande will one day cut through them to carve the canyons of West Texas and define the borders of nations. From time to time, chunks break off the reef and roll seaward or lagoonward to pile up as a chunky breccia. This gets embedded in layers of sandstone, limestone, and dolomite. Corals and calcareous algae — algae that deposit limestone-forming skeletons, much as corals do — all colonize their own debris pile, and the reef swells below the surface of the sea. The life of the reef will come to an end only when the whole region tilts and is lifted, high and dry, into the air.

That happened two hundred and thirty million years ago. Since then the reef has been high and bare, or dropped and buried in overlayments, and submerged for short periods and tilted and lifted several times, the latest time being between one and three million years ago. With every shrug and dip of things the massive reef limestone cracked and the sediment layers around it cracked. Rock layers in a moving earth are like crockery in a mattress trampled by elephants. Everything cracks.

Uplift was followed by erosion. So, nowadays, erosion having exposed them, pieces of the reef lie high and bare again. There's Glass Mountain near Alpine, and the Apache Peaks north of Van Horn, and the Guadalupe Mountains that span the Texan border of New Mexico. The Guadalupes are a fifty-mile-long range of pure Capitan Reef limestone. They're the highest mountains anywhere around. They're riddled with caves: Carlsbad Caverns, New Cave, Lechuguilla Cave, and Black, Hell Below, Dry, Sand, Endless, Little Sand, Virgin, Pink Panther, Three Finger, Spider, and McKittrick caves, and more, some still undiscovered, some already broken away.

The caves are there because of the cracks. Whenever the reef rose above the water table, beginning back with that first emergence, water seeped downward through the cracks. This water was mildly acidic, having dissolved a little carbon dioxide from the atmosphere, just as acid rain does. The limestone dissolved into spongework, then into hollows and loops and domes and chambers and Swiss-cheesy "boneyard" corridors. It wasn't running water that did the work, it was acids dissolved in it; the carbonic acids, at first. Later — after the most recent uplift caused natural gas to migrate from the oil and gas fields of the Delaware Basin up into the reef — sulfuric acid formed in the water and dissolved the limestone, massively, like sun heat melting ice.

Water moves. Tubes widened where it punched upward from deep springs, scallops were eaten into walls by eddying flows, rooms more than two hundred feet across ballooned inside the body of the reef. The raw shapes of these solution caves are like the shapes of melting icebergs, inside out.

The caves formed as the Guadalupes rose. As the mountains pushed higher the water table dropped away, leaving damp caves full of air. Groundwater seeped through these, and, dripping or spurting, flowing, evaporating, leaving deposits behind, this solute-filled seepage made — still makes — what are known as "decorations."

This is only the first of many cave words that express an odd exuberance, though the people who discover caves and name their contents brave darkness and danger and get filthy, and may be excused for feeling awe. Perhaps a cave becomes an extension of one's own interior. As the deserts above stretch one skyward, the caves are a penetration to the core. Decorations may not be the wrong word. Most of them are old now, dry, finished, stained dun or reddish by dust and iron oxides. For all their fluid shape they have the look and feel of desert-varnished bone. They are what is known as "dead" — and look it. Here and there a few are still "alive." Water drops hang from and over them like jewels, and the live decorations are cloaked in a calcite that sparkles like cold snow.

There are calcified siltstone cave rafts, and calcite stalagmites and stalactites that join in places to make columns. There are gypsum blocks, rinds, flowers, popcorn, hair, coral pipes; there are silklike travertine flowstones and delicate draperies of calcite and aragonite. Sometimes one finds aragonite moonmilk and frostlike anthodites, epsomite cotton and soda straws. Most caves hold spar crystals and sulfur crystals, lenses of chert, breccia, cobble gravel, red clay, gray-green clay, and pools (not many) of water. Helictites sprout from cave walls, twisted and knotted like stone string. On the ceilings are war shields formed by a spurting fissure, perfectly round, fringed with stalactite ermine tails and eagle feathers.

The shapes of these are wonderful, but not beautiful. They are an interior desert, a landscape of viscera. One has the sense down there of creeping through the gut of a large and sleeping animal.

Carlsbad Caverns has miles and miles of rooms, columns the size of houses, draperies like the contents of a hundred fabric emporiums unrolled and dipped in fluid marble. It's all too large, too deep, formed in too much silence and darkness, with the passage of too much time. I come out of the caves to the surface again like a diver gasping for air, for some familiar dimension.

Even the Carlsbad Cavern bats are out of scale. They are small lives multiplied into a mass composite phenomenon, like the reef itself. In the evening they coil out of the mountain like smoke and defy all description except in terms of numbers: there are more than 250,000 of them here. At a maximum rate of 5,000 bpm (bats per

minute) it takes two hours for them to emerge for their nightly hunt.
Bracken Cave, also in Texas, is summer home to twenty million
bats; Carlsbad (in comparison) is village, suburb, a moderate dot on
the bat map. Each bat weighs a half ounce, as much as three nickels,
and lives ten years on the average — though ages of fifteen to eighteen
are not uncommon, and one has been known to survive to twenty-
seven. They will feed for twelve hours — from six P.M. to six A.M. —
logging 360 air miles in a single night. In that time they will fill their
bellies with insects and empty them via guano a total of three times.
They cruise at 25 to 35 mph, ranging up to 45 miles from their roost.
They're known as Mexican free-tailed bats in part because their tails
are longer than the flight membrane that stretches between their hind
legs, and in part because they migrate six to eight hundred miles
south, to Mexico, in the fall. They'll get to their winter homes in
Mexico in two or three nights of flying time. They'll spend their
summers as far north as South Dakota, Colorado, southern Oregon.
In the East they'll summer as far north as Ohio, but for the most
part they do their insect eating and baby-raising (one a year) across
the southern tier. They've summered in this cave for seventeen thousand years. Their guano heaps are as much as fifty feet high, though
one hundred thousand *tons* of the stuff was mined for fertilizer in the
first two decades of the century. Guano composts to the color of
warm sand, is as crumbly as stale cake, and odorless, except for the
newest layer. Embedded in it are countless brown sticks like tooth-
picks or pine needles. These are bat bones.

Their cave entrance is in a hollow of the Guadalupe Mountains,
and at dusk the bats swirl counterclockwise as they come, gaining
airspeed and height, then they trail off across the orange face of the
moon with a noise like leaves in a wind.

At dusk I build a campfire on a ridge. Dusk is long in the mountains,
the moon brightens in a deepening sky. West Texas desert rolls out
like a storm sea, the texture of silk; here and there hollows gleam
white with gypsum and salt. Here and there are hogback ridges and
punches of bluffs. One can see for a hundred shadowed miles. I sleep
uneasily, traveling, as if I dreamed on the back of a dreaming animal.

I am moving by dawn. I find a canyon that is shady and narrow
and walk in to a flittering tremolo of bird song. A pyrrhuloxia (can't

think why such a medical-sounding name) sings from a treetop in musical chips; it looks like a northern cardinal but is gray, with a heavy yellow beak and red patches on its face, under its wings, at the tip of its topknot. It's as ripe-colored and mouthy as a parrot. A family of cactus wrens are ratcheting *ruh ruh ruh ruh* from the flank of the canyon, big loud speckled birds cocking an eye at me and rummaging noisily. There is a canyon profusion of plants: cholla, sotol, little-leaf sumac, catclaw acacia, algerita, juniper, Texas walnut. Not far along there is a spring, and a pool of water where fox sparrows are bathing, flipping droplets into the air. Near the pool is a room-sized shelf with a dome of roof blackened by smoke. There are spiral petroglyphs on the stones, clear as last week's doodles or graffiti.

Having spent days now living and thinking in deep time — the millions of years it took the reef to grow, the millions of years ago it grew, the thousands of years' worth of seepage it took to form a stalagmite — I think that my species — Native American or non — has a toehold here the width of a pencil.

Now the pool is a magnet for deer and peccary, according to the tracks, but it's also a magnet for other things. A brown towhee comes, two painted-lady butterflies, a monarch, and lots of wasps and bees that hunker on damp mud to suck their fill. I watch them gladly, happier than I've been in days. In the end this is where life is — in single lives lived — quirky and tenacious and individual; though this whole reef was like that, once. Corals, coralline algae, fish, shellfish; each one held territory, mated, ate, built, died, all that. Even in the bellies of the caves this was good to keep in mind, but it was difficult.

The canyon floor is a rumpus of white stones rounded by flash-floodwater, each one wearing the marks of its makers. Most look as if they were made of packed chalk marbles: the deposits of calcareous algae. Others show round starry shapes, like sections of bone: the remains of corals.

A coyote has left his dung on a stone, several times, as a marker. The dung is packed with green glittering insect wings, walnut hulls, bird feathers, seed hulls, rabbit hair. Sometimes his diet ran entirely to juniper berries.

A canyon wren hunts among the stones. A low pointed bird, very

small, with a needly working end, a gray head, white bib and belly, a rusty tail streaked with pen lines of black, very elegant. She flirts her tail, bows, peers under stones, goes under stones and out the other side, goes on peering into every crevice and shadow, flitting, hopping, vanishing and appearing again, making little rusty squeaks. She is flirty, but calm.

The canyon keeps its cool through midday, though bulges of heat press in from the whitening land with the desert smell of hot stone, a smell spiked with juniper and herb. I stand frozen in the stones watching the canyon wren with wholly attentive delight. She comes toward me and cocks her head; she thinks this is an odd species of tree; she pokes her bill busily under the treads of my boots.

Sunset and Moonrise in the Guadalupe Mountains

Perhaps in the end what we call knowledge is only a kind of ritual, and naming and numbering have the values of a chant. Certainly my notebook has filled with this; details of geology, maps of time, intricate charts and lists. Perhaps these are ways to know the reef-that-is-now-mountain, perhaps they are only the preparation for knowing. There are other ways of knowing, too. Maybe I am learning to trust them.

After all, *being* is only the present instant, and I have learned to know harmony when it is here.

PART TWO

Winter

10

local color

The Mojave Desert, California

Color can do this: shake you into the world, make you be born over. At sundown the whole sky is one enormous trampling of color. It's all done with mirrors, you say: this time you're right. Every mote of dust in the air reflects light like a mini-moon. Clouds are fabulous reflective canvases.

The whole atmosphere acts like a filter, removing some wavelengths gradually so that others stand revealed.

The desert is a simple space, like the sea, and can so easily be filled with light.

This is an explanation, but nothing is an explanation.

You will have to get away from people or at least away from anyone you feel you have to talk to.

You will have to get where there is nothing between you and the air. Away from buildings with their chatter and lights. Away from cars. This desert has no trees.

The horizons are clean-cut as if razor-carved.

Plural horizons. And the sun has just vanished over the last of them. Perhaps those last mountains are made of glass, of clean plate-glass slag. They are the color of a large breaking wave, the color of jade. The nearer mountain range is lapis blue. The nearest range is copper.

The round little hills close and underfoot are cinnamon brown, like toast, warm with the reflected heat of the sky.

The clumps of calico cactus look carefully set out by a gardener possessed of exquisite judgment. The yucca is an explosion of swords. Overhead is a rampage of crimson and smoke. The sky is clear turquoise at the horizon, veined with red-gold, a soft thick red-gold with the texture of clean wool.

So the heart catches fire and answers with colors of its own.

Afterward, the colors deepen. Night is made in the mountain roots and flows up out of the canyons and springs, but never quite overtakes the sky, which, as you know, is always luminous.

While the colors deepen you will walk back to your camp on Bureau of Land Management land out on a wide plain with as much sky over it as possible.

You are not alone here, because like any desert this one has its nomads. You have joined them. You are one of them.

Three days ago there was a man standing beside a desert track. He had white hair, a white beard, a white T-shirt, chinos so ancient they were more crooked than the legs they covered. He was leaning on a palm-wood staff. He beckoned. I stopped.

"Looking for a campsite, are ya? Come and jine up with us now. We've got the best now. Jine up with us. Won't cost a nickel."

He tipped me a wink and gestured with his staff and wagged his beard like the prophet Isaiah, and told me how to find a certain nomadic encampment known to its inhabitants as Rollins' Ranch.

"Name's Gordie!" he said. "See ya!" he said, and popped out of sight behind a bush and emerged astride a bright red three-wheeler going full tilt, walking stick tucked under his arm like a lance.

Rollins' Ranch is a cluster of maybe a dozen RVs parked among mesquites along a dry wash. If you approach in daylight you will notice that larger pebbles have been gathered and placed to mark the edges of driveways. Lines of pebbles do the work of picket fences, too, as well as curbs, marking off private yard space around each RV. Tarpaulins shade trios of folding chairs, the odd toy-colored motorized three-wheeler, a cooler or two; a bucket of plastic flowers on a square of bright green indoor-outdoor carpet does duty as a garden. Empty cans of Bud have been sliced and splayed cleverly to make garden whirligigs; a creosote bush has been decorated with Christmas tinsel and red glass balls. Empty milk cartons have been fashioned into birdfeeders. Flocks of house finches and white-crowned sparrows flip in and out and scratch underneath, as they do in any suburb. It doesn't matter that the feeders are disposable and the suburb temporary. By mid-April the nomads will be gone and all that will remain as a sign of twentieth-century humanity will be the lines of pebbles and a thread or two of tinsel.

This is Rollins' Ranch. The inhabitants are all retired. They all own homes somewhere; as far away as Minnesota or as close as Arizona. They spend the winters camped out here, together. They are part of the growing migratory legion of white-haired ex-north-erners who call themselves, aptly, snowbirds. The group at Rollins' Ranch has evolved over time, gathering itself around Chet and Allie Rollins from Boise, Idaho. When necessary, they help each other out. At night they have a campfire. They bring their folding chairs and sit around the fire, in the brazier smell of mesquite smoke, and talk about the corniest things imaginable.

They see the colors, too. They told me where to go to see them best, and left me to see them on my own. Sunrise and sunset — even as cold as it gets, now, with deep night frosts — there they are, rugs tucked around them, in their folding chairs outside their RVs, eyes on the sky. When the heart catches fire the dross is burned away. I believe this.

Gordie Gold, at eighty-seven, is the oldest member of the group. After his wife, Annie, died he kept on coming, and why not?

And why not, indeed? Why not?

Out here in the desert night the smell of creosote is clean and strong, tarry and medicinal, and the stars are sprayed across a grand unlimiting sky.

Kangaroo Rat and Night in the Mojave

Kangaroo rats are completely nocturnal. There are several species of them ranging from Idaho and Oregon to Colorado and south into Mexico. This is a Merriam's, a common kind in the Mojave and through all the "hot" deserts. At night they sometimes came into our camps. This one took bits of tortilla from our fingers and was fond of beans. It was gold and white, smaller than a chipmunk, and it popped in and out of the circle of firelight at our feet, zipping off to carry its prizes back to its burrow store.

Once the sun had set it became very cold; when you looked up there were the silhouettes of ocotillo, teddy-bear cholla, and creosote against the stars. You will have to imagine the stars and the tarry camphor smell of the creosote, the smell of desert night and desert rain.

11

after the flood

The Salton Sea, California

This is a funny story if you tell it right. It's a backward version of most modern tales of natural things, all of which tend to have the same plot in which Man figures as the villain. So, I want to tell a story about a flood in the desert.

When I first heard this story I was reminded of that biblical flood in which Yahweh erased villainous folk by means of too much water. Too much, ironically, of a good thing. Closer to home, the Tohono O'odham Indians of Arizona and Sonora (their name means People of the Desert) had a similar figure in the hero I'itoi, who survived a morally cleansing deluge to be a father to his people. Perhaps it was the same deluge.

It's what came afterward, after the flood, that interests me. You have this virgin landscape. Muddy, true; but empty. Desert. Uninhabited. What can happen? If you let loose the animals two by two into this *tabula rasa* what will happen?

The flood that came to southern California was recent and relatively small. The causes of the thing were familiar human frailties: greed, short-sightedness, ignorance, and the like, along with bad luck, and the result fell short of disaster; we weren't drowned for our sins, we were made to look like fools. Afterward, some interesting things happened.

A bit of history: in the 1870s and 1880s the Southern Pacific Railroad built its southern route through the part of California that lies

just north of Mexico. Between the Chocolate Mountains bordering
the Colorado River and the buttresses of the coast ranges, the railroad
crossed a broad low salty basin. Exceedingly dry, with less than three
inches of rainfall per year, horrifically hot in summer, lying as much
as two hundred and seventy-three feet below sea level, it was known
as the Salton Sink. A tiny saltmarsh at its navel was all that remained
of what had been (a dozen thousand years ago, no more) a modest
inland sea. This sea had lain in the arms of the rift that is slowly
tearing this western piece of continent; the San Andreas fault runs
through the Salton Sink and is one reason for its low-lying nature.
In its day, the inland sea, called Lake Cahuilla by geologists, had
been surrounded by rustling forests of desert fan palms. It makes a
pretty picture.

The pretty picture dried up along with everything else as the glaciers and their bordering jet streams retreated northward, and by the
time the Southern Pacific Railroad brought its first dusty hopeful
settlers into the Salton Sink, nothing was left except that little marsh.

What to do with this overhot, rainless, and enormous basin?
Someone started a salt mine in the sink in 1882, but that was small
potatoes, and in 1896 some aggressive development muscle focused
on the real possibilities of the place. In that year, the California Development Company was organized to finance and control the construction of irrigation canals from the Colorado River to . . . well. You
can't really call the place the Salton Sink anymore now, can you?
Need a name with a ring to it. Something with size and, and . . .
what's that? Aha! Yes. We'll call it the Imperial Valley.

By 1904 there were seven hundred miles of canals in the Imperial
Valley and seventy-seven thousand acres under intense cultivation,
and twelve thousand people settled in the place, when some unruly
silt from upstream happened to block the headgate of the main irrigation canal. There was, suddenly, no water at all. It was 108 degrees
in the shade of wilting date palms, orange trees, cotton fields, grape-
vines. Twelve thousand people screamed bloody murder and the
California Development Company dredged a temporary bypass
channel, and, lo, there was water again in all the miles of canals and
acres of Imperial earth, and while the company pundits were mop-
ping their brows and telling their engineers that, yes, get the headgate

fixed folks but no hurry now, it rained in the San Juan Mountains of Colorado. Then it rained again, and then it rained more.

So the river rose. And as the river rose, more and more water poured into that temporary irrigation channel. And the channel widened. And pretty soon the whole Colorado River up and headed west and spilled down into the Salton Sink cum Imperial Valley, and there it was. The flood.

Farms, railroad tracks, saltworks, and towns were under water. The powers that were in Mexico were hopping mad, the Norteamericanos had stolen the Río Colorado; the only thing that ran into the Gulf of California was a river of sand.

The sink is an enclosed basin. With the whole Colorado River pouring in, it began to fill up right away and kept on filling up. Once decided on a course of action a major river is no easy thing to turn aside. The Colorado River ran into the Salton Sink for *three years.*

By the time the Southern Pacific Railroad had spanned the flow with trestles and dumped eighty thousand tons of rock and debris into the gap, and the water consented to travel on down across the international border again, it was February of 1907.

Where the old palm-ringed sea had lain in the time of the glaciers and the mastodons lay a new and glittering sea. It was forty-five miles long, seventeen miles wide, and was eighty-five feet deep at its deepest point. It was named the Salton Sea. There it lies to this day.

Since the flood, this sea has been discovered and colonized by a peculiar patchwork of creatures. It has the feel of creation half finished, of something new and wonderful under the broiling sun; chance and opportunity beckon, it's a world in the raw, ripe for exploitation.

It's full of fish, for starters. Mosquito fish and the mollies familiar to tropical aquarium aficionados patrol the shallows along with squads of native desert pupfish. Longjaw mudsuckers from the San Diego area and threadfin shad from the South Atlantic states breed in astounding numbers, along with sargo from Mexico and tilapia from Mozambique. There are orangemouth corvina that hail from the Gulf of California, and these have been known to grow to a bigger gamefish in the Salton Sea — to well over thirty pounds —

than has ever been seen in their native waters. In the early forties
someone introduced the humble barnacle, probably by mistake, and
the bars and beaches of the sea are made almost entirely of the shells
of barnacles, shells that are uniquely large and pink.

Aside from the barnacles, the most visible pioneers are birds. Unlike the fish, all these birds discovered the place on their own. Mind
you, this is near the southern terminus of the Pacific flyway, so it's
on an avian route to begin with. In season, sandhill cranes and dunlins
fly down from Alaska; common terns and snow geese come from
the Arctic coasts of the Northwest Territories; canvasbacks and pintails fly in from the East; wood storks, magnificent frigate birds, and
blue-footed boobies come up from the Gulf of California. This is a
sampling. More than three hundred and seventy-five species of birds
have been sighted in and around the Salton Sea. Between November
and February this is the winter home for as many as thirty thousand
geese and sixty thousand ducks. Most of the winter goose pasture
consists of alfalfa, sudan grass, and winter wheat and rye; the farm
fields of the Imperial Valley.

North and south of the sea are four hundred and seventy-five
thousand acres of agricultural land made possible by a Colorado
River tamed, shunted, respectfully controlled; the Imperial Valley to
the south and the Coachella Valley to the north. In the winter one
can sit on the shelly beach looking over a bogus sea in a bogus
landscape — there are rustling date palms planted in rows, the species
imported from Arabia — and the whole gleaming surface of the
water is sprinkled with birds. There are thousands of eared grebes,
with fluffed tails and red eyes. Each one dives down with a curl like
a folding wave.

Before the Gadsden Purchase made it part of the United States,
and this officially became the Salton Sink, the Mexicans had named
this part of their desert La Palma de la Mano de Dios, the Palm of
the Hand of God. Now it's filled with the lap of wavelets, the *keeek
keeek* of black-necked stilts, the *kwaaawks* of ring-billed gulls, the
peepings of killdeer, the throaty *kitikee* of willets. This is the sound
of the industrious adaptability of fish, bird, man, and barnacle, proof
positive of the shifts and quick turns, disasters and victories, the
everlasting neverthesametwice Glory of the Flood. Amen.

January Spring
Birdcage evening primrose in the Algodones Dunes, between
the Salton Sea and the Chocolate Mountains

12

wild palms

Anza-Borrego Desert State Park, California

The coast ranges are the wall at which the desert ends. Here east of them the land is dry as bone, cold in the winter nights and as majestically empty as a country scraped by ice. This lowland desert of southern California is the home of the wild desert fan palm, but you could pass through here a hundred times without seeing one. They have something of the elusiveness, rarity, and power of big game.

The great bordering faults — the San Andreas, the San Jacinto — have cracked the continent through here as if it were a vase, shattering the rock roofs of aquifers, so that water pricks up here and there along the fault lines, coming up cool and glass-clear or hot and salty; in any case coming up.

Wherever water springs to the surface there are wild palms. Suddenly in the corner of a canyon, in a crevice, a hollow of the broken wilderness of rock there is a clutch of thick columns of trunks leaning this way and that as if they were so many birds in a nest, with lively puffs of scissored green at their tops. These are very big trees, and the basket-colored petticoats of old fronds trail sometimes to the ground, making each one house-sized in girth. These are the only palms that keep their dead fronds all their lives. Unless the cylinders of thatch are burned or cut away they are prime habitat for king snakes and lizards and western yellow bats and countless insects, and every oasis is announced at a distance by the cooing of doves, and in some places by a tweetling chatter of house finches or orioles, as loud and contained a noise as if it were an aviary.

There are one hundred and fifty-one known oases of desert fan palms in the world, most of them in California, with a scattered few in Arizona and southern Nevada, and more in Mexico. In the Mexican oases the desert fans are mixed with sky dusters, Mexican blues, even with wild dates, but somehow one does expect palms to be there, the arcing fronds and their tropical rattling, part of a lush more equatorial place.

The real home of the desert fan palm is this so-called Colorado desert that lies between the river of that name and these coast ranges, south of the Mojave. Most of this country gets less than three inches of rain a year and daytime temperatures run well above 100 degrees from May through October. It's the hottest and lowest extreme of Sonoran desert. For miles on end the whole vegetation seems to consist of bush-sized puffs of gray dust in the runnels of eroded hills.

In one deeper canyon under the coast ranges, some of these puffs, tangles of chuparosa, come into red tubular bloom now in midwinter, and these are a favorite of the Anna's hummingbirds that scoot and thrum and hover through the dry watercourses. There are thickets of cheesebush and clumps of ocotillo and desert lavender. As one moves up-canyon, catclaw and honey mesquite appear in the wash; these thorny (and now in winter leafless) shrubs have taproots that can reach a water table more than a hundred and seventy feet away, but they do not grow to tree size without a water table there.

Among the stones of the slopes are scattered creosote and bursage shrubs and the odd cholla and barrel cactus. The first two shed leaves and even branches in dry times, the second two store water in waxy and thorn-protected stems. The parsimonious exigencies of desert life; spiny, sticky with resin; the passivity of the things gets on my nerves. They're desert nerves, don't tell me, I know, it's the light that does it, the eyes get gritty and the skin goes stiff as paper, even patience loses its resilience. The cacti are paler than stones. I want to kick one, out of spite.

After all this stubborn vegetation and broken rock, shimmering air, too much brightness everywhere, the first palm comes as a shock to the senses. It is square in the canyon bottom; a burst of green accordion-pleated leaves reflecting sunlight like a fractured mirror, leaf edges frilled with curling fibers. Then there are more, tall ones with spiky bursts of rush around their bases, then more, and a noise of trickling, black pools, a waterfall, a patch of cattails, a thicket of young palms as dense as grass. And *shade. Deep shade.* And a smell of earth and water. And the clean basket smell of the dry fronds, and a rattling and rustling and liveliness, a ponderous overhead swaying of green heads.

Fan palms are rooted with a shallow fibrous ball; they have no taproot, nor do they have any means of water storage in swollen root or stem; they do not shed leaves in a drought; they open flowers and set fruit in the hottest months of the year. They do not seem to be desert plants at all. They need their feet wet. They are relics of a California of two to twenty-two million years ago, before the coast ranges rose (as they're still doing, now, in tectonic agonies) to wring the moisture from Pacific storms. They surrounded lakes, marshes, river courses, inland seas. They have retreated, as moisture has. They survive in the wild now by having the audacity to stand in any available water source and shade out or shrug off everything else.

They are stout and long-lived. They can grow as much as seventy-five feet high and some of them have trunks more than three feet in diameter. A prime tree in a good year can yield over four hundred pounds of fruit. The fruit has a large stone in the middle, something like a date; it's round and black and sticky when fresh in the fall though it wrinkles like a raisin as it hangs and dries. The Cahuilla Indians here once stored these fruits and ate them by grinding the whole thing to mush. The coyotes eat the palm fruits still, shitting out the hard indigestible seed, which then has a far better chance of sprouting: an interdependence — or anyway an inter-good — of animal and palm that's well established here, though coyotes, of course, will eat anything.

The Cahuilla Indians and the desert fan palms go back together, no one knows how far. Three quarters of known palm oases have the evidence: rock art and stone circles, rock shelters with sooty ceilings, patches of blackened soil, flakes of stone tools, and every-where the round bedrock mortars made by and for the grinding of palm fruit. When the Spaniards first came through here on the way to the missions on the coast, most palm oases had permanent Cahuilla villages nearby. Walls and roofs of houses were thatched with fronds, palm leaves and fibers were used to make sandals and baskets, the long palm fruiting stems were made into spoons, shovels, walking sticks, fire-starting tools.

Fire. This was the language of their relationship. Fire connected people and palm. Those thatch petticoats will burn hotter and faster than paper. Once lit, the whole palm flares like a torch and subsides to a black and smoking stump. Then green fronds grow back. With water-carrying tissues scattered in bundles throughout their trunks, palms are resistant to fire. Not so the other desert plants that like to find rootholds in oases; mesquites and catclaws and other desert shrubs are killed (or pruned to the ground) by fire, and flames consume the trash of fallen stalks and fronds, all of which makes walking through the palms (and gathering of fallen fruits) difficult, even abusive. Palm stalks are curved in such a way that stepping on one end brings the other end up quickly into one's nose. Rattlesnakes like to hide in the trash, too. And fire kills some of the giant palm boring beetles that feed in and weaken the trees, and a number of other insects as well. In the year after a fire, palms show their appreciation by nearly doubling their yield of fruit, because of nutrients released into the soil or because of decreased competition for water. Whatever the reason, for the Cahuilla and for the palms, fire worked for them both.

Nowadays, horticulture has replaced fire as the language that people use, the medium of the relationship. Desert fan palms are amenable as well as big and handsome; nowadays they grace garden spots and avenues from Hollywood to Vegas to the resorts of the Caribbean and the cities of Africa. They are maintained by the fake oases of sprinkler systems. Whenever I see them there (they're hard to miss) in the self-conscious tropic landscape of a Palm Court Motel, for instance, gracing the general gracelessness of city streets with their birdlike leaning, as if they were sentient, lending an ear to us mortals below, it's like seeing contented lions in a zoo.

If you take the time to stalk them into the broken hills, you can see them wild. That is something else.

Wild Palms

There are two palm oases here, both in the Tierra Blanca Mountains in Anza-Borrego Desert State Park in southern California. They are really more than a mile apart. To give a sense of scale, there is a self-portrait in the lower left.

13

honey, juice, badlands

Anza-Borrego Desert State Park, California

The Tierra Blanca Mountains in the foothill country of the coast ranges are made of crumbling white granite. If you should ever doubt the extremes of temperature here, note that the rocks are peeling away in layers like giant onions shattered by shotgun blasts. This whole landscape is made of broiled and busted stone.

Below the last slopes a white gravel plain is inhabited by lumpish shapes of cholla, lace bushes of creosote, and bunches of gray sticks. It is not a comfortable landscape. It is strangely arresting, like a kind of art form: Strange Shapes on White. The white ground is pocked, as all desert landscapes seem to be, by varmint holes.

In the distance there are mountains with badlands harsh around their knees. The world ends in mountains everywhere; the low mounds of the Fish Creeks, the Vallecitos to the west, the Coyote peaks to the east, but the foreground is badlands: meaning that it is country eroding so fast that nothing much gets a foothold, that it is so hard to travel in that hardly anyone tries.

In the pale stone, the spareness of event means that each event is magnified. *Event* being all and anything to do with life.

At dusk a coyote crosses just below camp. He is slim, pale, with a dark tail tip, his pelt more gold than gray. His pace is an even trot. He stops now and then to look, listen, breathe. Then he goes on with his light gliding trot. The varmint holes are (or were or will be) home to mostly rodent but sometimes reptile coyote food that can be had, perhaps, by diligent patrol. The next night the coyote comes through camp again at the same time in the same way. The impression he leaves is of lean body, thin nose, scant pelt, long legs fine and fragile as porcelain sticks, eyes almost white.

Canyon Sin Nombre leads into the badlands. The name means canyon without name, a kind of joke. This canyon is steep-walled and flat-floored and, at first, nothing much grows on its alluvial floor except for neatly spaced groves of smoke trees. These trees are cloudy in form and their twig ends dissipate into the air. Like the paloverdes of the uplands they have no leaves to evaporate quantities of water, the twigs and branches are where photosynthesis goes on, and each twig ends in a thornlike point. As protection against ferocity of light the whole tree is a waxy reflective gray-green; in different lights it turns into a cloud of silver or gold.

On the flanks of the dry watercourse there is an odd catclaw acacia, leafless and black. These trees stand out against the pale gravels and in their naked state you can't miss this: they are infested with desert mistletoe.

Desert mistletoe is related to the kind that grows on live oaks or junipers, the familiar mistletoe with green spoonlike leaves and white berries sold for Christmas decor, but the desert kind is functionally leafless and its berries are red. It is a parasite of ironwoods, acacias, mesquites, paloverdes.

The smallest mistletoe clumps look like a posy of dark sticks. Something wrong, one thinks; no tree would grow that way. Larger ones look like heaps of twiggy trash or collapsing nests. Sometimes trees are so weighted by these clumps that their branches have broken.

Red berries decorate this mistletoe from November through April. If you squish one in your fingers you find out that the juice (they are full of juice) is as sticky as hide glue.

A number of birds eat these berries — mockingbirds pluck them, Gambel's quail scratch for them under the trees — but one bird, the phainopepla, depends on them for food and water all winter long. A phainopepla looks like a cardinal except that the males are glossy obsidian black and the females are the color of gray flannel. Their eyes are as red as the mistletoe berries. Wherever you find desert mistletoe you'll find one of these birds in the top of an infested tree, keeping watch over his or her resource. Their song is a sorrowful rising whistle: *Whoooeep . . . whoooeeep . . .* , and when they fly from tree to tree they flash white panels of wing feathers. One year, when an early frost killed most of the crop of mistletoe berries, phainopeplas died by the thousands.

Mistletoe seeds come out the far ends of phainopeplas nearly as sticky and red as they went in. Since the birds spend most of their time sitting up in trees, many of these seeds land and stick on branches where they can sprout and burrow into their host.

There is this neat symbiosis of mistletoe and phainopepla, with the tree in question pumping the water up from a deep aquifer and providing the physical support. To come on this arrangement, entire, complete, self-contained, tree and mistletoe and bird, in the middle of a badlands wash in January, is to see one piece of life cut out clean and simple. At first. And then . . . just when you think you've got it neatly figured out there is . . . the unexpected. What's this? . . . a thick sweet lovely smell in the air! . . . and you follow your nose . . . to the mistletoe. It is in bloom. The flowers are flecks of yellow, the wash smells like a May morning in an apple orchard, the collapsed-nest clumps are being rummaged by thousands of ecstatic bees.

Here it is: Sensuality on White. Cloud of scent, hot buzzing and cool song, yellow bees and ebony bird and red berries, and the winter sun warm on your head.

Desert Mistletoe
With mesquite tree, male phainopepla, and bees

14

elephant tree

Anza-Borrego Desert State Park, California

I've heard of them and I've read about them plenty, but I've never seen one. I wake in the dark with my sleeping bag hauled over my head until there's only just a hole for me to breathe, I'm practiced at this, the desert winter nights are long, quiet, and cold. Too long, too cold. There is despair in my heart; the only thing I can think of that might soften the edge of misery is hot *El Pico Café* brewed to espresso strength in my little pot, but that means climbing out of bag and into starry chill of predawn. It means the beginning of the last day I've allowed myself to hunt for the elephant tree.

The elephant tree belongs to a small, eccentric, tropical family of plants. It grows farther north than any of its relatives — into "isolated desert mountains in southernmost California and southwestern Arizona," says one field guide — but "only in places where there is never any frost." In short: it's reclusive, beautiful, and big. I've looked, all right, but I haven't found. The elephant tree has taken on the status of a grail.

To make it harder on myself I've refused the easy way out: a trail by a road with a signpost that says "Elephant Tree Discovery Trail," with a parking lot next to the sign and dune buggies parked in the lot. I wince at my snobberies but I want to find the thing myself. I don't want an elephant in a zoo. So I'm camped by a canyon that, according to fine print in an old Anza-Borrego publication, "is home to a few isolated individual elephant trees, relics of bygone times."

Relic meaning a living thing, or an isolated population of living things, pinched off from the main body of its kind by some anarchy of climatic change.

This suits me fine. The coffee pot burbles and sighs and while the grounds settle I hold my tin mug expectantly in gloved hands, and the eastern sky goes rose over the white plain. A last holdout star glitters over mountains.

A desert dawn is beautiful beyond description. And it is brief. And while it is achingly brief and beautiful beyond capture I want desperately to see just *see* the whole of the rosy, purpled, gilded landscape in a single glance, but this is impossible. Dawn, in short, is orgasmic. Afterward the sun comes up. I pour myself a second mug.

There's something in this, this search, that goes beyond mere naturalist's curiosity. There are more important things in this land-scape. There are plenty of living things that have a greater impact. There are issues — like dune buggies, or threatened and endangered species, or sinking water tables, or arroyo cutting (caused by paving over, or overgrazing, or agriculture, or dune buggies, or other habi-tat changes, such as climate) — and these affect water tables; and there's an endless rich trove of Native American lore and history; and wonderful trivia to do with gold rushes and the desert expeditions of Juan Bautista de Anza in 1774 and 1775–76; and dozens of bizarre and wonderful plant and animal adaptations to desert life; but the elephant tree has become an obsession.

I've come to realize that one's inner life cannot be separated from the outer one. Whatever road the spirit travels is reflected in the outward journey. Only by traveling honestly — not where we think we should go but where we *know* we should go — do we get some-place.

Where? Who knows, the trail beckons. Fold the map to its appro-priate square and put it in its Ziploc bag and put that in the pack, full canteen, granola bars, jerky, dried fruit, camera, notebook, two pens, extra film, binoculars, leave out the field guides — too heavy and besides field sketches sharpen the eye — first-aid and snakebite kits . . . check. Check. Hat, shades, zip the tent, we're off, the sun is on the peaks, the white fan of alluvium guides me up into heaps and scarps of broken rock.

White, white land. There are palm oases up this trail, too. Meanwhile only stones, and in the stones the scattered tortured shapes of
desert plants. They are separate, like wildly expressive sculptures in
a museum. They are not like plants; they are like beings dredged
from a dark subconscious. The leafless ocotillo is bunches of thorn
rods. The chollas throw many-armed punches in their beige nets of
spines. The khaki lace of the creosote bushes filters the light and
gives back a scent composed of more than forty-five kinds of volatile
oils. The burrobush, the brittlebush, the blackbrush, are variations
on textures of gray. The barrel cactus leans like a demon.

   Then in the first small palm oasis, something strange is going on.

Two people are there. One is a thin very young blonde wearing a
great deal of makeup and a not much of a bikini. She is huddling on
a rock in a bright red and silver ski parka and the rest of her is
covered in goosebumps. Her makeup apparatus is spread out on a
stone: black and gold and aqua and pink and tangerine. The other
person is a portly balding photographer who is struggling with a
tripod. The rest of his apparatus is spread out on another stone. I
pause long enough to find out that these people left L. A. at two A.M.
so the light would be right to shoot a scene of paradisiacal near-nudity
in order for someone to sell swimsuits to somebody else. As I go on,
the girl gives me an embarrassed tangerine smile. The photographer
grunts. The palms lean with their green crests scissoring the sun and
their great frond skirts trailing in white sand and stones, but it is
January, and two unhappy people are waiting for the goosebumps
to go away.

   I like it that the desert is full of strange things. If there is one
phrase that sums up life in the desert, it is: the predictability of the
bizarre.

   So I follow a wash. The wash is narrow between rotting granite
hills. A mile on in the wash, saltgrass, telltale growth of alkaline
seeps. Beyond, a small amphitheater filled with a semicircle of palms,
clumps of rush, the ground whitened with a crust of salts. And
on the hills around, nothing but burst pale stone. I walk and look
everywhere, moving on slowly and quietly as if what I wanted could
run away.

   Then high on a crest of broken rock there it suddenly is — there it is, suddenly for me, though it's been here quietly, sturdily, for centuries maybe — one wide and golden tree. There she is, she is here, marvel of marvels after all, more huge and magnificent than I ever imagined, perched on the dry and crumbling scarp. Fat limbs clad in brassy satiny bark roll snaking out of a swollen trunk the size of a barrel. Twigs hold up a nimbus of green. The Elephant Tree. Old, huge, in healthy golden prime, swollen with water, hung with berry-sized fruit. On one low branch is a single white-winged dove, singing.

Elephant Tree

The dove has just flown away and is sitting in an ocotillo, with its mate, off to the right.

15

tortoise, tortoise

Colorado and Sonoran Deserts,
California and Arizona

Desert tortoises live in burrows, and each dark entrance has a near-Gothic arch like the shape of its maker. Between February and April — depending on local climate, but when the desert is least like a desert — the tortoises come out to graze on flowers: the purple phacelias and orange mallows, apple-green cactus shoots, white forget-me-nots, pink gilias, and so on, some of them perennials but most of them annuals, the growth that appears almost overnight with the chancy falls of winter rain. In the northern parts of their range their diet tends more toward grass, but in any case what they eat is soft, succulent, temporary, and in some years nonexistent.

In the heat of midsummer they return to their burrows until the monsoon brings a new crop of annuals into bloom. They go back to earth to hibernate in September or October. During the few months that food may be available everything of importance to tortoises has to be done: traveling, mating, digging burrows, laying eggs, hatching, growing, fattening for the winter and summer fasts. Because of this, the tortoise's whole life is an exercise in stubbornness.

A male tortoise matures roughly at the age we do, somewhere between fifteen and twenty, at which time he becomes irritable and aggressive. He rushes at other males, ramming them with his gular "horn," the bifurcated ridge that projects from his lower shell. The gular horn is like the medieval lance or battering ram, or the modern hockey stick, or — given the solidity of the carapace and the verve of its inhabitant — the bumper car. The loser of this duel retires to his shell with a clunk (a submissive signal known in the behavioral lexicon as "shell drop") or in more dignified style walks off or, often, gets tipped over. It takes a tipped tortoise some time to right himself. By then who knows where the winner's got to or what he's managed to do?

Slow by nature, a tortoise has a savvy, cautious bag-lady look from the moment it hatches from the egg. It isn't (or wasn't) uncommon for a desert tortoise to live for seventy or eighty years, and some may live more than a hundred and even as much as a hundred and fifty. In any case their feet are as thick as an elephant's and their skin is wrinkled and their mouths toothless — the turtle clan has been toothless for the last one hundred and fifty million years — and their shells may bump on rocks as they haul them along, but the desert tortoise is nobody's fool.

They have rules and manners to regulate life among themselves, just as we do. When one tortoise meets another they bob their heads up and down in a ritual nodding as stereotyped as our bowing or handshaking; a means of subverting aggression and of sussing out the vigor (or limpness) of an opponent or partner. An open-mouthed gape is a threat signal used by one male to another in the lists of battle or by a female defending her nest, or by a male announcing the force of his lust to his intended ladylove. Such a "courting" male may try to bite and ram a female into sexual submission, and may succeed — his goal is simply to get her to stand still — but females have been known to initiate courtship, too, and to do some hearty ramming of their own, forcing unwanted males to go away and leave them be.

When mating does take place it is by all reports distressing to watch. The male mounts the female from behind; with his forelegs propped on her shell he thrusts away, eyes half closed, making those moans and gusty sighs we thought were unique to our own love affairs.

Afterward, the female digs her nest in sandy soil, using her hind legs to dig the nest, arrange the eggs, and cover them up. She may make three nests of up to five eggs in a season, the season for feeding, mating, and egg laying running from late May through July. The eggs will hatch maybe a hundred days after they are laid, depending on temperature, and when the hatchlings emerge they have no bony support for their fingernail-thin shells; they are some two inches wide and flattish, roughly the size, shape, and texture of chocolate chip cookies. Numbers of young tortoises are eaten every year by coyotes, skunks, ravens, hawks, bobcats, and foxes. Especially by ravens.

By the time they are five to seven years old the flexible shell has gained underlying bone and has hardened and has grown to be some four inches long, half the length of an adult's. A five-year-old tortoise is no longer an easy snack; though eagles may take some, this is a resident animal that knows its way around. The savvy look goes more than skin-deep.

In the heat of midsummer and again during the cold months of winter, desert tortoises live in their burrows, which are deep enough so that the temperature and humidity down there are stable, comfortable, and safe. These burrows may be anywhere from ten to thirty feet in length and may have side chambers and branches; a clan of tortoises may use a common burrow and other creatures use these shelters, too. Insects and spiders, lizards, geckos, rattlesnakes, burrowing owls, packrats, roadrunners, quail, kangaroo rats, mice, even cottontail rabbits, have all been found sharing the tortoise's retreats.

Like us, a desert tortoise becomes more influential as it matures past middle age. Older larger females lay more eggs, older heavier males win more mating duels and subdue more females than their lighter-weight competitors. Besides, the old gents know from years of experience exactly where the females' burrows are and will lie in wait there, with single-minded devotion to their cause.

Most older animals have lived through several bitter droughts even before they're mature, and greater size does help an animal through lean times. A tortoise will eat to obesity if it can, becoming so pudgy that it can't retreat anymore inside its own shell, and this saving up has survival value in the desert where drought years are as much the rule as the exception. Most of the tortoises' water is absorbed from their food, and when this is low they can reabsorb water from their bladders, excreting their urine as a semisolid. When the salt buildup in their blood becomes too high they will go to earth until it rains. They have an uncanny ability to tell when it will rain. They'll come out then and stand by an empty tinaja — a natural stone tank or catchment basin — and wait for the rain to come and fill it up. Before there's a cloud in the sky, mind you. And when the tinaja does fill they will drink and pee at the same time, rehydrating themselves and ridding themselves of excess salts all in a rush. Once tanked up they'll go back to the business of eating well.

The tortoise's gradual nature makes it a kind of animal version of a tree; or — here — a desert shrub or cactus, since most of these are drought-resistant, too, and long-lived, low-profiled, durable in an environment of temperature extremes and water and food scarcity. Treelike, tortoise reproduction tends to be a year offset from climate; the year after a rainy year is when most tortoise eggs are laid, the year after a drought year is reproductively lean; the lag time here is part of the unhurried way in which a tortoise, physically, works.

In general, a tortoise's life is long and its reproductive rate is slow. This is a conservative style, a life of gradually maturing investment. The home base, the burrow, is built at some cost, lasts years, is as vital to survival as our own houses are. Smaller shallower burrows for a noon or night snooze may be built as "camps" nearby. The home range around this base is perhaps fifty yards in diameter for a youngster and as much as a square mile for a patriarch. Some males in courting trim may cover more than half a mile in a day, though a quarter mile of daily travel is more common. Either way, an animal will know its range. It will know exactly where to go for good cover and good feed, mineral licks, the tinajas where water pools after a rain. The movements and status of the neighbors can be read in the scent of their trails or feces, and the odor of threat and command is clear in the urine of the locally dominant male, an idiom understood by all. Neighbors are nodding aquaintances if not old mates or old bugaboos with whom bashing battles have been held often enough to consider them intimate enemies, undangerous because well known.

What is dangerous to tortoises is any disturbance to this status quo, "disturbance" being just those things that people seem most prone — out of ignorant self-interest — to do.

People pick up tortoises and take them home. After a while these captives are neglected to death, or they escape (or are loosed) into yards or parks where the food or climate is likely to be wrong, and where if they do survive they're doomed to live without mates and without community. People also let pet-shop tortoises loose in the desert under the illusion that they are giving the gift of freedom, though often enough the pet-shop critter suffers and dies of starvation or cold (or heat) but only after giving the local animals some exotic disease to which they have no resistance. Thousands of wild tortoises are now infected with an illness that is more than snotty noses and general depression; this one is as deadly as a killer strain of flu. Another plague of pet origin has infected the tortoises' shells. The result of these epidemics is that hundreds of square miles of prime tortoise range are filled with ill and dying animals.

One can plead ignorance for this state of affairs, but not for other things. Game wardens anywhere know about "plinkers" — those gun-toting folks, mostly urban, young, and male, who will shoot at anything that moves. In the deserts, urban centers are growing. Plinkers are legion. So is the evidence: tortoise shells that have been shattered by bullets. In some places these are easier to find than used burrows, or worn paths, or the tramped circles where a pair of animals has mated, or any other sign of tortoise life.

In other places, livestock has crushed desert shrubs and introduced weeds, and as a result, much country that was once desert scrub is now a kind of weedy waste. Fires sweep through the dry stems of this waste, destroying native plants, since desert species have no tolerance for fire. Whether tortoises can adapt to this change in cover and food no one is sure.

Then there is development — agricultural, urban, mineral, energy, anything — which generally means the un-development of tortoise habitat. Roads bring in the collectors and plinkers, and the off-road vehicles that are quick death to all creatures not quick of foot, as well as plain old cars, and tortoises are plain slow in crossing roads, and there you are.

If one looks hard enough in the right places and at the right times the tortoises can still be found, and unlike most beasts they do not mind being watched so long as you mind your distance; tortoise wisdom says (erroneously) that once they're grown they have no enemies. There are several subspecies of them, populations separated ages ago by barriers such as the Colorado or the Yaqui River, and one or another of these tortoise varieties can be found in the desert valleys (bajadas, really; in the basins rather than the ranges) from southern Nevada and Utah into western Arizona, and through the deserts of California down into northwestern Mexico.

Sixty or even forty years ago there were parts of this country where there were as many as two thousand tortoises per square mile. You could find twenty or thirty in a half-hour walk. You might see more than a hundred in one place at one time, at a mineral lick, or on the path to a spring. Nowadays you will have to walk all day, in the same places, to see two or three.

It's the kind of desert anyway that you wouldn't think was worth much. Scrub, mostly. Creosote and burrobush, maybe some Joshua trees up in the Mojave and scattered chollas and prickly pears; the kind of place that has no sign of life except for varmint holes and a few chuckwallas in the rocks and some coyote tracks in the wash. Most of this kind of country is covered with gravel and rock and sand, exactly the bare ground that gets blanketed by flowers in certain seasons.

Whatever the reasons are for the desert tortoise's decline, it is now officially an endangered species, a flagship for the preservation of scrub desert, a rallying cry, the object of much research, a hot emotional touchstone, another flare gone up out of a crumpling relationship — modern man to desert — that doesn't always seem to work too well.

More to the point, it would be good to know why we cause most havoc with creatures most like ourselves, the largest predators and the most long-lived and social of beasts: the lions and wolves, gorillas and whales and elephants, and tortoises, too.

Desert Tortoise and Spring Wildflowers

16

cattleman and mesquite

Green Valley, Arizona

He is a strong square man bristling with wariness. He is so wary that his face hardly moves at first and he doesn't meet my eyes.

William A. (Bill) McGibbon is the president of Santa Rita Ranch, Inc., a business not inherited but grown by him from grassroots. It's a family-run outfit that employs and feeds five families. He hires the odd cowboy or two or three at roundup time, though the roundup hands no longer sneak up the mountain ranges from Mexico, as they did in the old days, appearing ragged but ready at the door, superb horsemen with a cattle sense that no Anglo seems to have.

Bill is also the president of the Arizona Cattle Growers' Association, so he's spokesman for an industry and for a relationship — cattle to man to arid ground — that goes back to the neolithic revolution in general and to the seventeenth century in Arizona, in particular.

These are some of the points he makes within the first five minutes:

Ninety percent of the people in Arizona now live in the Tucson and Phoenix metropolitan areas.

(Note: other desert states — Nevada, Utah, Texas, New Mexico — are also top-heavy in outsider/metropolitan folk. These desert states all have nearly 90 percent of their population in urban centers, more than twice the percentage that other states have, and there's a good reason for this: desert cities are oases. They are not the desert.)

Four-fifths of the people who live in Arizona are "from away" and have no experience or knowledge of ranching. Ranching (as Bill makes clear) is this: food and fiber production in the southwestern desert environment. Most people's view of cowboy life is unadulterated Hollywood: anachronistic, in other words. Unimportant in the here and now.

Ranchers are on their own. There are no government subsidies for the beef cattle industry, no support prices set, no artificial market manipulators.

The rural economy is fragile. A drought, a drop in livestock prices, the closure of a local timber industry, can dry it up for good.

The rural part of the state is being raped for the benefit of urbanites.

Water supplies once used for cattle, sheep, orchards, groves, fields, are now funneled to recreation areas and high-priority urban demands.

There's plenty of evidence of these demographics around, Bill makes clear, though he's still hardly moved; and I realize he's less wary of me than he is in earnest, slapping facts down like cards on a table. These are the facts. After holiday weekends, trash is scattered on the range, fences have been cut to let in off-road vehicles, people have gone swimming in waterholes and have left the water running in water tanks, materials left out to build things (timber, wire, cement) have been stolen, mesquite corrals have been taken apart and trucked off for firewood or charcoal.

Then there's sabotage.

Windmills have their bolts loosened just enough so that when the wind blows they'll self-destruct. Cattle guards are pried out of their foundations. Cement is poured down wells to give the pump a fatal case of congestive heart failure. Fences are systematically wrecked, the wires cut between every other post for miles.

There is a small, vociferous group of people who want cattle off all public land.

There are vast quantities of people who don't care.

He stops. Pauses. He's finished his litany — the list of angry truths delivered in a soft voice — and he looks me square in the face.

I've heard the like of this before. It reminds me of something else. It's a status report of sorts, and it reminds me — the fragility of a system, the thoughtlessness and ignorance of the urban majority — cattle ranching in Arizona reminds me of an endangered species.

Bill McGibbon raises Hereford and Barzona cattle and ranch horses on one hundred sections of desert grassland in the Santa Rita foothills. In a normal year there may be eight to nine hundred mother cows, in drought years less; in some dry years they've run as low as six hundred head. The bulls go out from March 1 to October 1; 75 to 80 percent of the calves are on the ground by the end of February and are weaned by October, coming off the range weighing four hundred and fifty to six hundred pounds apiece. With the demand for leaner beef the steers and low-end heifers go into feedlots better grown than they once did, with more time spent on the range before they do go, and then they have more bone and size on them than was usual only a decade ago; they stay in the feedlot only long enough for a grain diet to give the meat good "finish."

This range alone produces enough cattle per year to fill the needs of five to six thousand people. As Bill points out, an increasing number of these are foreign; in other words, abroad. Agricultural exports do a great deal to combat the imbalance of trade, and this is an item often forgotten in arguments about the pros and cons of cattle. It is not an argument that Bill forgets. All in all, more than four and a half million people are fed by Arizona beef. Pound for pound, most of this comes from range. From desert.

The first cattle came to the foothills of the Santa Ritas with a Father Kino entourage, sometime in the latter half of the 1600s. Looking around even now from Kino's mission of San Xavier del Bac, his "white dove of the desert" below Green Valley and just south of Tucson, you can see the wave of grasslands rising to the east. Desert grasslands are what you find when you climb above the scrub and gravel of the valley floor; they come between scrub below and forest above, in moisture and altitude. If I'd had charge of herds back then, the Santa Rita foothills are where I'd have put them.

If I had cattle in Arizona now, that's where I'd like them to be. In winter, with the mesquites no more than a leafless haze, the grass shows through thick as a golden pelt. With summer rains it all goes green. In Kino's day, native bunch grasses ran here like a clean sea:

rothrock and side oats and subtropic gramas, three-awns, tanglehead grass and windmill grasses. In the arroyos there were oaks, for shade.

Nowadays the native bunch grasses have been replaced on the lower slopes by Lehmann love grass, a rugged import from southern Africa. Neatly spaced mesquite trees cover the ground almost entirely, as if this were an orchard. The oak groves are there in the uplands but most of the oaks lower down were cut and used by pioneers for building materials, and have been replaced — since Kino's day, even since the late 1800s — by mesquite.

Desert grasslands all across the Southwest have been invaded by mesquite. No one knows exactly why. Some folks accuse cattle of having changed this world for the worse. The bottom line is: if you love cattle, you don't think so.

Father Eusebio Francisco Kino came to San Xavier del Bac in 1692, seventy-two years after the Pilgrims stepped out of the *Mayflower* onto Plymouth Rock. He arrived as a missionary in Mexico City in 1681, every inch an educated European and a man of the Spanish God, and ten years later he set off on the first of forty expeditions into the desert hinterlands of Pimeria Alta — now northern Mexico and Arizona. This Spanish outback was the home of desert tribes known generally as the Pima, though the local group here was later called the Papago; Spanish and Anglo nomenclature of Indian tribes is a tangled skein. In any case, the native people here are now known by their ancestral name for themselves: Tohono O'odham.

In Kino's day the Tohono O'odham lived in camps along the few perennial watercourses, they farmed some and hunted and gathered some and pursued a life of unremitting generosity with one another. They traveled light, the more they gave the more they got, stinginess being the sure way to starvation; in any case they knew the value of giving all unnecessary things away. This is a desert understanding. They also knew the value of clean and plentiful water. Because of this, they did not think too much of cattle.

A hundred and fifty years after Kino's bandwagon of provisioners brought cattle in to the Santa Ritas, the Tohono O'odham were still trying to run the cattle (and the cattlemen) out of there.

Nowadays the Tohono O'odham are cattlemen themselves.

They run their cattle in the old system of open range. There are no fences; the cattle are let loose on reservation land to graze until they're rounded up. This was the system used all across the public lands of the Southwest, fifty and more years ago. It led to severe overgrazing, extreme abuse of landscape. The Taylor Grazing Act took care of that; ranchers nowadays have specific — fenced — leases on public land. It isn't in their interest to damage their rangeland resource. They have to stay and make a living here. It's no surprise to anyone that the rangelands of the Tohono O'odham are in rougher condition than anyone else's around.

Bill McGibbon's pickup bangs over the rutted ranch roads through the yellow grass; the desert basin lies pale below and the Santa Rita range — Mounts Hopkins and Wrightson — rise forested above. Bill drives with his shades on and his cowboy-style rancher's hat on, too. In the back of the truck are dogs: a black Lab named Thor and a young enthusiastic Australian shepherd named Bucky. Between the bumps and clattering, Bill McGibbon talks:

"Cattle are a useful management tool that can be used to improve the condition and biodiversity of the range. What we use on this rangeland now is a technique developed by the Holistic Resource Management Foundation. It was developed by Alan Savory, a Zimbabwean wildlife biologist who grew up in the South African rangelands. He transplanted the idea of native migrations — the migrating herds of elephants and wildebeest and so on — here to our rangelands. Here we are."

The pickup stops at last in a cloud of dust by a new metal corral. Bucky jumps out. Bill finds a stick and starts to draw in the dust. What he draws is a wheel. The center, the hub (this is where we are, here, now), is a corral with water supply, weighing scale, sorting alley, squeeze chute, loading chute. Around this hub are a series of eight to sixteen paddocks, each one between six hundred and a thousand acres in size. The whole "cell" worth of cattle grazes one paddock at a time; about every three days they're moved (through the hub) into the next paddock, mimicking as they go the wildebeest (or buffalo, for that matter) impact: a short period of heavy grazing and trampling hooves followed by a time of long untouched regrowth. The herd has passed by. So.

The system is expensive to set up, but once it is in place the land is more productive, the cattle healthier and easier to manage — they're handled more often and so become less skittish — and Bill finds he can get along now with one less employee. The Holistic Resource Management concept is still in the experimental stage, it hasn't caught on widely yet, because it's new and because of its expense, but here it is: arid lands ecology, applied. Bill has two cells working now, and three on the drawing board.

He is a pragmatic man, he's no idealist, and it's clear right away that he loves what he does; that he does it with imagination, commitment, care. Cattle to man to desert is a relationship he's in, it's where he wants to be, it's as gritty as a marriage; a relationship to be lived in and worked out, a way of living to be defended against those others who, for whatever reasons, wish to take it apart.

Lesson learned, it's time to go. "Back in the truck, Bucky! Bucky! Buck!" he says, and seconds later the hub of the wheel, the Zimbabwean waterhole transposed, disappears in the dust.

A half-mile away we come on a pair of mother cows, each trailing a calf. The cows are brown and white, glossy, solid, with the bug-eyed wet-nosed bumptious look of healthy animal. The spunky calves have legs as thick as girders. We watch them and they watch us until the mother cows, with a feral maternal lowering of necks, lead them off into the mesquite.

"The mesquite? There are a number of hypotheses. No one seems to have the final answer on that one," Bill says. And this is true. No one does. The widespread mesquite invasion of desert grassland is a controversial biological mystery.

One theory holds that the first mesquites were imported up into desert prairies as a source of firewood. The trees grow fast and their hard wood burns long and bright, so this isn't unlikely, but doesn't explain the trees' lightning-fast spread through the grass. Mesquite beans are eaten by livestock and wildlife and survive, somehow, even through the macerations and fermentations of a cow's gut — coyotes eat them, spreading seed up the washes they patrol — but the beans do also sprout from cow dung, giving credence to the "cow-flap hypothesis." Old photos do show groves springing up around corrals and along the routes of cattle drives. The old grazing system, whether of open range or of fenced pastures in continual use, tended to weaken the native grass; grazed and grazed continually, like a savings account drawn upon above its interest and never refilled, the perennial grasses had no time to reinvest in rootstocks or set seed. Weakened or dying, they left ground open for invasion, and mesquite invaded, and there we are.

Then there's the theory of fire. Ecologically, these grasslands are what is known as a fire subclimax. This means that desert grasses grow where shrubs or even trees would grow if they were not destroyed by periodic bouts of fire. Once started by lightning, wildfire will sweep unchecked through the thick tinder of dead grass, through the mattresslike leaves and stems that lie, in this dry climate, unrotted for years. Fire will kill seedling trees — it kills young mesquites — but will not kill grass.

Pioneers and cattlemen and land management agencies put out fires. And cattle, if they are grazing more heavily and regularly than wild game, will reduce grass tinder to a frail fabric. So however they did come, the mesquites came, and stayed, and grew, and — once grown large — they could not be killed by fire anymore.

The largest theory of them all, the one that hangs over all these others like a sky, is that these deserts are still inexorably, visibly since the end of the last century, drying out. Part of this is due to climate, part of this is due to increasing demands of people; all through the Southwest, water tables are dropping like stones. And mesquite can withstand deeper drought than grass.

Nearly everywhere, even on land never grazed, desert scrub is expanding at the expense of grass. This is a universal phenomenon in American deserts. How much of this has had to do with cattle? With other human impacts? With natural succession? No one knows.

The truth is that none of these theories can be dissected from the others. Whether change has been brought by culture or by the global shifts of jet streams, the mesquites are here and Bill McGibbon is here and the calves are here, too, proof that the relationship does work, for them.

As a cattleman, Bill McGibbon is part of a shrinking minority. The hard-worked pickup, the obedient happy dogs, the wool felt hat, the risk-taking management styles, the sound relationships with banks, the long roundup days in the saddle — these are slim defense against the tide of popular myth and population growth. Nowadays, the cattle-raising industry is under fire, and no amount of cowboy romance — or reality — can change that.

"Most of these ranchers, especially the old-timers, just want to go back to their ranches and raise their cattle like they've always done. And leave the world alone," he says, tipping his hat back with his fist, "but the world won't leave *them* alone."

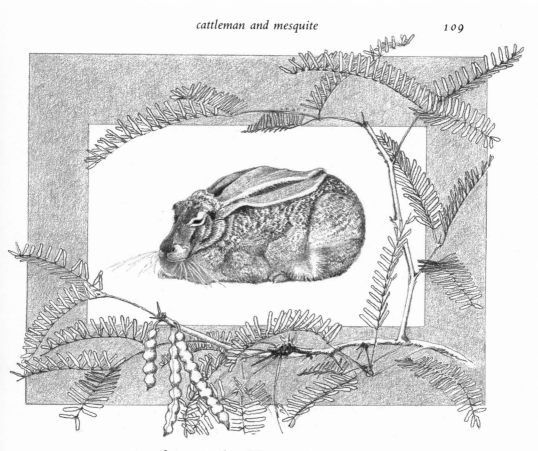

Antelope Jackrabbit and Mesquite

You could write a whole book about mesquite. It has a thousand uses and its beanlike fruits are eaten by almost everything, even people, and they're sweet and nutty and nutritious. The trees themselves are used as shelter by another thousand things, including antelope jackrabbits snoozing through the hot daylight hours in their shade. The thing to notice about the antelope jack is his ears: they are so enormous that he has to fold each one in half and then stack them on top of each other when he goes to sleep. At dusk he unfolds himself and goes foraging. If he catches wind of a predator he will take off at high speed in dizzying zigs and zags and then his big ears serve as radiators to get rid of the heat he generates in his stupendous run. Most hot-blooded animals cannot sweat as we do to get rid of excess body heat, so big "radiator" ears are a common desert adaptation.

17

patriots

White Sands Missile Range, New Mexico

When I went to White Sands Missile Range there was a war on. American troops were moving into Saudi Arabia to stop Iraqi forces from taking that, too, Iraqis having taken Kuwait already. If they took Saudi Arabia, they'd be sitting on half the oil resources of the planet, which was not a good idea.

This war was very much on people's minds. One felt that anything could happen; there was a sense that the world could suddenly change in unpredictable ways. Things that were the same seemed out of place.

Out in the desert, everything was the same. I was driving through New Mexico mountains taking note of cliff rose and Torrey ephedra, my botanical obsessions somehow unaffected by the fact that millions of Arabs and Israelis were in the line of fire and that hundreds of thousands of young Americans and Europeans had put themselves in that line, too. Chihuahuan desert mountains, I thought. Higher, colder. Still mesquite, I thought, cholla, saltbush.

I had my son, Coulter, in tow for a week; it was school vacation and he'd flown out to Phoenix to meet me. There had been comics in his backpack, an airport full of folks in shades and shorts, a motel in Las Cruces for the night, McDonald's for breakfast. These things were the same. But I had discovered that I did not trust them.

Maybe this is the meaning of war: that what can be trusted in peacetime — food, warmth, professional pursuit, the people one loves, one's own life — may be taken away. And one is powerless to stop it.

It was an interesting time to come to a missile range. I had not planned it this way. The appointment had been made many months before. And there we were.

We went through the gates at nine A.M. after signing in, thinking how much the guards were like National Park rangers, thinking that the missile range base looked like any desert town, only bigger and duller and with more wires, awed by the ranked museum of white missiles ranged on the roadside in "typical firing attitudes" aimed at a space in the air over the Tularosa basin. Some were aimed a little toward the San Andres Mountains.

We'd just come through the San Augustin Pass on down into the Tularosa itself. The Tularosa is a tube of a valley most of which is missile range. The range is two million acres strong, forty miles wide and one hundred miles long; larger than Delaware and Rhode Island combined. It contains White Sands National Monument, and the monument is closed down whenever it's in the line of experimental fire, which is not often. The basin is bounded on the eastern side by the Sacramento Mountains; "this was chosen because it was *enclosed*," we learned soon.

White Sands Space Harbor lies in the missile range, too, just north of the National Monument. NASA space shuttle pilots train there on a modified Grumman Gulfstream II jet, and the runways of packed gypsum are kept within three hours of readiness all the time in case a real shuttle needs to land there. *Columbia* did land here once, in 1982, when Edwards Air Force Base in the Mojave Desert of California (like White Sands, Edwards is on a dry lake bed; dry lake beds being the most absolutely level places on the surface of the earth) was temporarily flooded — a hazard of desert lake beds anywhere.

White Sands Missile Range came into being on July 9, 1945, and was called White Sands Proving Ground at the time. It was needed badly and right away, there being a war on, and some of the ranchers that lived here were hustled off with less than two weeks' notice, the Army Corps of Engineers seizing the place by right of eminent domain. This desert being what it is, with about ten inches of rainfall in the average year, things do not rot fast — though they may rust and blow away or be buried in white gypsum sand — but a lot of those ranchers' homesteads are still here. Cans are still on shelves, washbasins in the corners, bedsprings on the floors. All the minutiae of peace. Horses got left behind in the rush, too, and they have gone about their business ever since, undisturbed by rocketry or the Army Corps. There are about twelve hundred feral horses on the range right now, there are clearly too many of them here, and no one knows what to do about it. They overgraze the place and take food from the mouths of desert bighorns and pronghorns, and this upsets environmentalists and people at Game and Fish, but there are animal rights activists who do not like the round 'em up for dogmeat option; so the public affairs officer has to deal with the thorny politics of horses, among other things.

Outside the Public Affairs Building, next to the sidewalk, is a round-ish object with boxy rocketlike flanges at one end. It's about the size of an old VW bug and is painted yellow. A sign next to it says that this is a spare casing for Fat Man. Fat Man was the first atomic bomb that ever exploded anywhere; it went off on July 16, 1945, at Trinity Site in the northern reaches of the White Sands Proving Ground, one week to the day after the Proving Ground had been established; the reason, no doubt, for the rush. Later, another Fat Man exploded over Nagasaki. The spare casing is a little rusty, and you can put your hand on it.

The Public Affairs Building is something like a school; the ceilings are low and the desks are old and are busy and crowded, the linoleum is worn. Every office has a wide-screen TV — this part is not like a school — and every TV is tuned to the same news station that features a twenty-four-hour-a-day newscast on the war in the Middle East. During the hours that I spent in that building conducting interviews, our eyes kept wandering to the screen: tanks, aircraft carriers, airplanes, trucks filled with soldiers in camouflage — partly desert and partly forest camouflage; they'd been in a rush, too — and fuzzy views of Scud missile damage in Tel Aviv, and clips of the President talking in front of a blue curtain with the Presidential seal.

Twice there was a clip showing a missile riding a comet of white fire toward the top center of the TV screen. The video camera had followed the missile in an uneven way, in jumps and stops, so the missile didn't seem to move much but got smaller and smaller until it became a ball of white fire.

When this news clip came on, the Public Affairs Building went quiet. You could hear cars going by outside. You could hear the *rurk* of a raven over the Tularosa basin. You could hear the announcer saying how the Patriot surface-to-air guided missile system "designed to acquire, track and engage multiple high-speed aircraft at medium and high altitudes" had been successful in intercepting all, or almost all, of the Iraqi Scud missiles aimed at Tel Aviv. The Patriot was saving lives. By spiking a big gun. By blowing up enemy incoming in midair.

The Patriot was tested and retested here. Originally conceived as a defense against enemy aircraft, it now worked fine against missiles, too.

The Patriot had taken twenty-two years to develop and perfect. Whenever the news clip came on, people looked at their hands, at their desktops, into space, more than they looked at the screen. They didn't need to look at the screen. They looked like they were listening to their own child delivering the valedictorian address for the graduating class of White Sands Missile Range.

This is a humongous outdoor laboratory, a white-coats kind of place. It is used as a test facility by the Army, Navy, Air Force, and by NASA, as well as by independent defense contractors. When a missile is developed it can be sent here to see what it can do, and what can be done to it. Under carefully monitored conditions the "product" is soaked in salt water to mimic oceans and rolled in mud to mimic battlefields, it is roasted, frozen, irradiated, shaken, bent, rolled, chipped, and generally tormented. This is a kind of boot camp for matériel, in other words, after which the test results — the report card — are sent home to the engineers and scientists who mastermind design. Often this means that the product goes back to the drawing board, for a while.

Then it comes back. After it's passed all these and other in-house tests, if it is a missile, it is fired.

Dr. Robert H. Goddard is generally considered to be the father of American rocketry. He patented the first liquid-fueled rockets in

1914; during World War I he worked on making rockets into weapons; in 1919 he wrote a paper concluding that rockets could be built that might reach the escape velocity of the earth, launch us into orbit, in other words, but this bit of whimsy was scoffed at or ignored. During World War II the Germans were the only ones who took his ideas seriously, and they turned them into weapons, including the infamously famous V-2 that almost cost the Allies the war.

In August of 1945, three hundred freight cars filled with captured V-2 components arrived in New Mexico, along with one hundred captured German missile experts and scientists. On April 16, 1946, the first V-2 was fired on White Sands Proving Ground, from Launch Complex 33 (this is now a National Historic Landmark, as is Trinity Site), and it flew to eighteen thousand feet.

Goddard had launched his early inventions from his meadow, back at his home in New England, and after a while these went pretty far, and the local Massachusetts fire marshal told him to stop — his gizmos were a hazard to his neighbors' corn. So Goddard moved to Roswell, New Mexico.

There was not much here that his rockets could be hazard to, and no one to mind much if they were. This missile range was established less than a hundred miles west of Roswell with that same reasoning, and — if rockets have to be fired anywhere — it turns out not to be bad reasoning.

I've heard this from five separate biologists (I didn't believe it at first, but I do now, having heard it since from three more): if you need to look at pristine desert, go to a military reserve. There are plenty out here: there's White Sands, and there's Fort Bliss (New Mexico and Texas) and Barry M. Goldwater Air Force Range and Yuma Proving Ground (Arizona); and Nellis Air Force Range (Nevada) and China Lake Naval Weapons Center, Edwards Air Force Base, Fort Irwin Military Reservation, Chocolate Mountains Gunnery Range, and Twentynine Palms Marine Corps Base (all in southern California). Not only do these outweigh, many tens of times, the size of the National Park system; the important thing is that the public is not allowed on them. And it turns out that the public — with their cars and dirt bikes and pistols and penchants for picking things up — is more of a damaging force to native desert than any amount of exploding ordnance.

There are flourishing herds of pronghorns here, as well as the horses, and in the mountains there are bighorn sheep and mule deer, and the lowlands are home to a growing number of gemsbok that were imported by the New Mexico Game and Fish (for some outlandish reason) from the Kalahari. There are mountain lions, bobcats, coyotes, kit foxes, and the usual desert array of golden eagles and quail and owls and other birds (barn owls have made a nest on the deserted gantry of Launch Complex 33), and plenty of small mammals, bats, snakes, lizards, insects, desert pupfish in the saline springs. More than three hundred species of animals have been documented here. A team of wildlife biologists is part of the base staff of White Sands Missile Range. Part of their job is to route and schedule missile firings to fit the breeding and feeding schedules of wildlife, to see that least damage is done.

The Public Affairs' (somewhat repetitive) cant that this range is a "National Treasure" is not entirely blarney. Eight independent biologists can't all be wrong.

The strange, contained, pristine value of this landscape goes beyond the natural history. It works for human history, too.

Bob Burton is an archaeologist, and has been on the White Sands Missile Range staff for four years now.

"Protection of archaeological sites is *policy*," he says. "It's expedient for them to find an area for the launch site, impact points, camera pads that won't have a negative effect on the archaeological sites. This place is a national treasure, archaeologically speaking. We have sites on this range that are maybe unique in the United States. The pot hunters haven't been here. No one's made off with the goods."

He's a large, comfortable man, and he's as excited as he should be by having the run of the place. As he ticks off the waves of peoples and cultures who have lived here, I'm struck, as I was in the Goddard story, by how thin and recent this history is.

Between twelve and thirteen thousand years ago the first bands of nomadic hunters came in here, and this paleo-Indian era lasted until nine thousand years ago, at least. There were lakes in the basin then, freshwater lakes surrounded by trees. These nomads, known as

Clovis people, hunted big game. There are mammoths' footprints fossilized in the now dry bed of Lake Otero: it is no trick to see what they hunted for.

Since their heyday the whole Southwest has been drying out and warming up, and within a few millennia of the hunters' arrival the big game was gone. People turned to other things. Some learned to farm. Those who lived here next built settlements and planted corn. By A.D. 1100 there were villages here made of hundreds of adobe rooms, some stacked three stories tall. The villages were built near permanent springs and the people planted their corn on the now dry lake beds where the water table lay close. In those days, there were more people living in this valley than live here now, including the more than eleven thousand people who work or live at the main post of the missile range.

Between 1275 and 1400 the drying and warming of the desert had gone so far that farming ceased, almost overnight; the Anasazi and Hohokam disappeared, as they disappeared elsewhere, the people moving en masse to the valley of the Rio Grande.

Then, around 1500, Apaches came in. Nomads again: "they lived lightly on the earth," Bob says, and it's easy to see that he likes this, that lightly is the way he believes this piece of earth is meant to be lived on; the only way to live on it, now that it is desert.

He's working on a site right now where a battle was fought, in 1880, between Apaches and the U.S. Cavalry. He's found the Apache emplacements, the stone fortifications built to shoot from and hide behind. He knows where the cavalry holed up; he's found the scattered cartridges. There was a war on here then, and the cavalry were surprised, outmaneuvered, and surrounded. They lost nine men, and most of the fifty were wounded. It was a lot like Custer's fight, Bob says, except that the U.S. troops were rescued by another troop of cavalry at the eleventh hour; after a token charge or two, the troops took their wounded and left.

"It was a battle where both sides won. The cavalry drove off the Apaches. The Apaches got the Army off their tail."

There's a silence after this; only the big-screen TV keeps up its exotic blather. All three of us — my son and I and Bob — sit bent forward with our elbows on our knees, as if we were gathered 'round a fire, TV light from the Middle East flickering on our faces, our faces blank, watching another battle forming up.

Now the Tularosa valley is dominated — when it is dominated — by high-energy laser systems running through their paces, by smart missiles shooting through their gantries, riding cones of white fire, from which boiling clouds of smoke roll up. The only thing that is not the same is this: just over a century ago, bows and arrows nearly had the upper hand.

White Gypsum Sand Dunes, Cloudy Sky, and the San Andres Mountains

18

borderlands and river

Lajitas, Texas

Against the rising sun a horseman crosses the Rio Grande from Mexico to Texas, the river like a sheet of fire under the horse's belly and the hatted man riding dark and straight. The horse clambers the bank and disappears. They are going to the Trading Post, I think. Where else is there to go?

A battered metal rowboat comes to the sand beach under the bank, the boatman in a rough workshirt shipping his oars and running the port side on the sand. A woman and her two daughters, all in their best clothes — white and blue and red and lace, neat white shoes — get in and are ferried across. I have the idea that they are going to visit Grandma in the Mexican village on the other side.

To say that the border is porous here is an understatement, and is close to unimportant. This borderland is a place unto itself.

Time was, this was a dangerous place to be. By the early 1700s — once they were equipped with stolen horses — the Mescalero Apaches drove out the indigenous tribes, tribes who had been living here who knows how long. The horse was the key to this country. A hundred years later, mounted Comanches gave the Apaches hell. When Texas was "annexed" by the United States in 1845, a string of forts sprang up, and the U.S. military — also a-horseback — gave the Comanches hell. The border was as unenforceable then as now, leaky as the dickens, and it went smack-dab through fluctuating tribal claims, lending the Indian wars here the aura of a game. During the

Civil War the cavalry had other things to do and Mexican bandits
attacked the ranches and border towns, and this went on for quite a
while, no one in Washington taking West Texas too much to heart;
so Texas Rangers and their horses took the heat.

After the Mexican Revolution of 1910, Pancho Villa's gangs made
"border incidents" pretty much at will, raiding ranches and ranchos
interchangeably; these are the moustachioed gents in big hats and
leather chaps, chests criss-crossed with bandoliers of ammo (there
are postcards of old photos in the Trading Post that show exactly
this; victorious banditos lined up for some gutsy photographer, he'd
set them up, some kneeling and others standing, all bristling with
guns) and it wasn't till the 1920s that this era came to an end. A kind
of end. Prohibition sent booze and guns flowing back and forth across
the river, and the smuggling business hasn't stopped to this day, can't
have, really, in spite of what the locals say.

Nowadays there doesn't seem to be too much of interest either
way, other than the Trading Post or Grandma's house or the odd
cantina. Serious wetbacks or bigtime smugglers wouldn't choose this
as a crossing place, this has been explained to me: strangers in town
are too visible in these here parts and it's a long four hundred miles
up across the desert to El Paso, the closest place for illegal employ-
ment or markets for smuggled goods or places to hide. Here Mexico
is mostly the place to go for lunch and the U.S.A. is the place to
buy burro oats. These are still two outbacks lying side by side along
the Big Bend of the Rio Grande, which is not grand now, in wintertime, and no more trouble to cross than a wide road.

The pale silt-dust of the river blows into dunes between the battered shrubs of the floodplain. A roadrunner comes to drink, pauses
at the bank, and stretches one foot and the opposing wing in the sun.

The Lajitas Trading Post has an American flag flapping from a pole
over a pen of goats, so you know where you are. You can smell goat
when you come to the door, male goat in particular, Clay Henry the
Beer Drinking Goat to be exact. He's the claim to fame of the place
(there are posters and T-shirts of him for sale inside), and there's a
cooler in there half full of Lone Star and Bud, for customers, of
course, but I'm reminded of the quarter-in-the-slot turn-the-toggle
pellet dispensers in children's zoos. The female goats like beer, too;

they'll climb the fence when they see you've got a can in your hand and look meaningful looks from their gilded slit-eyes, but you have to hold it up for them to drink. Clay Henry will take the whole thing from your hand, gently, adjust it against the ground until he's got the working end firmly in his teeth, then tip his head back and let it all pour down. He's out there surrounded by empties, their colors neatly echoing the flag overhead.

Inside there is a single long dark room, high-ceilinged, with burro panniers and pails and boots hanging from the rafters, and picks, spades, and grain sacks keeping company with grocery shelves and the cooler and racks of candy. Some of the more outbacky items look a trifle dusty but I have to believe that the dust's there because they're leftovers, not because they're bought for show. There are the T-shirts and a rack of weekend campers' gear: Swiss army knives, plastic canteens, golfer-type hats; overall, a mix of twentieth century with nineteenth. The post has been here for more than a hundred years and things haven't changed too much. It's the kind of place where you can get yourself a drink and sit at the rickety table and wait for someone to come and get paid. This is what I do.

After a while a man in a plaid shirt and with a blond ponytail down his back does come to the counter. His name is Norman and he's thirtyish, maybe; later his wife comes in, wearing overalls, cradling a baby blond as a cherub. Meanwhile Norman tells me what he does here, why it is he's here.

He's here so he can spend the summer nights — beginning in May — running the roads and hunting for snakes.

At dusk he fills his gas tank and stocks the cab with Cokes, jerky, Maglites, bubble gum, cigarettes. Three million candlepower is already mounted on the front of his Jeep. He hunts for himself or for other collectors, and keeps meticulous data on every find. He's discovering the minutiae of behavior: the effects of rainfall, humidity, weather, temperature, time, habitat. Lizards like it really *hot* but the ideal snake temp is 72 to 88 degrees F with 30 to 70 percent humidity, he says. When he finds an animal he notes the species, sex, length, pattern, scarring, parasites, coloration. These are delicate, extraordinary creatures, these are individuals. Every summer he spends three to four thousand dollars for gas for his Jeep. It's worth every nickel.

Last year he ran the roads for one hundred and seventy-nine nights straight. The year before, for two hundred and thirty nights straight.

"I do it for the high. It's the ultimate high," he says.

He collects data on the lizards, too; the Big Bend geckos are extremely sensitive to habitat and weather, he says, but after years of data collection, "I can pretty much tell you when they're going to burp."

Then there are the "nimmies," the whiptail lizards, the fastest lizards in the world. They've been clocked up to twenty-two, twenty-three miles per hour. Some species are "normal," meaning that there are males and females. Other species are composed entirely of females. These are the "liberated lizards," he says. They're parthenogenetic, there are no males at all. Some of these lay eggs, some give birth to live young. One species lives at the flats at the base of the mountains; there is another species in the first five hundred feet of slope, and another above that. There is no interbreeding between or among them, of course.

He finds Big Bend milk snakes, trans-Pecos rat snakes (a race of blond trans-Pecos rats lives only in Boquillas Limestone), Texas lyre snakes, mottled rock rattlers, Mojave rattlers (the Big Bend variety is as venomous as Mojaves elsewhere; I'm glad it's not summer now), and, sometimes, given time and luck, he finds gray-banded king snakes. These are strictly montane, he says. They live in ancient seabeds punched up by volcanic action above two thousand feet. Once he caught one that was baby blue with chocolate rings and fire orange saddles; a gorgeous animal. A friend of his caught one that was sky blue with thin ivory white lines bordering bands of jet black, the saddles bright red. He was offered fifteen hundred dollars for that snake by a professional collector that very night, and wouldn't take it:

"Looking at that animal . . . Christ. I can't even tell you. Beautiful . . . ? I wouldn't have let her go for a million, myself."

Norman leans on the counter, I'm into my third Coke, we could go on like this forever — my listening to him talking — customers wandering through, goats and burros whickering outside, the screen door banging. So I ask him what it is he trades in, what he does at the Trading Post when he's not looking for snakes.

Turns out what the Trading Post does is cross-borders barter, mostly. They buy cactus plants, the little nipple cacti and the claret cups, the ones that look like bunches of lacy stones and have grand flowers. And cholla — Europeans like cholla, and much of the market for cactus is, eventually, European. Cholla skeletons, tubular and gray with rows of holes, come in as raw material for napkin rings and southwesty decors. Then there's Mexican vanilla, the real thing, and pottery, and antiquities — with permits, of course — and candelilla wax. Most of this gets bartered for beans and flour, a pickax, matches, oats. The Mexican traders tie their horses and burros up by the goats outside.

The candelilla wax is made in "wax camps" across the border. It's not legal to produce it here, the candelilla plant being more delicate or rare, protected anyhow, on this side of the border. It's a Chihuahuan desert plant that frills the limestone ledges in plasticky-looking bunches like clusters of gray pencils. It is leafless, and it coats itself with wax to reflect light away and keep its water in, something like a waxed rutabaga in the grocery store; in matters of damage control in hostile environments we haven't invented too much. The wax of the candelilla — little candle — is one of the highest quality waxes in the world.

Norman gives me a chunk of candelilla wax to hold. It's the color of maple fudge and is smooth and heavy as marble and almost as hard. The wax camps — I see one later along the river — are a brush shelter over a stone hearth on which bunches of candelilla are boiled. The wax is skimmed off and set to harden in pans. When all the candelilla in reach has been harvested, the camp is abandoned. The raw wax is sent north some ninety miles to Alpine to be refined, then it's sold to a dealer in New York City to be used in specialty items: chewing gums, shoe and car and floor polish, sealing waxes, lubricants, waterproofings, but soap and ointments and cosmetics, mostly. I think of those city racks of lipsticks the colors of cactus blossoms, and neat boxlets of expensive desiderata with their Frenchified labels, and of the goat pens and the limestone ledges; and it is strange to me how the world has been connected up.

For connections here the river is the greatest force there is. The connecting that it does is more natural than its work as border, which it doesn't do well. Governments do that, or try to; that's their job; the river is a route, a thing unto itself in the midst of something else: the desert.

Río Bravo is what Mexicans call it; Bravo, meaning brave and strong and also hurrah, is a word we don't have anything like. The river is the through channel for Rocky Mountain snowmelt and — through the giant tributary river, the Conchos — of storm rain from the Sierra Madre Occidental, the Western Mother Mountains of the Mexican state of Chihuahua. All the water in the river now is Rio Conchos runoff, the Rio Grande having been tapped pretty thoroughly for city use and irrigation through New Mexico and Texas.

Today the Río Bravo's running four feet deep in its main channel. This leaves plenty of clearance for a raft. A raft is what I use. A gray inflatable raft with a veteran river-runner named Tom.

Time for a luxury cruise is what I think. Enough of long marches and rough camps and instant soup. The rafting company has said it will send steaks and a bottle of wine, and salmon salad makings for next day's lunch, and a blue water barrel the size of a bathtub. Tom will bring his private oars, heavy enough for a Viking ship. There will be rapids. We will go through country inaccessible any other way except by foot tramp fifteen miles one way up over Mesa de Anguilla; I'm not in the mood.

In the morning we tie the baggage on and shove off, and all we have to do is take the river in. Mesquite roots trail in the water like cinnamon-colored hoses, thick as hair, like pipes. A great blue heron rises from the bank with a squawk like a door hinge. A sandpiper wobbles along the bankside like a single animated shoe. This is early migration time. The river is a road north, for birds. True spring won't come, Tom says, until the turkey vultures get back here from Mexico. Turkey vultures let the borderlands know they've had the last frost.

The water is as sleek and gray as silk. It mutters softly under us, being agreeable, comfortable. The desert can be comfortable, too, when you have a water barrel the size of a bathtub. It isn't always like this. Last fall the river rose in its bed to the height of twenty-three feet and washed the rootholds from under those mesquites and carried out whole groves of cottonwoods and swung a long arm around the village of Santa Elena, Mexico. For a while the whole Rio

Grande/Bravo looked like it might decide to follow this arm and dig itself a new main channel. There was a whoop-de-do in Santa Elena — it was cut off from everywhere then like an island — because they thought they might be U.S. citizens just by staying where they were.

The usual fall floods reach twelve feet or so, so that was a doozy, but summer rainstorms being what they are, the watershed being what it is, a sudden flood can happen anytime. A debris line comes before you've noticed any rise in water; junk picked up from once-dry banks. Then rocks begin to move in the rapids and you can hear them rumbling, even in the night.

Now black phoebes dip and flit from low branches, scooping insects. A flock of ducks flies on ahead. Big Bend turtles, red-orange patches behind their eyes, lie hauled out on stubs of wood and stones by the dozen, sometimes stacked three deep like bowls in a drainer. Hard-core baskers these ones are, not plooping in until you're at arm's length. Sudden loops of orange bob and wobble in the shallows: these, Tom says, are carp lips. Carp slurp foam where water back-eddies and foam gathers. What you see are lips. Tom says that a friend of his has caught carp here by baiting his fly rod with marshmallows.

The water is chalky in the sun. Texas color. Candelilla, prickly pear, hedgehog cactus, lechuguilla, on the ledges. Banks trashed by last year's flood. Wide high empty sky. Limestone mesas city-building-sized with black volcanic intrusions filling in a story or two. Dust-fine river grit everywhere. This is what my notes say. And: canyon light makes the dissolved and polished rock as smooth as cream. And: except for water noise, at midday, silence.

In the evening I walk a side canyon and climb ledges to the top. From there, the river looks like silver melted and poured. Can't see what all those horsemen fought over. That's my blindness, my myopia. I'm no Comanche, no river rat either; just passing through. What was worth fighting for unless it was the emptiness? That's still here.

There are resources: turtles and fish and ducks to eat, and beaver — we found the tracks of a beaver on a river bar, we could see where he'd come back again and again to bite and drag away branches of catclaw acacia; we could see the gray stubs on the catclaw where he'd bitten branches off last year; he'd remembered where they were. He lives in a hole in the bank (Rio Grande beavers live in bank holes; no way and no reason for dams here, and he'd survived that flood). In spite of beavers' foraging there's plenty of firewood along the river. The rise of the Chisos Mountains is furred with grass — great horse country there and game forage. And there's water in the mountains and the river. And there are a hundred thousand places to hide in the volcanic Chisos and the faulted limestones, too. But for all the galloping back and forth, it's been left pretty much as is.

There's been a little overgrazing — more than a little, the Mexico side is threadbare — and horses and cows and goats cross over all the time. Mexican horses made the trail I followed up here. They give the Big Bend National Park rangers a hard time. Rangers catch the horses and return them to their ranchos, then the horses come back. Of course they do. I would. The old story over again; the river's no barrier at all.

Maybe it's the emptiness. Maybe people needed that — need it now. I don't mean a romantic need for wilderness to soothe the soul or a need for contemplation space — Christ went to the desert for temptation, that's a thought. I mean the space to be away from other people's judgment. Perhaps they're all one need rolled together. Some people have the thirst to live without mirrors or their equivalents, the pressures to conform to *rules*. Wherever there are people there are rules. Whoever makes them or whenever they've been made there've been laws of behavior and appearance, codified expectations. Rules. Laws. Nice to get away.

The rangers do their best to keep this side pristine, but the unpristineness is part of its charm. Horses can be outlaws, too.

Above the woodlands and canebrakes of the river, desert comes back. There are two places here for the eye: huge distance with its spill of silver river, then close focus: the pale clustering of cactus at my feet would fit in a flowerpot. Each stem is the size of a golf ball. Red buds just poke through white spine mesh. This is beauty of another size. It will have flowers in March, in spring; it's still winter now. You can feel it ending, though.

Rubbery red jatropha plants, and candelillas pale as shredded moonlight, perch in the limestone. And brindled green lechuguilla.

Lechuguilla is the symptom of Chihuahuan desert. It grows nowhere else. It's an agave, it has that familiar fleshy rosette, each
foot-long leaf tipped with a black spine; but lechuguilla has a fiendish
sort of *will*. It grows in colonies, blanketing the ground, each rosette
curved like a claw. All those spines are thick as awls and as sharp
and hard and they all, somehow, seem to point uphill.

Not so bad maybe when you're afoot, you can walk around and
choose a climbing place so they're nowhere underneath, but if you're
on horseback then they're something else. Uphill's fine: that's the
sneakiness of the things. Coming downhill there they are. They can
cripple horses, pierce their ankles. If you fall on top of them you lie

Sunset on the Rio Grande

To the left, at the mouth of Santa Elena Canyon, the river narrows and plunges in rapids between sheer sandstone walls. Across the river in Mexico is the Sentinel, where the Mexican revolutionary Pancho Villa posted a lookout to warn his bands of approaching enemies and to communicate important news, by smoke signal or mirror flash. During his revolution there was a continuous system of such lookouts from Mexico City to the border. According to people in Lajitas, the lookout network brought the news of his victory to Texas before the telegraph did.

impaled. Tom calls them "lemme getcha" and that's right. You wonder how they did it, all those horsemen, fighting. Why?

For the emptiness, I think. Can't see what else. Like the lechuguilla, they fought for keeping others out. For the right to the emptiness itself.

The river is red now like a spill of paint. Nothing moves that's visible. Nothing man-done is visible, and no one, and no live thing, though that's an illusion, too: these rocks are limestone boulder jumbles, great snake habitat. And camp is down there and the fire must be ready for those steaks. I'm just passing through. I'm going. I'll be gone. I'll watch my footing all the way down. I'll be back.

PART III

Spring

19

Awatobi and the tota-achi

Hopi Reservation, Arizona

Coulter and I have come back here to visit Alex Kasknuna, and this
morning he brought us to the ruins of Awatobi. There are potsherds
all over the place, each fragmentary design now a new design in
itself. I trace the patterns with my fingers, turn the shards in my
hands, not so much willing them to be whole as wondering about
their use and about the hands that made and used them. Then I put
them back in the dust and stones. I am acutely aware of where they
belong. I am sure that the potters painted their glazes on with this
same sense of balancing.

There are stripes, checkers, parallelograms inhabited by dots; variations on the zigzag, partial spirals, hooks, flecks, and fragments of
large complex designs broken away. The glazes are all shades of
cream, orange, brown, red–brown, rust, black, and gray. Some colors are chalky soft, others bright. There are finer clays and coarser
clays, thinner and thicker shards. In tracing the patterns with my
fingers, committing them to memory, I realize I'm repeating the
strokes of the potters, the potters of the ruined town of Awatobi,
and I am repeating them in part, not in totality, because the totality
is smashed.

While we are walking there, it comes to me that people are moved
to try, in one way or another, to define the meaning of civilization,

perhaps because it seems to be the only thing we have achieved that other animals have not. And in defining anything one creates a boundary: on this side *this* and on the other side *not-this,* as all animals do in defining the bounds of territory. Mammals for the most part enclose extended families within theirs; coyotes and beaver patrol their bounds and scent them afresh, insisting on definition.

The notion of boundary is the oldest notion of life, it seems, one definition of *life* being this: the possession of an enclosing semipermeable membrane. When the integrity of the membrane breaks, life is over. Such a membrane encloses each one of our two billion–plus body cells, the semipermeability allowing some things in and walling others out. In varying flexible ways and sizes such a "membrane" encloses each of us, and then our family with us, then our community, tribe, nation, civilization, species. These are the ring walls of identity.

I've heard the boundary of civilization defined as cleanliness; as godliness (meaning the belief in certain myths and codified practices; of totems, in other words, and taboos). Others subscribe to the notion of a stratified society as the earmark of civilized beings, one in which there are aristocrats, politicos, artisans, and the downtrodden, or their equivalents; anyhow, a coherent and interlocking structure in which people — strangers, even — can live and relate in peace within collective city walls. Others prefer to point at inscription, the written word, as the symptom of civil life. Others point at art as the prerequisite.

These shards are remnants of the latter, I suppose, though not as that word is in use now by us. Artists nowadays sign their names to their creations; they expect what they create to be an object of emotional impact, more decorative than useful, more important than decorative. The Awatobi potters were not, I think, like that. Human hands not only made these pots but filled them, emptied them, cleaned them; used them, in other words, in the business of living.

A wind is blowing, hard, sending sifts of dust along the ground and tossing the silvery rabbitbrush like surf. While Coulter explores, Alex and I sit side by side in the shelter of a broken wall. He tells me that this village was deserted long ago, he does not know when. Or why.

Or if he does know, he does not tell me. I am aware by now that some questions are impolitic, even dangerous, and I do not press him. Later, in books, I will find out that Awatobi was deserted in A.D. 1700 and has been empty ever since. Now it is a humpy landscape inhabited by hundreds of rabbits. Why so many rabbits . . . perhaps half-collapsed hollows of old houses and kivas are ready-made rooms for them, underneath. Like the English badgers that live in cellars of long decayed and forgotten Roman villas, they take advantage of human ruination.

Later I read this: in 1700, the men of other Hopi villages came at dawn and trapped the men of Awatobi in their own kivas, and threw burning branches in on them, and guarded the doors until all live sounds had ceased and the kiva roofs had collapsed in flames.

Then they took the women and children of Awatobi back with them across the plateau. On the way there was a quarrel about the divvying of spoils; some women and children were killed in the ruckus, but most were absorbed into other villages.

Since that morning, Awatobi has fallen into ruin and silence. Unless you know your way through the rutted tracks of the Hopi grazing lands, you will not find it.

The Hopi have a reputation for being peaceful, almost passive. They keep a low profile and keep to their way. They had this reputation from the beginning. The Spaniards had contact with them before the *Mayflower* docked at a rock in what was to be Plymouth, Massachusetts. They have this reputation now. They are secure in these mesas, in which they have lived as settled farmers for more than eight hundred years.

Physically they are different from the surrounding Navajo; shorter, stockier, finer featured, more closely related to the Aztecs than to the taller Athapascans of the north. In the sixteenth and seventeenth centuries the Hopi villages were a kind of Switzerland to other desert tribes; in those years, when Spanish governors and Franciscan ecclesiasts were busy with the work of subjugation, members of other tribes showed up as refugees on the Hopi doorstep. They were given living space, room to build, fields of their own. They were welcome, as all people of any faith are today, at the dances of the kachinas; the masked spirits of ancestors, animals, men, clowns. It is a tenet of the Hopi Way that these dances are good for everyone to see, that they are for the benefit of all people.

So: I am trying to understand what it was that stirred them to massacre their own kind and destroy their own village, and I wonder myself — and it is my own wonder, from within my own cultural boundaries; I cannot inhabit any other — I wonder if the raid of Awatobi was something like the trials of witches at Salem, or the burning of heretics at the stake, in Inquisition days. It was the burning of heretics, in point of fact.

The story of the ruin of Awatobi began on August 20, 1629, on the feast day of San Bernardo, when three Franciscans and twelve Spanish soldiers walked up the mesa paths into this village. It was the first Hopi village that Spanish priests had ever come to, and they fell on their knees in prayer. When they got up they resolved that the mission of San Bernardo de Awatobi would be grand, magnificent, for the proper enlightenment of man and the glory of God.

The Franciscans went on to other villages, too. They founded the missions of San Francisco in Oraibi, Visitas in Walpi, San Bartolomé in Shongopovi.

They were not welcome anywhere. The priests, backed by soldiers, methodically destroyed Hopi altars and railed against Hopi customs and made the Hopi work to build the missions. Immense beams for the mission churches were dragged from the mountains tens of miles away. The ruts visible in the mesa stone of Oraibi were, the Hopi say, worn there by the butt ends of dragged mission beams. According to one book that I read, the Hopi word for Franciscan priests in those days was *tota-achi,* meaning a grouchy person that will not do anything for himself. It was a word otherwise used for cranky crones or spoiled children. It came to mean more than that. In the end, the tyranny of the tota-achi was too much to bear.

In the Pueblo uprising of 1680, the Spaniards were thrown out of the villages of the Rio Grande and out of Hopi country, too. Some missionaries were killed and the missions were razed, but that wasn't the end of it. That wasn't the end of it at all.

One day in 1700, twenty years after the Franciscans had been thrown out, Fathers Juan de Garicochea and Antonio Miranda marched back into Awatobi, having walked and ridden for many days from the capital of New Spain — now Mexico City — and once in Awatobi they fell on their knees and raised their arms in the air and preached and prayed and baptized the faithful all day long.

Terrible personal risk and terrific hardship and fanatical belief must have refined these two Franciscans to bright flames of pure zeal; the faithful of Awatobi were a fuse they set alight.

Their revival meeting attracted quite a crowd. There were some people in Awatobi whose conversion to Christianity had been genuine, years before, and who had hidden their faith all the years between, and who welcomed the fathers back into their midst.

Tapolou was the chief of Awatobi in those days. He was not among the Christian faithful. The glad response of his own people was more than disturbing; it was heretical. After the Franciscans went back to their home missions, to gather soldiers and matériel for a longer stay, Tapolou plotted with the chiefs of Oraibi to destroy his own town. The Oraibi chiefs managed the rest; rousing the warrior societies of other villages, coordinating battle plans, organizing the making of bows, arrows, heavy shields.

There was no place in the Hopi world for Christians who were loyal to the king of Spain. These were infidels, to be destroyed. The membrane had been breached. The infection would be cauterized and the breach would be closed.

Years later, Oraibi itself split in two over the question of whether or not their children would have to go to the white man's school. This was in 1906. It was the same question over again: our civilization or theirs. The anti-school faction walked out and formed the village of Hotevila.

Everyday life goes on here, now, without having changed much, in some ways, from the time of Tapolou. The Hopi Way is still the Way here. When you go to a Hopi village you have to sign in at the town hall and go through the village with a registered guide, and take no photos and make no sketches. You are treated, carefully and kindly, like a guest; a guest who cannot quite be trusted to behave too well.

The Hopi Way is like a desert shrub: the invisible roots are many times greater than the visible part. The leaves are small and the branches may be small, but the tenacity of the whole is astounding, it is durable and strong almost beyond belief.

Now, today in Awatobi, a flock of horned larks is flying and twittering and chipping; they rise singing over our shoulders in the wind. Now this is a humpy landscape of saltbush and rabbitbrush and tumbleweed, wildflowers and rabbit dung. The fine gray soil has the texture of ash. Away from the ruins is a nubbly yellow-silver sea of grass with junipers dotted like dark flames.

Picture a country with soil the color of cream and ochre. Add ring muhly grass like rough rings of just-tarnished silver. The far hills, rust and yellow, are freckled with juniper. The whole landscape is the colors of the potsherds, blurred and unresolved. I stare and stare at this country as one does at the horizon of the sea, or at flames of a fire. When I look at him, Alex is staring, too; and Coulter is standing looking out, with an orange jasper arrowhead and a black marble of volcanic glass in his hand, the findings of an hour's forage among rabbit holes. He will leave them behind when we go.

"They belong here, Mom," he'll say.

He knows by now whose treasures they are.

Later, back at his house, Alex carves a kachina while I make notes on the day. The kachina in his hands is still attached to its natal curve of cottonwood root. He shoves the knife forward with his thumb and curls of wood fall away.

He is making a wolf doll to go with a set of antelope dancers. The wolf will have a white mask with two red eyes, a red mouth, a fur ruff. The antelope dance is a hunting dance; this wolf is the predator.

"How do you know how to make it, Alex?"

"I look at something and I soak it in. I remember it. Like a photograph. It's a part of me."

The wolf has high pricked ears, a long snout, a rattle in one hand and a bow in the other. One foot is lifted and the skirts flow back from the lifted knee.

"When I carve, I change the thing. It's how I feel it, from in here. I have to feel how it should be." He thumps himself on the chest.

Then he looks up:

"You remember those potsherds you liked, back there?" He tosses his head, meaning Awatobi. "A lot of those patterns, we still use," he says.

Then he says that a neighbor of his has begun making pots again. She started two days ago. She uses a round pebble to polish the clay smooth. Right now, he says, her hands are sore from smoothing pots.

And I wonder if my will to remember is as strong as his. If the coherence of my world is as strong as his. I did not wonder these things before.

Later, when I read the story, I can't forget that in Awatobi we were sitting in the ash of a heretics' pyre, that this was a price paid to keep a people whole.

I think: what happened to the natives of Massachusetts, the Wampanoag who gave baskets of corn to the *Mayflower* Pilgrims at Thanksgiving time? They were friendly, ameliorative, and willing, and — except for a remnant few on the island of Martha's Vineyard — they are gone.

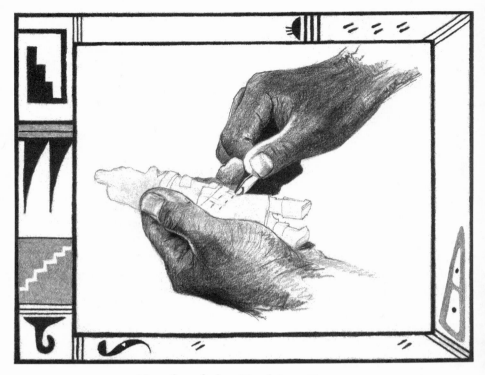

Hands of the Kachina Carver

The mask, the kilt, the leggings are taking shape, one foot is lifted in dance.

The border designs are taken from Hopi pottery, ancient and modern. Over time there seems to have been little change in the design elements themselves or in the earth colors used in the glazes, though every potter makes use of them differently and every pot is a unique creation. Since the elements have symbolic meaning, each pot is also a kind of poem, or statement.

20

pilgrimage

Canyon of Rainbows,
Tohono O'odham Reservation, Arizona

Plants and animals change as one goes up the mountains, and so, apparently, do people.

I have been noticing people's faces as they come down. They are flushed and hot, but there is something else in them, too: a happiness. Maybe because they're down again, back in the bosom of the extended family, and it's almost time for the big meal. Maybe not, I think, later.

The people arrived last night in a phalanx of pickups that banged and roared into the canyon, over the wash, the crowds in the beds of them yelling with the loudest jolts, then there was chatter and lights for an hour as they settled in. There was a dog or two and an army of children. This much I could tell, in the dark.

Well before dawn there was a cracking of twigs and the crack-thump of ax on wood, and giggling, and the smell of smoke and then boiling coffee, then cross-borders polka music from a radio, and the children and the dogs got going. An extended family of Tohono O'odham had arrived in the canyon camp for a reunion.

Even before their breakfast had been served from the mammoth black frypans and two-gallon camp kettles, I noticed that groups, two or three and more, came by me up the canyon toward the mountain trail. They wore sneakers and jeans and T-shirts and baseball-type caps and carried bottles of water in plastic bags. I thought they

were going up a little way to get a view, or a peaceful place away
from the maelstrom to chitchat and visit. Later I wasn't so sure.

I had come for something else, for the mountains themselves, or that
was my intention. Ecologists are interested in biotic communities, in
their inhabitants and boundaries, and as one goes up a mountain slope
these change. The ranges are islands; each one isolated from the next
range by miles-wide bajadas, great alluvial outwash plains that stretch
between them like bowls so gently curved they seem flat. In the way
of islands anywhere each range is unique, though here each one holds
roughly the same concentric rings of Sonoran desert community.
Beginning with the basins — the markless expanses of cholla, paloverde, and barrel cactus — one can climb through gravelly slopes
dominated by saguaros, then through upland scrub, semidesert grasslands, Sonoran evergreen woodland, into the oak forests of the encinal (*encino* means oak in Spanish), and beyond that to forests of pine
and fern, even spruce and fir. If the climate changes these communities can swell downward or retreat up, and can wait isolated in their
mountain islands for millennia.

The encinal has waited a long time. It hails back five million years
or more to the time before the glacial ages began. What's left in the
Mexican uplands and in these few border ranges are relics, swatches,
forests from the past.

Climate changes with the altitude, becoming cooler and wetter in
general as you go up, though the way the slope faces matters too;
the south sides of the canyons are drier, lighter, more extreme. Here
these are desert slopes of saguaro, mesquite, gravel. Cactus wrens
start their burbly muttering there even before dawn, and flocks of
Gambel's quail scutter between the washes. The north slopes are
more temperate and shadier, damper; there are crevice-forests of oak,
Arizona walnut, netleaf hackberry, canyon grape, filled with flocks
of red cardinals and yellow warblers, and mourning cloak butterflies,
big and velvety, heavy as shadow.

Mountains being what they are, with creases and canyons, raw
bedrock and tumbled scree, the theoretical neat layers of biotic community are hopelessly scrunched and scrambled. There are endless
microclimates, possibilities for pockets of wildflowers, jojoba, or for

an exceptional species — elephant trees, the tiny fiery wild chilies called *chiltepínes,* or something else — bird or coati or wildflower.

I had come in here the afternoon before, promising myself a day of rest, of reading and writing and eating well. I was tired, and confused with traveling. I'd gone a hundred miles out of my way to find a store; I'd bought a bag of oranges, real meat, fresh tortillas and peppers. The canyon of rainbows had been a balm before and I wanted a day of rest before climbing the range as high as I could go. The mountain communities were something that I needed to see. And botany and birding and the glimpses of animals, or the signs of them, are the best escape from one's own dreams and confusions and the general drama of human life, but now a new drama had arrived in the form of this big family of Tohono O'odham, whose country this is, after all. So in the morning I made my own coffee and kept my head down and met no one's eyes; I was self-conscious, and they seemed happy enough at first to ignore my presence.

Coming in, I had stopped for water at the post office in the last of their villages before the mountains. There were hardly any houses and no stores but there was an old Spanish mission building, painted white; there were children in the playground wearing neat uniforms. There was a spanking new post office and a water spigot outside the door, but no way to turn the thing on. When I asked inside I found that the postmistress kept the tap in the drawer with the airmail stamps. She examined me with that impassive X-ray stare endemic to the fiercer breed of third-grade schoolmarm before allowing me to borrow this talisman, this key to kingdoms, this threaded bronze wheel. I screwed it onto the spigot, filled my water bags, and returned the tap to its guardian with profuse expressions of gratitude.

Such is the effect of water on the desert traveler. Then I followed a track into the range, and made my camp in the canyon.

Now after breakfast the children have gathered around my camp. The boys climb all over the rocks, the girls sit and stare and smile and laugh; the most un-shy children I've ever met. I get my bag of oranges and cut them up and they eat and giggle — there's Olivia, and Renata, and more names I don't catch.

All morning they appear and disappear, as flocklike as birds. I run out of oranges but they still come. They look through my books and recognize birds and animals, pointing. Late in the morning the father of one of the boys comes to sit awhile, he's just come from the mountain, and his feet hurt; he's wearing a pair of new boots that the Park Service gave him for his summer job as a firefighter. When they call him, he'll go, wherever the fire is, as far as Nevada.

He says he likes the Sierra Club and other conservation-minded folk who leave no signs of themselves, and who love and respect nature.

He was in the U.S. Marines for four years. When he came back — from the Philippines, Australia, New Zealand, Singapore — he knew so much, had so much understanding, he would try to tell people. He would tell them about the treasure of their natural resources. He counseled them to control their cows, to keep them from overgrazing the range. He would try to lecture them against drinking. They didn't listen. They called him White Man.

He says that teenage pregnancy, alcohol, diabetes, and the self-destructive tough-guy mentality and so on — these things are rampant. And no one will listen.

"Now in the schools here they teach Tohono O'odham language, and traditions — why can't they learn this at home?" he says.

"Here, Renata," he says, and talks in a slow, low, soft, choking language. Renata shakes her head, giggles, hides her mouth behind her hand.

"Children are ashamed to speak O'odham," he says.

There is a familiar ring to this. In the clash and mingling of cultures unexpected things are discarded and adopted, but often enough no whole fabric has been made. People fall between the meshes. On the other hand, in unexpected ways they are buoyed up.

"Have you been to the mountain?" he asks.

When I say no, not yet, he says:

"This is the sacred one." He points up. "The mountain of our God. His cave is there. If you go there, you must leave something."

Half an hour later a tall white-haired priest arrives in the canyon. Someone has fetched him in a pickup, and he comes to the groaning reunion table in full Roman Catholic regalia. Everyone has gathered;

fifty or sixty people. Suddenly there is silence and bowed heads. I see Leo's graying head, and Olivia and the others kneeling on the ground, the little children's heads in their mothers' laps, and the priest raises his hand and gives a long blessing, the words inaudible. The fire smokes, the pots steam. His hand is lowered at last and everyone begins to talk and eat. The priest stays awhile, then some- one takes him away in a pickup. Someone else turns the polka music back on. After the meal, more people begin to walk, in little bunches, up the mountain trail and out of sight.

By nightfall the whole family has packed back into the trucks and is gone, no one is left but me. In the dark there is a poorwill poor willing for all he's worth, a great horned's somber staccato hoots from upslope, the wails of coyotes rising, falling. A crowd of coatis comes through camp, shadow shapes with tails like walking sticks, to rummage the trash cans the cows have dumped over; in the morn- ing the ravens, their wings in the near-dawn like heavy breathing, pick over what's left. Legions of camp goons, here.

True to the spirit of the spigot, in which all things of importance here seem incomplete, puzzles to be resolved, just above camp in the canyon, as I set out at dawn, I find a busted wooden sign nailed to a stake. Whatever it said once it now says "MOUNT." Signpost or commandment, it stands beside a narrow path.

The path goes up through fat green saguaros, their tips white-gold with meshed spines; they're like enormous candles. There are wild flails of ocotillos, in leaf now — though they'll drop them in any drought, put them on again in any rain. There are clumps of nipple cactus, white netted mesh with dark hooks, complete with enormous yellow blooms. There are prickly pears in bud, new pads like beavers' tails with small wedges of upcurling leaves. These will drop away soon, and permanently; now they make the new pads look like larval porcupines.

The Tohono O'odham make fences out of ocotillo. The bodies of these fences are ocotillo stems cut to size and packed vertically like palings. Ironwood is used for the fence posts, saguaro ribs for hori- zontal supports. Ribs are what's left when a saguaro dies and the flesh rots away, and they're naturally smooth as though they'd been sandblasted. You can't see through these fences and you sure can't get through. O'odham ocotillo impoundments are made from a nice cross section of Arizona upland flora, and are as through-proof as close-woven barbed wire.

When I stop for breath a broad-billed hummingbird sits on a mesquite twig ten feet away, then on another twig, closer, turning, as if to give me the view: of fire-red beak tipped with black, his breast grading from central purple through parrot green to pale lemony green at his flanks — a jewel. Then he burrs away.

There are smatterings of spring annuals: orange Mexican poppies, blue stars of phacelia, purple pixie hats of paleface delphinium, lupines. Where cows haven't trampled them whole slopes are tinted orange and blue, though it has not been a rainy year. In rainy years the colors rise in these hills like a Technicolor shag rug.

The scene begins to change. I am not sure when the cacti fall behind. The air goes bluer with the day.

There is a slablike funnel of a canyon between rounded rocks — trees with bonzai footholds, ferns in north-facing crevices. A yellow warbler flirts through branches, sings, is gone. In the shade is a single false mock orange in white bloom.

The path climbs, steadily screwing itself upward. In one pitch after the next it switchbacks up through raw stones.

The air begins to change. The swifts that nest high in the rock whirl and chatter against their cliffs like live smoke.

There are scattered oaks and pinyons; there are meadows of mountain yucca, clumps of desert ceanothus. In the stones are pale circles of rainbow cactus, the muffin-sized cactus of the mountains, cream and red and pink and silver, delicate as dreams.

At a bend in the path a single oak holds on to a crevice of red stone. Today in the hot sun the tree is a mass of golden pollen, and is alive with bees. The noise of it is huge; a thrum that communicates through rock.

Then the path goes goaty, steep, with a near-vertical drop on one side and rubble and cliffs rising naked on the other. All on one side as if the earth had gone wrong is the mass of the air: below and away like scrunched cloth whole ranges wrinkle the landscape, the gray plains lie between the mountains as far as far with no scratch of road or patch of field visible anywhere, no sign that human beings have crept onto the planet at all.

Then the trail climbs over a rim and arrives in the encinal, a yellow grassland dotted with ancient trees.

The grassland laps against red knobs of rock. Scattered in the grass are oaks, thick and short and spreading, here and there clustering into forest. Around them the grasses are tall and the path is no more than a grass-covered dent through them. The cows have never come here; this is above cow line, above usage, beyond anything but the feet of pilgrims; and there haven't been too many of those.

There are emory oaks, gray oaks, Arizona white oaks, their leaves glossy, dark, small. There are one-seed junipers and Mexican pinyons. Gray-breasted jays move in loud flocks through the trees, their dark eye lines giving them a jazzy look, big blue birds cocking me a cocky eye.

The path goes on through the grassland and the forests. A coyote has left her dung, as usual, beside the trail. She has been eating juniper berries and small rodents — there are tiny teeth, rib fragments, a tiny broken femur — and there is hair: bighorn sheep wool and rodent fuzz; there are grass stems, berries. There are deer tracks in the path, and the dry flattish pellets of a cottontail.

The desert is below all around like a distant sea, with stains of cloud shadow, and faraway mountains like old teeth. It is all a faintly freckled texture roughened by the ranges like tree bark. Here and there a dust devil wanders, a pale pencil of a djinn balanced on one pointed toe. Overhead there is very dark blue sky full of flat-bottomed clouds. The clouds are close. Ahead is a last rusty pile of stone streaked with lichen and desert varnish like a corroding hulk. A real peak, peaklike and final. The path ends on a tilting shelf of forest and beyond it there is only red rock on which nothing grows.

Here is the place. A narrow precinct of stones walls it off. Behind is a hole in the rock, in a cleft; it looks exactly like the entrance of a vagina. No wonder, I think. A hole like that would stop anyone in their tracks.

The hole has been rubbed smooth. I go in feet first, touch ground, ease my shoulders in with my arms over my head. Inside it is dark and smells of old smoke. It's a while before I can see anything. Then it arches up, the size of a room, the walls blackened, everything dusty, there is a kind of altar alcove, and all around the walls and in this alcove there are things.

There are empty cans and bottles and bottle caps. A rhinestone necklace is stuck to the wall with a wad of gum. There are half-made baskets, a toy truck, a teddy bear, a ball, a comb, a football trophy, photographs, hair bands, cobs of corn, votive candles, bandannas, a piece of sandpaper, seed pods, a lot of baseball-type hats, a few sneakers, and an enormous hand-forged medieval sword standing on end, piercing a black-and-white photo of a Roman Catholic priest in full regalia.

I take an empty page out of my notebook and a jay feather out of my hat and wrap them in the band from the end of my braid, and put that by the wall, too, as if I'd been thinking about it all the time, which I hadn't.

This is the cave of the god who first found the path of life that all Tohono O'odham follow from their birth until they die, and they leave the simplest pieces of themselves in his house.

Then I go out, squeezing head foremost into the light.

In the winter, Leo said, you can walk here in the encinal through six inches of snow with no shirt on. The light is as strong up here as medicine.

The Old Mission and the Older Mountains
Tohono O'odham Reservation, Arizona

21

bechan

Desert Laboratory, Tucson, Arizona

Bechan is a Navajo word meaning big shit, and there is a cave by that name in an obscure canyon in southeastern Utah, and that is what it is full of. Other caves across the Southwest contain some, too, but this one holds nearly three hundred cubic yards of the stuff. It blankets a roomy cave of red Navajo sandstone that is one hundred and seventy-three feet deep, one hundred and three feet wide, up to thirty feet high. Some of the dung boluses are still intact, and they are similar in size and shape to those of an African elephant. They were left by mammoths.

Twelve thousand years ago — and this is following clues, mind you: dung and hair preserved in this dry cave and others, fossil footprints in lake beds, skeletons preserved in alluvium and tar, radiocarbon dates from bone and boluses, and the behavioral patterns of African elephants, mammoths' close relatives — twelve thousand years ago a herd of mammoths used the cave as shelter from the sun. Larger than the woolly mammoth of the tundra and northern forests, the matriarchs of this clan stood more than ten feet high at the shoulder. Their tusks were lyrate, incurved. In those days hundreds of thousands of these Columbian mammoths ranged from coast to coast, from north of the Great Lakes to as far south as Florida. They were grazers. Their main feeding grounds were the grass prairies that stretched from Nebraska to Texas, west through New Mexico, Utah, Arizona, southern California, down into the Mexican plateau.

There is other dung in the cave, too. Maybe two kinds of ground sloth rested or bred there between mammoth visits, the Shasta and the big-tongued, most likely; huge plant-eating creatures of open brushy country, slow-moving, solitary. Horses and deer and other hoofed animals used the cave as occasional shelter — camels, perhaps, mountain deer, brush oxen, stout-legged llamas — anyway, from goat-sized to the stature of moose. Packrats made their nests in there, too, sheltered from the snow and rain.

Outside the cave a stream ran through the canyon bottom — there is an ephemeral stream there now but in those days it ran all year — and along the stream and its plunge pools were thickets of blue spruce and water birch, elderberries and wild rose, wet meadows of sedge. Flanking the stream were dunes furred with ricegrass, saltbush, clumps of prickly pear. Then as now the packrats hauled in pads of cactus, as well as twigs and bits of everything else, to armor their messy houses. Beyond the dunes and water meadows were gray slopes of sage. The mammoths grazed the sedge meadows and salt-bushes and the ricegrass slopes, then they moved on.

All of these plants — their stems, thorns, twigs, leaves, seeds, sifted from the dung and the packrat middens — are living species. Some are still growing outside Bechan Cave, others have retreated two or three thousand feet up the mountainsides, or north as far as Idaho; they have shifted ground. It was cooler in those days but not much cooler; wetter, too, but not much wetter.

Now, instead of sagebrush, the slopes above the cave are spotted with blackbrush. Blackbrush is tolerant of drier ground and higher temperatures. The evidence is, that since the mammoths left, the deserts have arrived.

Other things arrived, too. Against one wall of the cave a group of Paiute or Navajo once made a shelter of juniper branches, and left layers of charcoal, chips from stone tools, broken metates. After they left, the packrats added corncobs to their middens.

These people came later; they came much later. The metates and the corn say that these cave visitors were farmers. But the first people

who came here to the Southwest eleven thousand years ago were
not.

These North American pioneers — whether they were absolutely
the first people or not is in question, but they were the first to leave
plentiful hard evidence — were big-game hunters. Their hunting
skills had been honed on the steppes of central Asia. They are known
by us as Clovis people. They were named for the site in Clovis, New
Mexico, where the assemblage of their campsite tools and artifacts
was first recognized as a culture worthy of a name. They are known
most of all for the delicate leaf-shaped blades of their projectile points,
an inch and a half to five inches long, thin and sharp. They followed
their quarry across the swampy ice-free corridor of the Bering land
bridge some thirteen thousand years ago, and a millennium or two
later they came down here into a country that we could never in our
wildest dreams imagine.

Where the deserts lie now there were open steppes of grass and
sage. Rivers ran from snowed and forested mountains. Meltwater
from retreating glaciers in the Wasatch Front of Utah and the Sierras
of California filled desert lake beds, beds that are now flat pans of
cracked and crusted salts and silt. There were elk and bison and mule
deer and gray wolves and coyotes, as there are now, or were till
recently; but they were the least of it. What the hunters saw here was
a country of huge beasts: herds of mammoths, herds of giant bison,
tapir, capybara, and more herds: several species each of horses, camels, llamas, four-horned pronghorns, deer, oxen, goats. There were
ground sloths the size of elephants. There were giant beavers and
armadillos. To prey on and scavenge these there were cheetahs,
saber-toothed and scimitar-toothed cats, American lions, short-faced
bears bigger than grizzlies, giant condors, dire wolves the size of
ponies. Now there were Clovis people, too.

Paul S. Martin is an ecologist, and his terrain is the landscape of the
past. His area of research is the end of the Pleistocene — the Pleistocene epoch ended ten thousand years ago; this last ten thousand years
is known as the Holocene, or Recent — so Bechan Cave is his turf,
so to speak.

This much is clear: in the final three thousand years of the Pleistocene epoch, three things happened here at once. One: the landscape grew hotter and drier, the glaciers retreated, fast, the deserts crept into the basins and up the foothills. Two: Clovis people arrived in the Southwest. Three: the great animals known as the Pleistocene Megafauna, thirty-three genera of them, disappeared. Paul Martin estimates that the biomass alone of these vanished animals, the sheer weight of them, was seventy-five million tons; roughly the same as all of the domestic livestock and big game now present in North America.

Nowadays Paul Martin is the Acting Director of the Desert Laboratory of the Department of Geosciences at the University of Arizona in Tucson. The lab was founded in 1903 by the Carnegie Institution; it was the first study center to focus on arid lands. From the beginning it took the long view. The desert needs a long view. A saguaro cactus that lives several centuries needs generations of researchers and decades of data to even begin to understand its life cycle, and many desert plants are longer-lived than that: there are creosote bushes whose seeds germinated ten thousand years ago, when the California basins first dried enough to give them a foothold. It takes a long view to understand the contents of Bechan Cave.

One room of the Desert Laboratory is half full of green steel cabinets. These are filled with boxes and bins filled in turn with labeled plastic bags, and they contain the evidence.

There are chunks of fossil packrat midden — dusty, faintly honey-combed, hard and heavy as rock, black and resinous in cross section, made of packrat garnerings cemented with their feces and urine. Since a packrat rarely goes farther than three hundred feet from its nest and gathers up anything interesting within that: animal bones, twigs, bits of insects, stones, cactus pads, leaves, seeds (some of this for food but much of it to add bulk and protection to its home), these middens are a sampling of the rat's environment. With time, the middens become as dark and glossy as tar. Protected in dry caves for millennia (the oldest fossil midden found was made more than fifty thousand years ago), they can be collected, soaked in water, their contents sorted, identified, carbon-dated. They are collections from the past.

Also in the green cabinets are chunks of Australian stick-rat midden, porcupine midden, too. Plant cell structures are preserved in these even when plant parts have been too finely chewed to be identified by other means, and pollen can be identified as well. There are pieces of dung of the Shasta ground sloth that were found in a cave in Arizona; these look like horse dung, only larger. There are boluses of mammoth dung from Bechan Cave; a large double handful each, brown on the outside, strawy in. There are sloth and camel and horse bones found in Gypsum Cave, Nevada. There's a piece of hair and skin of a ground sloth, found preserved in bat guano in a New Mexican cave. The hide and hair of another ground sloth, a fragment found in South America, is seal-like but very thick; buried in the skin are pebble-shaped bones, dermal bones that served as body armor, though there was plenty of room between them — at least on the belly of the beast — to slip a Clovis spear. There are pellets from Harrington's extinct goat, a mountain goat that lived in these mountains as bighorn sheep do now. There are human dung and basket and bone fragments. There's a piece of horse hoof that was found in Rampart Cave, in Arizona; it came from a small horse, burro-sized. Perhaps the carcass of that horse was dragged in there by one of the big cats, one evening in the height of the Wisconsin glacial age, long before the threat of extinction; when simple life and death still ruled the day. The hoof in question was trotting on the plains of Arizona "26,300 years ago, plus or minus 760 years," the label says. Carbon-14 dates are accurate, within a range.

That's just it: the most recent dates of all of the remains of the Pleistocene Megafauna — all except the human remains — cluster within a range. Horses evolved in North America north of Mexico, and lived here for a long time. Some crossed to Asia over the land bridge during some pulse of glacial advance: the ancestors of zebras, burros, onagers, the modern horse. But there were half a dozen species ranging here till Recent time, from burro-sized to the stature of a thoroughbred. All of these are gone.

The final dates are telling. Horse: 10,370 years ago, give or take 350. Giant beaver: 10,230, give or take 150. Camel: 10,370. American mastodont: 10,395. Mammoth: 10,550. Tapir: 9,400. Fugitive deer: 9,940. Shrub ox: 8,250. Shasta ground sloth: 10,035. I've left out the give-or-takes. The fact is that the last evidence of these animals was left here between fourteen and eight thousand years ago, with the peak of last appearances eleven thousand years ago.

Paul Martin believes that this is no coincidence. The rivers and waterholes were drying out, the ranges of feedstuff were shrinking — becoming islanded by desert — but the animals had survived interglacial dry spells before. The arrival of one new predator, one who could stake out a waterhole and wait, who could organize, in fact, might have been the last straw. The animals were climate-stressed, then exposed to a new, unknown, highly efficient predator. They disappeared in a coast-to-coast wave (their extinctions parallel the wave of Clovis migration), went down fast, within centuries, in what Paul calls a "blitzkrieg."

The evidence is convincing. It has convinced him, but not everyone. Other paleoecologists cite Pleistocene extinctions on other continents, too; even Africa lost 15 to 20 percent of its species of big game. Asia lost more, Australia still more. But North America lost everything, almost.

What we think of as having been the animals of the pristine Southwest — the buffalo and elk, the bighorns, the puma, the gray wolf, the grizzly — were ragtag remnants of an emptied land.

Holding the little bags of evidence in my hands — compressed chewed grass stems, terribly dry; a mummified hoof — I find myself, suddenly, almost in tears. I can almost see them, they're so close, almost here, almost alive in my hands — shitting is such an intimate live act, and extinction is so final, more final than any death, though just as natural, it turns out.

Paul sits at his desk, leans back in his chair. Long windows look out on the bright landscape of Tumamoc Hill; saguaros and creosote, a scattering of spring wildflowers even in this drought year, but nothing a mammoth would want. Two walls are floor-to-ceiling books and papers, the other two are windowed stone. Several of the books and papers are on the desk and the floor.

"It makes a difference in the way you view the world," he says. There's a pause.

"That there were these extinctions. And so many of them. And that these animals have escaped history," he says.

"They have escaped — " I begin and can't go on, perhaps what I mean is that they have escaped me, but the sentence like so many things hangs there unfinished. Maybe finished enough. Paul nods. Says:

"Escaped. Exactly. Yes."

Peccary and Prickly Pear

A peccary looks misshapen until you realize that its head is what it works (and plays) with. The skull and jaws are massive and the nose is as sensitive as fingertips. Peccaries eat prickly pear, the fruits and the young pads, plus whatever else they can find on or below the ground, both animal and vegetable. They live in families and they're playful and quick and very good to eat, and they can be aggressive, though this one looks sleepy because it is midday: nap time. Their coarse brindled hair helps them to disappear in the shadows of rocks and canyon scrub whenever they want. They live in the Sonoran desert of Arizona and throughout most of Texas.

Pahranagat

22

fossil water

Pahranagat National Wildlife Refuge, Nevada

When you come from the south there are the fluid shapes of mountains reflecting in dark double form, and the double brightness of — must be water, couldn't be anything else — set like a mirror in a frame of dusty no-account hills.

It is so strange to come on open water out here that at first it looks as if pieces of sky had fallen on the ground, and the frills of greenery around them look entirely false.

This is Pahranagat, an oasis that lies along a crease of the Mojave desert some eighty miles north of Las Vegas. At the south end is a wildlife refuge that runs for ten miles, including in its boundaries quantities of desert scrub, grasslands, meadows, cattail swamps, crops, pastures, and *seven hundred acres* of open water. Farther north, rich farm fields stretch for thirty-five more miles along the line of ponds and marshes, lush round shapes that lie in their crease of the hills like a string of pearls.

The water is pearl-colored in the evening light. Cottonwoods billow on the shores. Above ponds and swamps and cottonwoods are hillsides of average Mojave, meaning rocks and creosote and bursage with sometimes a spiky yucca. In a "normal" spring there would be wildflowers clothing the rocks and dust in ephemeral color, but this is the third and worst year of drought so wildflowers are out of the question. Their seeds are in the dust, monumentally patient.

This year only dark green yuccas stand out against the pale hills and bleached vegetation. The Mojave yucca tends to grow in clusters, little ones and big ones in cartoonish family bunches, each faceless member made of a substance like pineapples and scissorblades. Every yucca seems to be twisted to one side, like a maimed figure.

I have never been able to get used to the raw rocks lying where they have fallen from some outcrop. There they lie, unchanged over centuries. Somehow this is discouraging; these rocks express a kind of futility.

There are very few cacti in the Mojave. The Mojave is a cold desert, cold in winter, anyway. Not now. The rusty creosote bushes, with their twigs wriggling up and out, look as if they were the skeletons of fires.

So, among all this, coming to the oasis of Pahranagat, one heaves a sigh of happiness; this is a miracle, a wonder, and a mystery. Where is this water *from?*

On the pale surface of the first big lake is a freckling of shapes like pepper sprinkled: birds. Stopping there, squatting under a cottonwood tree, feeling the dance of water-flecked light on my face, I watch a muskrat paddle by in a wake of silver ripples. I hear the clurks and low mutters of mallards, the clicks clucks, squeaks and rattle-squeals of coot, the bright loud warbles of a marsh wren, the watery flops as one coot chases another, head down like a black awl.

A wren is making a nest in an island of bulrush. He is full of self-importance and his tail sticks straight in the air. He sings with the passion of a diva. There is a caldron of turkey vultures boiling up over the north end of the lake, the dark birds circling slowly in their thermal tower to gain altitude. There are hundreds of cormorants and white egrets perched in the cottonwood trees.

By the time I make camp I've seen numbers of ring-necked ducks and northern shovelers, gadwalls, several pied-billed grebes and a half-dozen great blue herons, and two gulls too far off to identify.

In October, so I hear, serious numbers of ducks come through Pahranagat on their way from Canada to the southern coasts. Then there are thousands of northern pintails, green-winged teals, canvasbacks, wigeons. In winter there are hundreds of swans and Canada geese. There have been white pelicans at Pahranagat, and white-faced ibis, grebes and egrets of all kinds, even greater sandhill cranes. Now it is the tail end of the spring migration, and the coot and mallard are setting up housekeeping.

In the evening I set up mine, on a rocky hill above a lake.

When the sun is down and the air goes lavender and gold, I light a fire. Sturdy dry cottonwood branches the size of my arms make a good bright hot fire; it's the first one in a long time, the first fire larger than microscopic in weeks. It's the first place where there has been fuel for the taking. Now the smoke is coming over my shoulder, one pants leg is warm and one ear, my rump, one arm. The lake is alive even in the dark; there are trills, whistles, rustlings, and splashings. There are coyotes calling from up-country.

Twelve thousand years ago I would have been listening for other things. I would have been worried about a herd of mammoths stampeding over me in the darkness. Or horses, or camels. I would have been concerned about a sabertooth cat or a pack of dire wolves scenting me out, or a three-hundred-pound Shasta ground sloth or a giant beaver the size of a black bear blundering into my tent.

In the valley of Pahranagat there was a river in those days, it was called the White River, and it ran all the way to the Colorado. This was a semiarid steppe with juniper trees and grasses instead of the yucca and the creosote.

Speaking of rains — this is the odd thing. The rains of that time charged the underwater aquifers, and gently canted impervious layers of rock have since guided that water for dozens and hundreds of miles, out at last into the light. A series of such ancient springs now feeds Pahranagat; there is no upstream of the White River anymore. What water is here now comes from long ago.

This is a fragment of Eden pinched off and saved.

The cottonwood trees have been saved, and the coots fussing, and the silver world of the muskrats.

This water has been down in the rock for a long time. According to experts in desert hydrodynamics, the water that fills Pahranagat now is from rain that fell twelve thousand years ago. It is known as fossil water. Here it comes. Here it is.

Pair of Ring-necked Ducks at Pahranagat

23

the color blue

Devil's Hole, Death Valley National Monument, and Ash Meadows National Wildlife Refuge, Nye County, Nevada

There is a species of fish whose breeding habitat is the size of a desktop. A desktop isn't much space in the world. A schoolroom-sized desk, too, the kind with the chair attached and a shelf underneath where you tuck your books. The habitat is a shelf, really; a lucky triangular bit of stone jutting just so, with two feet or less of lucky water over it. The shelf looks yellow-green with algae and has coppery blotches that may be algae also. One has to look very hard to see that there are fish there: inch-long dark shapes, sometimes curved, sometimes moving.

The fish are Devil's Hole pupfish and this is Devil's Hole. Beyond their shallow habitat is the hole itself, a kind of underwater cave that is, so far, immeasurably deep. Scuba divers have gone three hundred feet down in there and never found bottom. Two scuba divers got lost down there years ago and were never found themselves.

The opening of the hole is fifty feet long and ten feet wide, and the shelf is on one side of it. Otherwise, it goes down. A little way down you can go sideways to a cave, not far from the opening, called Brown's Room, filled half with air and half with water and utterly dark. The fish do go down as far as eighty feet themselves, so the scuba people say; why, no one knows. Only the shallow shelf seems to be useful for most feeding or mating, and beyond that shelf the rock curves out of sight into the depths of the hole like the fundus of a toilet bowl.

In midday that deep water is sapphire netted with black, a clear impossible blue. It lies in a deep setting of gray rock. It has the cool lucency of a jewel. At one edge is that triangular patch the size of a desk, like an imperfection at the edge of the jewel.

All of this — shelf and hole — lies at the bottom of a deep, nearly sheer cleft in the rock and you'd never see it at all unless you came close enough to nearly fall in. I fooled around with this, trying to tell how close you'd have to be to see something here besides the gray stones rising at the base of a hill: twenty feet, fifteen, ten, five . . . if a fence weren't here you'd have to stop yourself teetering on the brink before you'd look down and see that color lying down there, and then you'd blink, not understanding what it was, for a minute or two.

The water renews itself all the time. It may come from the Spring Mountains forty miles off, or from as far as Pahranagat; from a hundred miles or more, all underground. This is fossil water, again. What it makes possible here is a strange archipelago of life.

Long years ago fish swam upstream through what is dry baking air — 95 degrees F in April now; presumably Amargosa River water then — and these fish made a home among the jutting rock shelves around the shallows of what was a lake. When the lake dried they were stranded in Devil's Hole as if it were a kind of tide pool. One is familiar with tide pools. One has seen minnows stranded in them. This one has been here with the pupfish in it for ten thousand years, at least. Left in their island of water they've evolved into a species that is unique in the world: here, and only here they are, with a smaller and more fragile habitat than anything has, anywhere, as far as anyone knows.

The gray foothill that wears Devil's Hole in its flank like a sword wound is between the Spring Mountains and the Amargosa range. Below and to the west the ground levels and pales: the old lake bed paved with alkali dust. Scattered in one corner of this lake bed are bumps of shadow; unmistakably trees. Trees in full leaf. Far away, at the end of the dry lake, are the dark bulks of the Amargosa Mountains. On the other side of the Amargosas is Death Valley, the dry heart of the dry Mojave, which is going into the third summer of drought, after the driest winter in its recorded history. On this foot-hill slope the creosotes are nearly transparent, their few leaves gone olive-brown. Between them the hemispherical saltbush shrubs are silvery snarls of leafless twigs. Perhaps they are dead.

Those green trees down there are just as strange as the color of water.

Stranger still: the man who is working there, near his blue Ford pickup, with his hands full of grass and a clipboard under his arm, is a fisheries biologist by profession.

His name is Doug Threloff and he's been here for less than a year. Ash Meadows is a new wildlife refuge as these things go; there isn't much in the way of funds for it yet, and what I've learned in Vegas is that no one there goes out to the desert much, they're far more likely to hop a plane to Boston than to drive an hour and a half out here, so there aren't many visitors. Doug does whatever needs doing most; he's geologist, botanist, maintenance worker, tour leader, re-searcher, file clerk, educator. The refuge was established in 1984, and includes just under twenty-four thousand acres of ground. The green trees there are ash, mostly; single-leaved ash, velvet ash.

"Ash Meadows is Nevada's version of the Galápagos," he says, right away, and that's what the story is. This is an isolated archipel-ago; islands of springwater in a sea of rock and alkali dust.

Devil's Hole is the highest water here, in terms of altitude; down-slope there are more than thirty seeps and springs. Where the Galápa-gos has tortoises, Ash Meadows has fish. They are fish that are unique in the world: three species or subspecies of pupfish, plus Ash Meadows speckled dace. And snails: six species of endemic spring snails, four species of tryonia. And insects: a riffle beetle and a nau-corid bug. And flowers: a sunray, an ivesia, a gum plant, a milk vetch, a blazing star, a niterwort, an orchid, a bear poppy; big showy flowers in full bloom, island flowers, flowers found nowhere else in the world. There are at least twenty-five plant and animal species in Ash Meadows that are found nowhere else in the world. That's a greater number of endemic plants and animals than are found in any other local area in the United States.

The story is that no one really knows what's here. It's an archipelago that has hardly begun to be explored.

"The orchid, for instance, until two years ago, no one even knew it was a new species," Doug says, "and three days ago some researchers came out here to see if we had desert tortoises. It was the first time anyone had ever *looked*. They found what they thought could be a burrow, but no one is sure. And pollinators, beetles . . . they'll find more beetles out here. Endemic pollinators. No one has really started looking."

We're standing by Crystal Spring, the biggest spring on the refuge. There are others: Rogers and Longstreet, School and Point of Rocks, Jackrabbit, Big, and Bole. All of them are full of fish. There are two small reservoirs: Peterson and Crystal. Crystal Spring is the size of a good-sized swimming pool and is as clear and blue as a blue eye, roiled by the force of water coming in. Water trickles off into a marsh rimmed by reeds and cattails. Three hundred yards away, four horses are grazing; two bays, a palomino, and a buckskin.

"Mustangs," Doug says, following my eyes, "wild horses. A few years ago they fenced off some of the little springs to keep the mustangs out. They graze the vegetation around the springs and get in there to keep cool, especially in summer, and they muddy the place up, I tell you! The assumption was that they were doing damage. So the horses were fenced out. And the vegetation grew in over one little spring and choked it solid and killed all the pupfish in there.

"We have to watch it with assumptions," he says.

Among other things, Doug monitors the levels of the springs and the numbers of fish in them. He does whatever other research he can, keeping careful notes on that clipboard. Though there are pupfish in springs and oases throughout the desert, even in Death Valley, each is isolated from the next and is a distinct, unique species. There are three species or subspecies of pupfish here: the Devil's Hole, the Warm Springs, and the Amargosa/Ash Meadows, in that order, coming downhill. As their lake receded, that was the order in which they were left, so to speak, behind. The Warm Springs species has several pools to live in; its habitat can be taken in, from here, by a wave of the hand. The Amargosa/Ash Meadows fish has more springs to its name; a wave of the arm's worth, from here. Of all the springs on the refuge all but two are warm, heated on their under-rock journey by geothermal energy. There are three kinds of water habitat: springhead pools, stream outflows, and marshes. All of these are small, by anyone's standards.

Crystal Spring is the biggest one. Three thousand gallons a minute surface here, in a steady push that keeps the pool surface nearly convex. At last count, last autumn, there were between five and six thousand pupfish here, plus twenty-five thousand mollies and three thousand mosquito fish.

Mollies and mosquito fish are aliens, brought in by the ranchers who owned the place and who thought they'd be useful: the mollies to sell, the mosquito fish to eat mosquitoes. The mollies are the plain household-aquarium-style black ones. They live, as the pupfish do, near the pool bottoms. The mosquito fish patrol the water surface. No one knows what effect either one of these have on native pupfish, but the assumption is that it can't be good.

One of the mandates of the refuge is to return Ash Meadows, as far as is possible, to its pre-human-interference state of being. This won't be easy. Creatures once introduced are hard to root out, and the transplants are happy here. There are crayfish in the springs, and bullfrogs. There are the old farm fields, and the weeds in there may prove more vigorous and seed happy than the fragile lovely bear poppies, sunrays, and so on, the wild endemics that have lived here in their island spring-world since the end of the glacial age. Then there are tamarisks — salt cedars — the water-hungry aliens with a way of spreading peskily from the roots. Every desert river valley and irrigation ditch and oasis is infested with spreading thickets of these Asian aliens; they're thirsty, efficient water-pumpers, something like mesquite, but can crowd in and drain a spring dry, so they're next to impossible to eradicate. Just the thought of policing the tamarisks makes me tired. It makes Doug tired, too, I can tell.

What this return to endemic purity will mean for the mollies and mosquito fish no one is sure, yet. No one really knows how the three fish species interrelate. No one knows the life cycle of these pupfish, their food sources, behavior. No one is sure of much.

I get the idea that Doug likes this. It's frustrating sometimes, but he likes it fine; he can discover things that no one has.

"For instance, the male pupfish turn blue," Doug says. "Well, anyone can see that. But when it isn't mating season, they're not blue."

They're blue now. In the clear water they glimmer like chips of aqua neon. They're an inch long, plump, zesty. They zip, scoot, hang still. I watch for a minute, two. The females are plain dun gray and seem to be drifting, eating, doing nothing much. The blue males zip, scoot, hang still.

"Are the males holding territories? Defending them, I mean?" I ask.

"Looks like it," Doug replies. He's beginning to grin.

"Are they defending nesting grounds? Mating grounds?"

"Don't know," he says. The grin is growing.

"So. When did they turn blue?"

His teeth are white in his tanned face.

"Six weeks ago. Exactly. To the day," he says, and laughs.

Merriam Bear Poppy

The dry cracked ground, level for miles, is ancient lake bed, the alkaline flats and dunefields of the Amargosa valley. The springs of Ash Meadows are real islands in this. Near them one can find this rare white poppy, here in bud, bloom, and fruit; its water-storing tuber is deep in the cracked silts, its leaves are furred by long silver hairs for protection against intense light and baking air.

24

thorns, spines, ecstasies, and itch

Colorado, Sonoran, and Chihuahuan Deserts

Some barrel cacti are completely covered by interlocking chain mail. The ones in Death Valley live in bunches armored with rosy pink; higher in the Mojave they stand alone but their spines are fiery red-yellow. Elsewhere the spines are gray. But they all have spines. And the younger they are the greater this protection is, only because the spine clusters are the same size all the cactus's life and what's right for a chunky adult looks immense on an infant. Whatever its size or age, the more the cactus dries out the more it concertinas together and the closer the clusters mesh, the long curved flattened spines fitting together like fingers interlocking in prayer, giving the greater protection the deeper the drought. Meanwhile, as another accident of form, the growing and flowering tip of the cactus — the dome of its head, so to speak — is always the most heavily defended part, that being the place where growth originates and only gradually spreads. The iron-hard spikes mesh so close there and lie so flat to the flesh as well as stick out that it's impossible even to winkle a finger through to touch the cactus skin.

When the barrel dies, its flesh softening to black crumbs and the waxy skin tearing and blowing away like flakes of paper, the clusters remain, scattering in the stones, darkening with time but sharp as ever, reminding me of minefields still active after a war has passed on.

Pincushion cacti and fishhooks and others of the nipple cactus clan have spines that make a kind of white fur. This works as modest chain mail and also reflects unwanted sunlight away, like a burnoose. Some of these tiny cacti are no bigger than Ping-Pong balls and are as pale as the rock in which they live, looking like puffs of linty cloth or knobs of lace. A tonsure of flower buds pushes out through the white spines somehow, in spring, without being punctured or scraped. The flower can be as large as or even larger than the stubby item it surmounts. The multipetaled skirts of pink, red, white, yellow, or purple, with their sheaves of ecstatic stamens, come as compensation for those motionless, colorless months of endurance.

One way or another, cacti do seem to possess a kind of intelligence. Except for the night-blooming cereus that grow from perennial water-storing roots, and all those chollas and prickly pears, cacti are generally dome-shaped, like stolid homunculi; their growth centers in the tops of their heads, a fontanel that never heals. The mat of feltlike hairs at the crown of the saguaro prevents heat loss on cold winter nights, exactly like a hat, protecting the most frost-sensitive parts, the flower buds and the live cells of the growing stem.

For impishness and sheer spite nothing beats the teddy-bear cholla, also known as the Bigelow or jumping cholla. I put them in my notes as T-bears; their spine coat does look like fur and their colonies do have a familial cuteness. You can't miss them and it's likely that they won't miss you. The first time I saw a whole slope of them together on a pass above Death Valley I wrote that they "look like a landscape filled with dirty mops" and I remember stopping the car to stare, not believing at first that anything could be guilty of such appalling ugliness.

The heavy pelt of T-bear spines is straw-colored in the new growth and as the spine ages it darkens through gold to black. This spine coat works, as the nipple cactus's lace coats do, to reflect unwanted light and heat away from delicate flesh, but that's not all. Each spine is covered by a frail papery sheath. Under this, the shaft is hard as steel and sharp and barbed. It will stick into and hang onto anything. If it sticks in your sleeve or your shoe *you* jump, not it, and when you do an entire joint of cholla will come away with you and will follow you until you pick it off with a comb or a fork or a penknife or a stick, not, please, with your fingers. Once you are rid of it, it will lie there awhile before sending down roots and setting up housekeeping. The ease with which these joints break off and sprout means that T-bears tend to live in colonies, some of them covering acres, and that each mamma cholla is surrounded by a family of golden children, any one of which would love to grab hold of your pants.

Spines, spines, you never know when you'll stumble on or into a new one for the collection. One species of prickly pear down in the Texas borderlands has four-inch-long coal-black ones. Some prickly pears have no spines at all. Most pears and chollas have patches of tiny hairs, bristles, some of them barbed, called glochids. These patches look as innocent as tufts of brown velvet but you should never touch them. The glochids get, literally, under your skin. They itch and annoy and by the time you've scratched and cursed at them they're too far in to get out.

Glochids and spines grow from a spot on the cactus called an areole. Flowers and fruits also grow out of these, roots and branches, too. Areoles are borne on the flanks of prickly pear pads, the ribs of barrels, hedgehogs, and saguaros, the ends of the bumps — nipples — of the nipple cacti. Each is an orifice, like eyes or mouths. That is where spines come from. Of all the genera of plants in the world, only cacti have areoles.

Thorns are something else. Almost every desert tree and shrub that isn't packed with resins, or aromatic oils, or bitter salts, has thorns. There are endless variations on the theme: the wicked talons of the catclaw, the black hypodermics of the mesquite, the pencil cholla's needles. On the leafstalks of wild palms are red rows of blades as sharp as canine teeth. The ends of paloverde or blackbrush twigs jab like fork tines. Thorns grow in leaf axils or as part of a leaf cluster, as they do on the ocotillo, and when the leaf falls that's what's left. Several yuccas have been nicknamed "Spanish dagger" with good reason, but the agaves are worse; each agave leaf has the size and potential of a harpoon.

Whatever their size or source, hundreds of species and dozens of genera have reinvented this defensive wheel, basic equipment for desert exigencies, like a scowl or gritted grimace, a sharp passive resistance meaning: don't push me, don't bother me, don't touch, don't you dare, keep your mitts off, don't think of it, I'll teach you a lesson you won't for the life of you forget. It's a stubborn grim scrapper's stance.

You learn to keep your distance. Out here, there are plenty of distances to keep.

Cactus Wren and Cholla

The cactus wren is a big perky noisy cocky bird, curious about everything. At a roadside picnic spot one flew inside our parked car through an open window and foraged under the seats and along the dashboard for crumbs. Then it stayed close, flitting impatiently and cocking its head at us, making it clear that it was time for us to have lunch. They often make their nests in cholla cactus and they burst in and out, diving in somehow through the thorns and using the cholla's protection as their own. They use these nests for loafing in as well as for raising families. Unlike other species of wren, their songs are not limited to the mating season and are not melodious in the least, but are a kind of laugh, a raw salty commentary.

25

strata

Death Valley National Monument, California

Dinted, cleaved, scarred with white, the cobbles lie in the high light and dust, as if someone had scooped truckloads of riverbed and run it through a damaging machine: the turbine blades of a jet engine, say. Before this damage the cobbles were almost perfectly oval, rounded by years of swiftly running water. Here and now the sound of that comes back: the gutteral clonking of a river rising over its banks, in flood, its water gone the color of milky tea.

Cobbles like these are what you see sorted into curves, according to weight, up on drying banks later in the year. Even shattered as they are and bunged up and wholly out of place they are river cobbles still. They are all colors; deep green, maroon, silver, gray, old-mustard yellow; they came from all over, washed downstream in ecumenical mix. As we go on around the shoulders of the range more of them appear, layers and lenses of cobbles line the road cuts and the walls of the canyons. They came swept down in tributaries over years. The deposits are massive: there was a big river here for a long time.

Now this is the dry northern buttress of the Amargosa Range known as the Grapevine Mountains, a worn multicolored fault block that forms the northeastern rim of Death Valley. From a distance one sees that these mountains are streaked with red and dark and pale like thick sliced bacon or badly carved layer cake, each layer and streak being a stratum, like a book page in the montane tome. Many of these strata are made of river cobbles. Like pages of translations, these came from somewhere else.

Here the earth is straining as you sit, like teeth bearing down on a bullet. The crust of the continent has cracked wholly through in more or less parallel lines, the side chunks thrusting up and the center chunk dropping away between them, thirty thousand some feet away — nearly six miles — filling as it goes with water and mountain debris but dropping (still dropping, now, tilting east as it sinks) faster than anything nowadays can fill it up. That isn't, really, Death *Valley* out there. "Valley" to a geologist means something that water has worn into being, or glacial ice, that being water of a kind. A dropped slab between thrusted mountains is known as a graben, suggesting that it has been grabbed onto and is being hauled to Hell by demon gravity.

The graben's bordering chunks have been shoved up, in a kind of bobbing motion, as the graben drops into the semifluid hot rocks of earth's upper mantle. These bordering chunks are now mountains: the Amargosas and the Panamints, respectively. Grapevine Mountain with all its cobble strata is well over eight thousand feet up, right now, but has been crumbling as it has been thrusting all the time, so who knows where it would be were it still whole; and who knows what "whole" is, or was, flux being constant in the world, as the cobbles bear witness. In all this hashing of bedrock it's no wonder that the river has vanished from what are now these mountaintops. Were there water enough to feed it, it would not run here.

Telescope Peak in the Panamint Range, on the far side of the Death Valley graben, is more than eleven thousand feet above sea level and is covered with snow. Through binoculars it looks moonlit; the iced slopes are specked with fir trees, linear and dark.

The graben itself has gone below what we're used to as being possibility. Much of its heartland is below sea level and some of it lies two hundred and eighty-two feet under the surface of theoretical waves. It also looks moonlit, dry and long and white, as if the planet itself had run through a damaging machine and been left with this gash, scarred with salt.

We start down from the Grapevine highlands by following the cleft of a wash. The wash drops between worn walls and narrows and its pitch steepens as we go: what is now Titus Canyon goes into Death Valley like a bobsled run.

All the way down I notice that wash and canyon are floored with cobbles. Some of them are the old ones washed from their strata and loose again in what is, sometimes, the bed of a flash-flood river. Where the canyon ends, cobbles and other debris spread like a fan.

This fan is a phenomenon. Fans like this one form in deserts, and only in deserts. Where there is more water in the world there are perennial streams that carry their load on down and on down; they deposit their debris in wide-bosomed floodplains or, at the end, in deltas. A delta forms at river's end. Here, all rivers end at the mouths of their canyons. There, the water simply . . . sinks. The waterborne debris is dropped as if from the tailgate of a dump truck: in a fan.

One trundles down this fan out into the pale floor of Death Valley.

This is the shape of the country. One sees right away that there are two kinds of ground here: bedrock and alluvium. Alluvium is bedrock that has been torn and worn away and is loose and trending downhill: everything, that is, from boulders to salts. The canyons and washes are strewn with loose gravels; where canyons enter the graben lie the alluvial fans; the graben is floored with level layers of sand, silt, and evaporites: borax, salt.

Bedrock, alluvium. The terms are relative. As the cobbles make clear, most bedrock strata were alluvium, once.

We woke in Death Valley this morning with mountains all around us in clean silhouette, well before dawn, on a bright planet that was as clean-featured as the moon. Close by there were neatly spaced silhouettes of creosote bush, sketches of branches as thin and tough as tungsten wire. Then the *rurk* of a raven and the black bird's deliberate passage across the stars. Then red light crept down bedrock peaks and alluvial skirts, the sky was turquoise, the clumps of bursage silver. We saw that there were tracks of crickets and kangaroo mice in the sand and a few darkling beetles trundling. Otherwise there was nothing to see but rock.

This is what there is to see: rock. Here there are countless geo-dramas written in fault block rising and fault block dropping down, in spews of volcanic ash the colors of muddy indigo, mustard, and peach.

Plate tectonics may be the power here, but the driest piece of this continent has been designed by water. In spite of the fact that the rainfall averages an inch and a half a year, water has carved cobbles, has ground sand, has routed out canyons, is the weaver of alluvium, is the tireless carrier of silts and dissolver of salts. It is the maker of landscape. The absent maker, like God.

26

ghost bedroom

Death Valley National Monument, California

You wonder how people ever lived here. How did they? In what kind of delirium? Out here the planet has been cooked and scraped to the bone. Even now in the spring the sun rises and it's all over: it's like being in an oven. It doesn't seem possible to be in it for long.

Golden Canyon runs into Death Valley from the east. Coulter and I walked up into it in the afternoon, with the tourists. It was very hot; we found a patch of shade and ate dates that we had bought at the ranch.

A big spring of water comes into Death Valley and runs down Furnace Creek; it supplies two hotels and a date-palm ranch. The hotels are pale stucco roofed with pot tiles; in style they fall somewhere between Moorish Spain and rococo Italy, and the effect of these in the bleached violence of the driest place on the North American continent is the same as if one had cut out a photo of the Italian Riviera and pasted it on a mural of a gigantic gravel pit.

The dates were very good. I thought to myself: this is what Bedouins carry in their pack saddles. In the Arabian Empty Quarter one can live for weeks on the likes of these. So I must have felt for a moment there something like Lawrence of Arabia: dashing, heroic, unpredictable, with a blue gleam in the eye. Perhaps this explains what happened later on.

Golden Canyon is entirely yellow. In the right light it is spectacular, like heavy brushed gold, though the texture of the place can be alarming. After a while out here one recognizes lake bed deposits on sight; fine-ground and as softly variously colored as chalk dust. These yellow hills are all lake bed stuff, over five thousand feet of sandstones, shales, and siltstones, some layers suffused with borax, all of it laid down in the bottom of a desert lake that filled and dried and filled and dried over and over again for three million years. Then the lake deposits were lifted and heaved at an angle, like someone jacking a car up from one side. The result looks more or less like eroded hills of yellow chalk or plaster of Paris, something between these two in hardness, and their surfaces are cracked where they have wetted and dried. Nothing grows on them.

After we had walked up-canyon with the tourists for half an hour we caught each other's eye and escaped sideways into a narrow wash. There we hustled along in the yellow emptiness. Footprints showed that people had come in here before. Soon we were beyond footprints, moving upward in a narrowing steepening defile. At last we squeezed ourselves by knees and elbows up an almost vertical cleft in the yellowness, Coult clambering ahead of me, then overhead, the climb becoming, quite suddenly, vertical, and suddenly terrifying enough that I lifted our general ban on cusswords; yelling the P word and the S word and the F word and some others for all we were worth we scrabbled and clawed and heaved until we emerged on our bellies onto the high country.

Along the ridge of this high country there was a trail. We followed the trail through more yellow eroded country until it crossed the graveled bed of a wash. There we caught each other's eye, again. The trail went one way, the wash went another; we took the wash. We knew the pattern of the country well enough by then to know that wash would lead to canyon and canyon would lead us back to Death Valley, so we needed no signposts; we went off downhill with our feet crunching in the wash gravel.

There was not a plant growing anywhere, except for the odd bush of desert holly. We passed half a dozen of these bushes during the entire afternoon. One of them was infested with ants; the others were not.

Desert holly is a saltbush, another of the hardy group that includes the four-winged saltbush, shadscale, all-scale, salt sage, and so on,

all members of a plant family related to garden spinach; but the
saltbush tribe has made a specialty of the most arid ground. Not just
dry ground, but earth that is chemically forbidding; soils fouled with
salt, alkali. And desert holly seems to be the hardiest of this hardy
bunch. Like the others, it has quantities of papery seed. Unlike the
others its leaves are large, flattish and thick and gray, warped and
curled, it seems, by heat and salt, and they do look something like
holly leaves, cast in a kind of velvety silver.

It was still very hot; now and then we stopped to eat dates and
drink water. We began to see mine shafts pecked in the walls around
us. We discovered that it was cooler in the mine shafts than in the
open, and we made a habit of sitting in there to cool off.

Prospecting and mining have followed a route through the desert
that is something like a roller coaster, as if the only possible scenario
were extravagance of boom and bust. In the early 1800s, gold and
silver were king around here. When the Panamint boom crashed in
1877, that was that for a while. In the 1880s borax began to be hauled
from the valley to Mojave by the famous twenty-mule teams, but
gold and silver got interesting again in the first decade of this century,
and gold was found and mined at Skidoo, Chloride Cliff, and Rhyolite, but these camps closed down in the nationwide panic of 1907.
Talc mining started up after World War II, and is still going on here,
and the mines themselves are just as raw, noxious, and untidy as any
mines ever were — to the chagrin of the Park Service, which prefers
mines (all mines, evidently) to be objects of nostalgia. Death Valley
is still open for mining and prospecting now. You are welcome to
come and stake your claim.

After an hour or two coming down that wash we saw several
tempting dark mine openings up a little side gully. When we worked
our way up toward them, we were in the ghost bedroom before we
knew it.

It was really the skeleton of a bedroom.

There were three mine shafts there; the deepest went twelve feet
through tilted beds of yellow stone. There was no bush or stick or
fragment of vegetation of any kind. Not even a desert holly.

There was deep blue sky and yellow rock. On a room-sized level
place beside an eroded gully were two iron bedsteads, with bedsprings.

That's all.
Nothing else.
We stood there.
"It's a ghost bedroom," we both said, at the same time.

Mining being what it is and was, ghost towns are all over the desert. Death Valley has several. When I first came out here, the words "ghost town" had the power to send a little shiver up the backbone, and I'd go out of my way to see one; there was excitement when I first sighted rubble, but those days are gone. Ghost towns are common as dust, for one thing. They are the discarded packagings of hope. They have been picked over, vandalized, generally left to flap and weather and collapse. They tend to be more depressing than interesting unless they've been touristed up, in which case they're commercial and not to be trusted to be true. Between one and another we've seen foundation stones of chapels and flophouses, streets paved with mine tailings, crumbling walls made of rum bottles cemented together, pieces of twisted iron half-dissolved by bullet holes, heaps of cans blackened with rust, fragments of Model T Fords, iron rims of wagon wheels, old signposts with a few letters: L EDV OST-OFFICE and the like, and bedsprings (bedsprings are durable) and

Ghost Car
Death Valley National Monument, California

broken glass all over the place. It's not hard to do forensics on the likes of this: back then around here it wasn't so much the thunder of hoofbeats as the plockety-plock of burro hooves; there were a few audacious promoters and hoodwinkers, they built Mediterranean fantasies; mostly there were unshaven men with bloodshot eyes, men wearing battered hats, men who didn't stay too long or make too much of anything.

In the ghost bedroom there was yellow naked rock. There were three holes pecked into the rock and two bedsteads under the terrible sky. The answer is: they lived like this.

PART FOUR

Summer

27

Owyhee

Owyhee County, Idaho

I

There are not many people here. Almost no one goes outside the irrigated land. There are some cattle ranchers who live so far out in some spring hollow that they come to town once in six months and visit Boise once in ten years. Then there are the others: the prospectors and trappers whose business is with the raw country and always has been. The greatest thing one hears, wrapped around their stories, is the size and mystery of the country itself.

There are other people out there, too, people who do not want to be seen. There are old Shoshone horse traps in box canyons, and rumors that the traps are used, still, perhaps for the purposes for which they were made; perhaps not. There are stories of gold strikes made and the gold hidden and the hiders shot and the gold never found. Satanic symbols have been painted on rocks in hanging canyons. Remains of bonfires have been found, surrounded with strange implements. A black Cadillac with black windows has been seen parked on a track leading to a washed-in mine. Women have disappeared, and men, under strange circumstances, into this dry wild country for which there are no good maps.

The whole state of Idaho, even beyond this desert corner, even including the watered and forested north and the rich farm belts, is almost the same in population density (or un-density) as desert

kingdoms like Oman. Owyhee County is the largest and least popu-
lated county in the state; it has one parking meter and no traffic lights
and was named from the beginning for lost men. It lies south of the
Snake River, its northernmost strip part of the Snake River Plain —
though *plain* is a misnomer; here it is riven by canyons and broken
volcanic ranges. Beyond the irrigated land there are no traveled ways
into the country except for a loose and unmapped (or wrongly
mapped) net of gravel roads, any one of which may be impassable
for days after a rain. Ten inches or less, on the average, may fall here
in any given year, and the rains are (true to desert form) unpredictable, local, and violent.

Together with the Harney Basin of southeastern Oregon and a
chunk of northern Nevada between Salt Lake and the Sierras — a
chunk four hundred miles from east to west and nearly as far from
north to south — Owyhee is part of the most uninhabited country
in the lower forty-eight. It is wilderness in the true sense, meaning
that it is mostly untamed and pretty much unknown. For most human purposes most of Owyhee might as well not exist, and to most
people it does not; it is a kind of North American *Ar-Rub' al-Khālī:*
an Empty Quarter.

"You never learn it all. Always something new. Something new to
find. Devil of a country to some people but it's home to us," Ed
says.

Ed Shultz has spent most of his life as a prospector and a miner.
He is an amateur archaeologist, a self-taught geologist, and for almost
all of his life he has worked in Owyhee County. He lives in Homedale at the north edge of the Snake River Plain, and a ditch full
of dam-held, canal-brought, mountain-born water runs behind his
house. He speaks in machine-gun bursts and hauls out by the bowl-
ful, fistful, by the shelf after shelf and case after case the artifacts and
anecdotes of a lifetime living here.

"We're desert people. We like it," he says, putting aside the bowl
full of semiprecious stones: orange Bruneau jasper, roiled Biggs jasper, desert rose picture jasper with its pink sunrise skies, rainbow
plume agate, Red Butte jasper full of flowery shapes, Idaho star gar-
nets that are the color of grape juice with central stars of silver light,
fire agates that look like live flames seen through black glass. He sets

out display boxes full of Paiute and Shoshone arrowheads as if he were setting the table. They're made of flint, chalcedony, jasper, obsidian. There are big ceremonial points with multiple flanges, tiny ornamental gem points, buttons, hunting points, darts, simple heavy triangular war points.

"The warheads were lashed to the arrow haft, see, with rawhide thong. Once it penetrated the flesh the thong would absorb moisture and loosen up and if you pulled on that haft it would come, sure, but the point would stay in there. That was the point." He doesn't quite laugh, he busies himself stacking the boxes away.

He pulls out others. Strings of Texas Comanche clay beads, amulets of faces and birds, nasal plugs, knives and scrapers. These were once part of the collection of one Johnny Meyers — "boozer buckaroo and range rider" — who dug Comanche mounds on the sly and peddled the findings for nights on the town. After Johnny died, what was left of his collection, "which was the best of it, you bet; he may have been a drunk but he knew his stuff," was in shoeboxes under his bunk. Most of it went to a museum. Some of it came to Ed.

The Comanche display is put aside and Ed spills a handful of beans onto the table. Some of them are white, others red, others mottled like pinto beans. I've never seen beans so large: nearly the size of pullet eggs. He handles them like jewels. They were found in an Anasazi pot that was, he says, six to eight hundred years old, according to its patterns and glazes. The pot was sealed with a bung of juniper bark hardened with resin. Ed planted half the beans last year, and ten percent of them grew. The second generation of Anasazi beans is sprouting in his garden now.

We go to see. His vegetables are weedless, the rows straight, the beans are just now germinating under a clean long mound of earth. Nearby is a flower garden filled with found objects displayed as if in a museum: an ore bucket, a bighorn horn, a cow skull with two bullet holes.

"Where do you think them holes came from?" He chuckles. "They used to hang men for rustlin', hereabouts. Some still do."

The lawn is flat and green as carpet. Everything around him reflects the same meticulous museum-ization of trinkets from a rough life and a rough country. There's a hunk of blue jasper the size of a pail, racehorse shoes, hay knives, wolf traps, a clawfoot bathtub overflowing with petunias, oil lanterns, iron-rimmed wagon wheels. There are petrified Miocene tree stumps between the cornflowers.

"When you're out there alone, you have to protect your camp, see," he says, this fact too a part of the collection of wild found objects neatly displayed, now, among domesticated things. "You lay out dead limbs all around. The crackle will tell."

Ed says that he rode a mustang named Ghost for years. He broke Ghost himself. You put double cinches on and hang panniers on the cinches and put blocks of salt in the panniers "just about heavy enough to crack their ribs" and put snaffle bits in their mouths and put them on plowed ground so they can't buck. When Ed was a kid, his dad broke horses for ten dollars a head. Breaking horses was nothing new.

The first "real rock" that Ed ever found in the woods was a black-and-white Nez Percé arrowhead. The second was a piece of red agate the size of a golf ball. These things went into a boy's pocket as such things go into all kids' pockets, but he hasn't forgotten them. At the end of World War II he was with the Army in Guadalcanal — he did demolition in the Army — and one day when they were swimming there he sat beside an outcrop and there was a ruby sticking out of it the size of a pea. A pigeon-blood red ruby. He picked the ruby out and put it in his pocket. Before he got back to his compound the ruby wore a hole in his pants and he lost it and pocketknife and all.

"I got fascinated after that," he says, "that was it, that changed my life."

Back in Idaho he placer mined for gold, working the riverbed gravels. He shot deer and elk for food. There was nothing much else to eat. He learned that grouse live and die within ten acres, that they live by creeks, that they generally have a birdish hankering for shiny things; if there is gold around the grouse can be trusted to have nuggets in their craw. Grouse were a diagnostic tool as well as dinner.

He learned that badgers quarry down six feet and bring deep gravels out for you to see. Squirrels burrow, too. When he lived in a cave on Three Fingers Creek he learned that a patch of unusual wildflowers means different mineralization in the soil. He learned that the first ground to thaw in spring is mineralized ground; metals heat faster than stone.

One day he worked up a ridge. He'd married by then, he lived in a house, he'd started a family, his wife and two boys were along. They'd brought a picnic. They spooked two bands of wild horses on their way into the hills; that was something, they all remembered that. Late in the morning Ed climbed the ridge to a pocket two or three hundred yards across.

"There was chunks of picture jasper lying around in there the size of bread loaves."

He brought in a Cat and bulldozed a road. He owned his own Cats and lowboys, and an Ingersoll rotary diesel drill. He drilled first with two-foot bits, then four, six, eight. He made four rows of six holes, each of them eight feet deep. The holes were packed with two sticks of 80 percent dynamite and a one-pound coffee can full of nitrate fertilizer. Primacord, caps, fuses.

"Hey! You could hear 'em blow clear to Boise!" he said.

They named it the Wild Horse Mine. His son still works it now. Wild Horse picture jasper is known around the world; the king of picture jaspers, a hard, fine-grained stone that cuts clean and takes a high polish, semiprecious stuff made of silts that once perked up volcanic vents: nickel formations making blue sky, iron oxides making browns and reds of landscape, manganese dendrites making scribings of dryland trees and brush. It's the picture of the country where it is: canyons and basins, desert distances, tumbled boulders, eroded multicolored volcanic scarps.

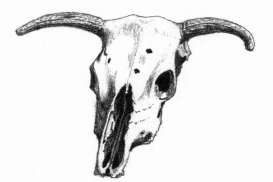

Cattle Skull with Bullet Holes

II

Cobby smells of woodsmoke when I come to his house, next door
to Ed.

"I'm making char-cloth. Come on through," he says.

Soon I smell of woodsmoke too. There is the fire and a lidded can
in it, a hole punched in the lid and smoke spurting from the hole.
Beyond is the shed, a heap of untanned hides, racks of bark-dyed
traps, a garden with corn and potatoes, the irrigation ditch and a field
and the pale Owyhee hills beyond, like an animal asleep.

Cobby squats by the fire with forearms across his knees. He owns
this house and his wife and family live in it with him — when he's
home — but he can live on wild ground and on his own with little
more than a knife and flint and steel. There isn't much about wildlife
he doesn't know, or wonder, and he's at home in the wilds so much
himself that the most complex arcana of campcraft are natural to
him; his membership in the American Mountain Men isn't as much
a hobby as an acknowledgment. He's a master tracker, of people as
well as animals, and folks come to know this after a while, and the
police have made use of his skills from time to time and place to
place. Most of the year he traps for a living, doing custom predator
control in summer and fur in winter. Trapping is more or less a
solitary pursuit, and accords with his nature. During fur season most
of what he traps are bobcats. A bobcat isn't shy.

"Shy is a very poor term. If you understand his nature . . ."
Cobby pauses, pokes the burning wood. "He's a stalker, he depends
on not being seen. He doesn't have a long running ability. He's not
a coward. He depends on sneaking up, on not being seen." Cobby
pokes the can, it sends up a final spurt of smoke. "And he's solitary.
Kind of like me. It's just his style of hunting."

Cobby grins, a good grin, and takes the can from the fire. No
more smoke can be encouraged from the hole. He puts it in the dirt
and leaves it to cool.

"Let's go," he says. "I want to show you Map Rock."

We go in the pickup. There are coils of snares looped over the
side mirrors. He takes a set of buckskin saddlebags with him everywhere — that and his leather hat — as some people take a credit card
and keys. He wears his hat every time he leaves the house, even to

dig potatoes; he's as naked without it as other people are without pants. He never goes into the hills without his saddlebags and his knife.

In the saddlebags are a piece of white flint and a steel. If you can't find flint then agate will do, even jasper, but flint makes the hottest and the whitest spark. The steel is a new-moon arc that fits in a fist and curves handily over the knuckles. Along with the flint and steel is a buckskin packet held with a bone button. In the packet is a metal case full of pieces of char-cloth: squares of pure cotton that have been blackened to charcoal in an airless can. When a flint-and-steel-struck spark lands on a square of char-cloth, the cloth will burn hotter than any match. In a pinch, char-cloth can be made from a shirttail or a strip from the bottom of your jeans.

Soon we're on a dirt track angling toward the river. The hills have come close.

"It's two hundred and sixty miles across to the nearest paved road," he says.

The truck bangs through ruts. There is a cliff of rusty rhyolite capped with twenty feet of black basalt, like chocolate icing on a cake.

Here water has a way of traveling, pooling, perking from underground, so the Owyhees are not entirely dry.

"There are some big springs in there." Cobby nods toward the hills. "Meadows. Ranches forty fifty miles apart."

More ruts; I brace myself.

"And rivers," he says. "Not like Nevada. We've got rivers. With beaver on them."

There's a pause. The beaver will lead to something.

"The mountain men came through here," he says. "The Snake was one of their main routes. Lots came in the seventeen hundreds but the main heyday was from 1805 to 1840 — Jedediah Smith, Hugh Glass, Bill Williams, Jim Bridger, those were the big names, but there's a lot of them no one remembers. They sent teams of trappers here to trap the beaver. All up the rivers. Once they sent out thirty men and two survived. That wasn't unusual. That was typical."

There's a bottle made of cow horn hanging from a knob on the dash. The wide end is sealed with a circle of polished wood held with brass nails. A notch around the narrow end is wrapped with a hide thong, the thong ends decorated with red and metal beads. In the small end there is a buttonlike bung of wood. The bottle is full of beaver castor: the contents of beavers' scent glands, a brown paste. It smells warm, tannic, resinous, musky, like summer woods. The mountain men used castor for stomach medicine, as balm for wounds, for baiting traps.

In 1818, Donald Mackenzie brought the first brigade of trappers here to the Snake River valley. The whole brigade was native Hawaiians who had sailed to the Northwest on a fur-trading ship: cheap labor. Mackenzie led them in here and left them with their gear, and months later he came to pick them up. He waited at the bend in the river and no one came. No one ever came. The whole brigade was gone. Hawaii was spelled Owyhee in those days — the pronunciation is the same — and now it's the name of the desert county where Hawaiians disappeared.

We come to Map Rock: a monster basalt boulder rolled from the rim and come to rest near the level by the river. Even from a distance it's easy to see the wriggles and circles scribed in the stone. Near the bottom, one winding line is deeper and wider than others, a snake in motion.

"That's the river, that part's clear enough!" Cobby laughs, tracing the Snake with a finger. "The rest, well . . . it's clear to anyone this is a map. They say it's an Indian map, see, but I have my own ideas. They could be wrong. Likely they are."

We climb on the boulder and crawl across the canted scrawls, tracing lines, patches of concentric circles.

"To my mind the circles are the locations of major Indian camps," Cobby says, "Nez Percé camps to the north and west of the mountains, Blackfoot on the east. At the bottom there is the Snake to where it dumps into the Columbia, with Paiute camps along there."

He points them out, larger and smaller bull's-eyes spaced in the Owyhee valleys.

"The Paiutes went into the timber in summer and came back down in winter. Where the Boise and the Snake come close were communal fishing grounds. Common grounds, for the tribes. Same thing with good arrowhead country. Common grounds, where they kept peace."

We crawl east:

"The edge of the rock is the edge of the Plains."

We crawl north:

"This one line, here, is the north trail to the upper end of the hills, up the great divide. Up here, see this here?"

Bumpy lines:

"On mountain man maps that means rough country. That would be north Idaho. Heavy timber country. That was avoided by the mountain men. It was dense and difficult. The Snake was a major trail for them to go north of here. There's no better place for a map than right here."

There's a pause. He stares at the patterns, thinking.

"Maps are a white man's concept. Foreign to this country," he says.

Cobby himself is part Iroquois and part Cherokee. He was raised to hide this; he doesn't hide it now. Ed told me — when I asked where he was from himself — that everyone from the West is part Indian somewhere no matter what they tell you, and he winked when he said it, and said that it was nature's way of making peace.

"I think this is a mountain man map," Cobby says. "That's what I think. That's who I think made it. They'd pass here and add a little line or two, some trail they'd found in here."

The Owyhee Mountains are, between Paiute camps, a maze of winding intersecting and conflicting lines.

"It hasn't changed much in there! No one knows all the roads in there." Cobby laughs, jumps down from the rock. "Look here. This is clear enough!"

On the side of the rock are animals. There's a mule deer, a bighorn ram, a bighorn ewe, a pronghorn antelope, an elk, a beaver. Below them is a wriggling line: a river full of fish?

"Yes, ma'am, that's their groceries," Cobby says. "Let's go."

"Every animal has his own nature. Once you get a handle on that nature, catching him is not a problem," he says, on the way home. In the evening light the wheat fields and mountains are equally gold.

"My wife claims I'm a psychiatrist of wildlife. It's hard to say. It's personality that interests me."

There's a pause. The packet of char–cloth, the unnecessary beauty of the horn bottle, the way that Cobby uses words, are the marks of a careful man.

"A possum has rocks in his head. He never learns.

"An otter is suspicious and particular. The kind of guy that when he comes home he looks in all the closets to make sure somebody isn't hiding there before he sleeps.

"A skunk has a big gun. And everybody knows it.

"A red fox is half cat, half coyote, but dumb as a muskrat. And he has a strange habit about him. A fox is a kind of scurfy character with a fairly predictable pattern.

"A coyote will do a little bit of his own thinking. He's unpredictable. A coyote is a terrorist; a cat is a hit man.

"Cats — bobcats and lions, too — are the same, more or less. Some days you're in a good mood, some days you're in a bad mood. There's a different style of tracks from these different moods. Some days you're playful. Some days you're plain grumpy. And damned independent!"

We laugh.

"And most folks don't know the first thing about it. The hard part is that animal. You've got to become a part of him, and see the world through his eyes."

Petroglyph Groceries on Map Rock

III

Basalt clothes the country: its icing is everywhere here on slices of high ground as if, since icing time, the cake had been much chunked up.

A single event started this icing process some seventeen million years ago, in southeast Oregon, just across the state line from here. A meteorite of considerable size came and punched a hole in the body of terra firma, something like a Shoshone warhead on a cosmic scale. And the wound has not healed. The meteorite (or its explosion) punched clear through the planet's crust — which is as thin relative to the whole as an apple peel is to its apple — and the magma below squeezed up and out. The meteorite crater became, quickly, a lava lake. Lava slopped out clear to northern Washington. Floods of basalt swallowed the valleys of western Idaho.

That lava lake was only part of it. The meteorite's impact made a split in the earth's crust clear from Oregon to Mexico like a crack propagating from a BB ding in a windowpane. A healthy bite of North America has since threatened to slip off westward, opening a rift and then an ocean through the heart of Nevada; and would, too, if the whole of the Americas weren't drifting westward fast enough to override the break, to keep the rifting closed, closed enough, but not wholly shut; the earth's crust here is pulling apart.

The continent moves. It floats west, over the meteorite wound. As the West Coast grinds out over the Pacific plate, driving it down, the Sierras crumple upward and wring all moisture from the Pacific wind. Here, the wound is still open. Once in a while this "hot spot" in the mantle rock bursts through the sediments and the ancient seabeds and river gravels and whatever has accumulated on the crust, and tips a load of hot new rock into the world. The wake of all this is the Snake River Plain. The wound itself is now under Yellowstone: the hot spot over which North America helplessly rides. Whenever it punches through, the crust continues to shatter, more cracks propagating southward from this string of BB dings in the continental pane. All the country south of the hot spot track, the Snake River Plain — all this country from the California Sierras to Utah's Wasatch Front and clear to Mexico — is breaking up. It is rifted, faulted country, extended and extending terrain striped with fault block mountains: basin and range.

Next midday we stop near a cave high in the country between Succor Creek and Leslie Gulch. We see the cave from the track we're on. It's hot up here and the cave may be cool; it's time for lunch. We stop the pickup and hike in.

Neither Cobby nor his wife, Carol, has been here before. Carol wears a black felt hat with the side brim held to the crown, Aussie style, with a raccoon bone. We carry lunch in plastic bags.

The cave is rhyolite: rock with the chemistry of granite but with a different history. Granite starts as a dome of magma, a molten push that never surfaces from whatever overlayment it comes up under; it cools, slowly, in place, crystallizing there with no one the wiser until the overlayment sloughs away, via weather. Rhyolite, on the other hand, *arrives*. It comes from molten domes that break, violently, through. On arrival, rhyolite magma is as thick as putty and soaks up water like a sponge, translating water to steam and expanding with it like a nightmare cartoon Alice in Wonderland who ate the cake or drank from the bottle: cubic miles of red-hot steam and magma shrapnel devour landscape like shock waves from a bomb. Shuddering to a stop at last, the magma shrapnel welds into rhyolite.

Some of this blasts to the stratosphere and falls elsewhere as ash. To give you some idea of scale here, the size of the Mount St. Helens explosion in 1980 put one-third of a cubic mile of rhyolite on the ground. Some of these Snake River Plain events have spread two hundred cubic miles of the stuff — in a single explosion, mind you. Afterward, at center stage, where the magma dome had been swelling over aeons, tumorlike, a surge of high and mounded ground, there is empty nothing: caldera, sinkhole, great collapse. Later on, calderas tend to fill with ash and trickles of basalt. The Yellowstone caldera is not hard to see. Right now, domes are rising there: the Mallard Lake dome, the Sour Creek dome. The Yellowstone caldera is more than fifty miles across. It has vomited a rhyolite disaster three times, at roughly six-hundred-thousand-year intervals, the last one being six hundred thousand years ago. There are plenty of signs over there of things heating up.

Here in this rhyolite cave, with its ceiling pockmarked like Swiss cheese and a level gravel floor, it is cool and dim and smells sweet, aromatic, like sagebrush and honey.

"Mmmmm! What's that! What is that wonderful smell?" says Carol.

Cobby moves in a slow rocking padding walk around the perimeter of the cave, staring down toward the toes of his cowboy boots, analyzing every scratch and dent and fleck of dung. He looks up once without expression and nods his head.

"Oooh, look at this!" Carol says. "And another one!" She bends, twice, and stands and holds out a palm: a flake of green jasper, a flake of pinkish agate. Both are slim bright chips sharp as scalpels, with the concentric rings showing where they were pressed off some Paiute's projectile point with an antler awl.

"Look, look! Obsidian!" Carol says, smiling, holding out a new-moon shard of volcanic glass, smoky and transparent.

"Obsidian is nowhere near here," Cobby says, "they brought that in, oh, tens of miles."

"It's packrat. And mouse," I say. "The ceiling is full of mice!"

"What is?"

"The smell . . . it's their middens dried up into this tar," I say, "that's what the smell is. Plant resins they just pee out. Hey!"

A white-footed mouse, big black eyes and little white feet and white belly and copper coat, peers from a ceiling hole and goes padding away through a rhyolite corridor. The ceiling and back wall of the cave are coated with gobs of molassesy tarry resin, hard as wood, fragrant as honey. I remember a story (maybe apocryphal, it's in one of those old explorers' diaries, though) of starving desert wanderers eating this stuff and finding it chewy and "sweetish, not bad," but they didn't know what it was, exactly. Which is just as well.

"Give him some cheese!" Carol says, and we do, placing a bit of Kraft American in the hole where we saw the mouse.

We sit against the back wall eating our sandwiches, watching the bit of cheese. History's more ghastly events have a way of becoming prosy and domestic, life breaks through, somehow, in wonderful ignorance, thank God. I think of film I saw of children in France after the last war playing a kind of handball against a wall that was pocked with bullet holes. Big bullet holes. An archway shattered.

Two boys leaping, a little girl scratching a bugbite on her knee. A colony of mice in rhyolite. An old colony, comfortable, secure, here for countless generations. They couldn't know or care less about the Armageddon that blew in here thirteen million years ago, burying a humid jungly forest in red-hot shrapnel. A mouse comes and whiffles at the cheese, then drags it back a little way, and eats, mouthfuls chewed then more mouthfuls, watching us as we're watching it.

"Oh, yes, the bobcats use this place, sure," Cobby says, when I ask. "One tom was in here yesterday."

There's a pause. He chuckles, looking up at the mouse warren, the packrat holes and middens:

"He can't keep himself away." And then he laughs, a brawny deep-chested laugh. "This place is *pure* frustration for a cat!"

Cobby

28

sage

Hart Mountain National Antelope Refuge, Oregon

There is a watery mirage between the hills, and in it there are shapes torn into globules by hot air. The shapes are copper with flashes of white and ebony; a herd of pronghorn antelopes looking as they did when Paiute hunters came toward them through the cover of the sage. Around them are wide felted plains and a mountain cone and bluffs with a few dark blots of trees. The sage covers the ground like a cloth, a ruffled green-silver, a color soft as silk in the distance. Close, it is rough and metallic and harsh.

The sage is hardly new. What is new is that here it seems to cover everything; *Artemisia tridentata,* three-fingered plant of the goddess of the hunt. It's known as basin sagebrush, common sagebrush, big sage, blue sage, black sage, wormwood; it's the Spaniards' *chamiso hediondo* (stinking chamiso), the Northern Paiutes' *sawabi,* the Shoshones' *pohobi,* the Washoes' *daabal,* Zane Grey's "Purple Sage," Twain's "fag end of vegetable creation." By any name it is the symptom of Great Basin and Colorado Plateau desert, the bush of dry steppe and coolish altitude, the blue-gray caulk between dryer hotter flats — with their bunch grasses and saltbush shrubs — and pinyon-juniper forest on cooler wetter slopes. It fingers into both, thigh to head high, even the size of a gnomish tree.

Sage is the most abundant shrub in North America, by some estimates. It does cover a lot of ground between Nebraska and California and on south to the borders of the hot deserts, where creosote bush takes over; too much ground for some people's tastes. It's the nemesis of ranchers, the horror of hay-fever sufferers. It's the state flower of Nevada, though its flower is gray nubbins carried in slender panicles, like asters without the blessing of rays of color. The pollen is wind-borne but the winds here have nothing much taller than sage to tangle with, and a big plant in a good year can make over a million seeds. The leaves are small, three-toed like fairy footprints, furred with white down against dry winds and intense light. They are born untidily pointing every which way along untidy brittle branches. The trunk is never vertical; on mountaintops it is even horizontal, and has the shape of a bundle of slats given a savage twist. The bark is the color and texture of frayed steel wire. It is not a thing of grace. After a rain and in the evening light I've seen the bark and twigs go black, and the leaves clearly silver, and the smell of it floats in the air then as if one had entered the herb gardens of the saints.

Here the midday light of June is reflected from miles of sage as if from a sheet of metal, and I screw my eyes against the blast. The tang of the sage is nose-wrinkling like whiffs of mentholatum; Vicks VapoRub, one thinks, or terpenes adrift in an artist's sunny loft. Somewhere back on the rise from Catlow Valley, on the curving dirt track along which I haul a rooster-tail of dust, was the border of Hart Mountain Refuge; two hundred and seventy-five thousand acres of southern Oregon set aside in 1936 for the use of pronghorns. Other things live here, too. But aside from the one herd of pronghorns I have seen nothing but the sage.

Hart Mountain is a vast fault block cracked loose and heaved thirty-six hundred feet above the Harney Basin. Punched upward to an altitude of more than eight thousand feet, it gets more rain than the basin does, between ten and eleven inches a year, on the average; an island only just jutting up, in terms of rainfall, above a desert sea.

Hart Mountain Refuge is a big place, and the veil of sage is a deception. There are seasonal streams here with water meadows and alder thickets. There are bony uplands scoured clean to the rock by wind, with fescue meadows in the cols and bluebunch wheatgrass on steep south slopes. Sheltered slopes hold thickets of mountain mahogany and bitterbrush. Coyotes, bobcats, and badgers live here, plus the usual big and the multiplicity of small mammals — five species of shrew, pocket mice and K-rats, cottontails and jacks. There are old lake beds white with alkali and fringed with ricegrass, and a hot-spring saltmarsh with yellow-headed and red-winged blackbirds chanting in the reeds. Bald eagles, white-tailed ibis, owls breed here; ducks and geese and a scattering of sandhill cranes, plus stilts and avocets, visit the swatches of marshland; there are ravens, everywhere. Magpies — elegant and sinister in sharp black and white, predatory in their way as any hawk, opportunistic as any crow — float prettily in search of carrion. And there are sage grouse. Sage grouse are the story here. Their numbers are declining, and no one knows why.

Sage grouse have the bulk and point-tailed shape of pheasants, and are big birds, more than two feet long. They fly like pheasants with a burst-up followed by long low level-winged float, though they will go distances; some are even migratory, others are not. The undersides of their wings are white in flight, their bodies mottled brown and black with brindling cream, their bellies solid black as though they had been dipped in ink. Their heavy bills give them a kind of Roman nose and smooth jet-plane silhouette. In winter they eat sagebrush leaves, in spring they like big sage to nest beneath, and even when they're foraging in water meadows and on alpine slopes they loaf in the sage and sleep there and use it for cover. There are two varieties of big sage here — mountain big sage and Wyoming big sage — and then low sagebrush too, a different species, a dwarfish version rarely growing more than eighteen inches high. Grouse in spring and summer seem to like low sage; it covers them as they move or feed but they can poke their heads up to see around. Their dark smooth periscopes sprout from the sage if you come too close.

The people I talk to here are knowledgeable, mystified, and upset about the decline of the sage grouse. Everything grouse need for a good life seems to be here, abundant enough, even in the drought of the last three years, and predators are no more predatory than they've ever been; the grouse just seem to be . . . sliding away. Nowadays the summer flocks of spinster hens are larger than anyone remembers. These are the hens that never bred or whose eggs didn't hatch or whose chicks died. These failures are rules nowadays, rather than exceptions.

Bill Pyle, Jenny Barnett, and Mike Gregg are all studying sage grouse at Hart Mountain. They live in trailers behind the main field station like construction workers living on site. They wear jeans, worn boots, and checkered shirts, even when they're working with their laptops. Radio-tracking collars hang bunched above their beds. They keep Ziploc bags full of the contents of sagebrush chicks' crops (pretty salads of yellow milk vetch flowers and black scarab beetles) in their freezers, along with the ice cream and cans of OJ. Bill Pyle is tall, the senior researcher, the authority. Jenny is slim, freckled, with straight-cut no-nonsense brown hair; she takes long-legged man-sized strides in her big boots and baggy jeans. Mike is squared off, dark, intense. This is his second year out here; it's Jenny's first. They do the bulk of field work, grunt work, the data-gathering perambulations with Ziplocs, binocs, string, notepads. They want to know where the hens nest and how many chicks hatch and how many hatchlings recruit into the flock come fall. Meanwhile they want to know what sage grouse chicks eat.

It turns out that chicks do not eat sagebrush. They do not eat seeds. Sage grouse, it turns out, never eat seeds. In spring and summer both adults and chicks eat insects — ants and wasps, dung and darkling and scarab beetles — crisp protein. What chicks eat most is flowers: milk vetch, foothill daisy, desert parsley, hawk's-beard, yarrow, mountain dandelion.

Early in spring Jenny and Mike go out after dark with a flashlight and a tape recorder and a pack of collaring gear. In March and early April the hens gather near the grounds, called leks, where the grouse cocks dance for their favors. Wading through the sagebrush there at night, one can easily find a hen resting from her daytime work as *bon vivant*. Once a hen is caught in the light the tape recorder is turned on high; it plays snow-machine noise, sheer motor roar, which covers the rustling of Mike and Jenny's approach. The sound-and-light-stunned hen is caught in a landing net, she is foot-tagged, and a collar of herculite cloth — stretchy, light, tough, weather-resistant — is strapped on her breast and back. The collar carries an antenna and solar cells to charge its nickel-cadmium battery. Last year, 71 percent of the radioed hens initiated nests, 60 percent of those broods were successful — that is, chicks hatched — and 11 percent of the radioed hens "recruited brood into the August population" (August meaning the month of the year; considering the esteem in which sage grouse are held here, one is tempted to think that it means something else). Eleven percent nesting success does not seem like a very large figure. Especially considering that 29 percent of the hens out there didn't even try.

There are twenty-four sage grouse leks at Hart Mountain, the dance and display grounds used year after year, and all but one of them lie in hollows of low sage. Some of them have been in use for more than a century, the evidence being a litter of Paiute arrowheads roundabout. The Paiutes prized this highland as a hunting ground, and then as now the grouse cocks' dance attracted more than hens.

Cocks come to the leks late in February and some stay well into May; the reason for the leks is for strut and display and sexual selection. The cocks do the former and the hens take care of the latter. The hens browse, lek to lek, before they'll make a choice. Each cock stakes a dance ground in a lek for himself and puffs his white breast feathers into a pouf — his dark head all but disappears — and in this pouf are two yellow naked patches of skin, like egg yolks. He fans his tail behind like a dark pointed star. He arcs his wings downward and riffles them, making himself enormous. Shuttling air in and out and amplifying the sound in his inflated breast, each strutting cock makes a loud plopping noise "like something dropping into a large barrel of water," according to Jenny. The noise of a lek full of dancing cock birds is uncanny, it sounds like what it is: an arcane ceremonial, traditional ritual, intimate, intense.

The hens find nesting places after they mate, and they're traditional in this as they seem to be in all things, nesting very close to where they nested the year before and raising their brood, too, in well-known territory. The hens may have traditions, but these vary from one to the next, and new traditions are pioneered all the time, and some of these are strange. For gatherers of data who need to quantify and find the meaningful average — good clean elegant science, numbers to use in a management plan — this is frustrating. For example: one hen brought her four-week-old chicks, still downy, for twenty-five miles across the country to reach her summer grounds. Another hen nested several hundred feet from her winter range and raised her chicks right there; in a year she ranged a total of less than a mile. A few hens brood high on mountain slopes — a good thing in a drought year but sure disaster when there are spring storms. Other hens nest in the shade and shelter of close-woven sage, hunkering in speckled shadows. If the eggs are eaten by ravens, magpies, badgers, or ground squirrels, or if they turn out to be duds (over 40 percent of the eggs are duds) the hens walk away, join the spinster flocks, take the summer off.

In summertime the birds stay close to water and the chicks (when there are chicks) need their provender of flowers; small streams and water meadows are important then. Wildflowers are the staples of their summer diet — the class of vegetation known as "forbs" — and these grow best in damper hollows. Some also grow in the protective shade of sage. They grow most thick and rich if a range fire has killed sage off for a while.

It turns out that antelope are forb-eaters, too. They eat sage in winter as the grouse do, and fatten in summer and raise their young on forbs in the damper hollows where the sage is not. The irony is that antelope numbers here, now, are at an all-time high, higher than they've been since the turn of the century. There are antelope everywhere in coppery herds, fawns at their flanks; animals oddly slim and African in shape with goat-pupiled eyes and ebony horns, the prongs curving back, more colorful and delicate than any deer. Don't get me wrong; there are plenty of forbs to go around. The grouse are just . . . declining. In some places now their nesting success is down to 2 percent, for no good reason anyone can see.

"Some hens just never seem to brood, or nest," Jenny says, with her eyes half-shut in the light of the sage, which comes from everywhere like wind. The wind is strong, too, blowing her hair across her face.

"Basically what I've been doing for the last two years is asking more questions," Mike says.

He squints, too, and looks away from Jenny over the folds of hills, but when I turn to write this down I see that they are holding hands.

Big Sage

29

lost water

Warner Valley, Oregon

For a long time this was the sea. Hundreds of millions of years' worth of rivers swept bits of mountains here to lie in level deep-water layers, until all hell broke loose and this slice of continent started moving west through the Pacific, the breaking loose being that schism from our European half. This split and drift and collision of continents is known as plate tectonics. Plates meaning chunks of earth's surface, tectonics meaning construction. Which reminds me of the slow-cooked soups I used to make, the low simmer moving bits of carrot and parsley to the pot's rim as if the gas burner was the roil of planetary mantle. The science of physics and the math of chaos teach us that laws abide in all the scales of things, soup or planets. Anyway, various things have happened since.

In all things we have to work from our experience; so, watch soup doing this if you can turn your stove heat low, low enough to make the broth just "smile," as the French say; low enough and you'll have plate tectonics just fine, the soup-fat globules with their bits of carrot embedded floating on that broth as granite does on dense basalt. Throw down a peeled garlic clove and then another, pretending meteorites. Popped loose by impact, the globules split and drift and then collide as continents do, flecks of celery bobbing into fault zones, globules wrinkling in mountain ranges: Himalayas, Alps, Sierra Nevadas.

Lighter-weight oceanic islands have scraped off onto our western edge as we move across the Pacific, little globules cumulating onto the big. That meteorite plunked in a little south and east of here, the earth crust cracking with impact and, even now, shattering apart; here the seabed layers split as if by knife slice and heaved groaning up, the vast fault block of Hart Mountain tilting like a chunk of carrot. The old sea layers stand naked now, a cliff running north-northeast in southern Oregon for more than fifty miles.

Midmorning in late June: the dirt track switchbacks down that cliff, screws itself down, and the plume of trail dust drifts off behind. I stop in the scatter and ping of stone. Sneeze dust, then quiet air.

Warner Valley stretches below and away with riffles of mountains fringing to the west, dusty gold dentition, but here at the base of the cliff the valley has the perfect physiognomy of marsh. There are round shallow lakes surrounded by swirl and swirl again, clearly here main water channel and there and there twist of meander.

That marsh is no mirage, but there is no water in it. It is the skeleton of marsh. It's as dry down there as baked bone. The ponds and bayous are dust, fringed with bleached grass. The greenery is greasewood, rabbitbrush. This is alkali desert with the *shape* of soupy old eutrophic wetland. I blink, I conjure skillions of geese and ducks and avocets and coots and little plovers wheeling, islands of cotton-wood and seething grass, and it's not hard, the shapes of marsh-land are graven clear as day. Only the water is gone. And everything with it.

Once I'm down I scuff my feet on a graveled shore as if I can't believe. I finger succulent needle leaves of greasewood, wishing blades of rush. I kick a rabbitbrush, which tosses, hissing like a wave. Dumb. The land is dumb, silent, flat forever. I take my chances now and turn up north on an unmarked road that is two wheel ruts through silence, dust, an immense plain.

The illusion is — and this lasts all the hours of the afternoon — that I've set sail.

Deserts are expanding nowadays at a rate of sixteen thousand square miles every year. That's all around the planet, not just here, and this mid-latitude planetary drying out argues for powers stronger than manhandling, though our misuse of desert edge can speed the process up. Grasslands can be sand dunes (as they have become in Texas) due to overgrazing, but they have been turning that way anyhow, for a while.

Climate shifts on an unthinkable scale. The hows of it are complex and *how* is what I'm asking, now, on this slow sailing flight through the Warner — what is it? basin? what was it? lake! — and big lake, too, seventy-five miles long and up to fifteen wide, with hilly peninsulas, a mountain range for islands, an eastern shore (that three-thousand-odd-foot cliff without a harbor anywhere, waves dashing the rock and all now so distant it's a misty line over there, behind, sunlit still) moving in a sea of shadowed brush the shape and color of wind-chopped wave.

Nowadays, this is a playa. That's the Spanish word for beach and is the word used for these ephemeral desert lake beds, here in North America, though playas are not rare in the scheme of things; there are more than fifty thousand of them in the world. Most of them are small. Some are not. Since water laid them down they are the flattest places anywhere on earth. They are the "pans" of South Africa, the *takyrs* of Asia, the *sabchas* of Arabia, the *kavirs* of Iran.

The Bonneville Salt Flats are one small part of the playa of a lake that was more than a thousand feet deep at its deepest point. It was the size of Lake Michigan. The earth's crust sagged more than two hundred feet under its weight. Ten thousand years ago it filled most of western Utah and fingered into Idaho and Nevada, and that was only its most recent high. This sometime Lake Bonneville has come and gone for the last five hundred thousand years. What's left of it nowadays is a puddlelike remnant a mere 10 percent of its former grandiose self, with a shoreline some six hundred feet lower than it was. We call this the Great Salt Lake. The level of that lake has fluctuated eighteen feet up and down since 1850, when folks began to measure. It will fluctuate some more.

Lake Baikal, the Caspian and Aral seas, the Dead Sea (once six hundred and fifty-six feet deep), Lake Chad in the southern Sahara (once seven hundred and fifteen thousand, eight hundred square miles of water), all of them are shrunken vestiges of what was. Ten and twenty thousand years ago there was a lake in what is now Bolivian desert, a lake that was larger than Bonneville. There were dozens of lakes in what are now the deserts of Nevada, California, Oregon.

Lake Manly filled part of southern California to a depth of six hundred feet, it ran down the Amargosa River to the Colorado and fish came up into it then, as they had before, and then the lake dried out. Three thousand years ago it filled again. Thirty feet deep and fifty miles long, it lasted a thousand years before it dried down clear to the playa floor. The bed of Lake Manly has built up over years to a depth of five thousand feet; five thousand feet of lake-bed silts, carbonates, sulfates, salts. This is called Death Valley. In 1969 it flooded again and water lay three feet deep over eighty square miles of its old bed, one four-thousandth of its ancient self. The truth is this: these deserts, and other mid-latitude deserts, too, were full of lakes. These lakes were not small, and they've been here more than they've been gone.

The climate change that brought the glaciers south moved the temperate zone storm tracks southward, too, to fill the lakes again. There was more rain here then and it was colder, but not much of each: seven to nine inches more rain fell each year, and it was five to nine degrees Fahrenheit cooler then, *then* being twenty-three to ten thousand years ago. It wasn't much different, but different enough. There were glaciers in the Wasatch Range in Utah, the California Sierras. The basins between ranges filled with melt and runoff. Geologists call this centripetal drainage: all things to a common center.

Temperate lakes have outflow streams. Extra water spills on down. Here, with the added rainfall, the lakes came, and stayed.

There were exceptions. Always are. Lake Manly found the Amargosa and ran on down it to the Colorado and the sea; Bonneville burst a way through Red Rock Pass and poured unthinkable tonnages of rocks and water through the canyons of the Snake, for a period of months, before it settled down. But these are the exceptions. The whole Great Basin has no outlet to the sea. Most basin lakes have no outlet streams. Rainfall fills them, evaporation empties them. Because of this, they are acute barometers of climate. Rainfall and temperature are *all*. So, playas are sensitive to changes of tiny magnitude. Climate doesn't shift in a smooth curve but jiggles and wobbles — on some trend, perhaps, like this drying trend, this present interglacial; it is, like all earthly things, irregular. Interglacials tend to last ten thousand years and glacial ages sixty thousand years or more (who defines these things? Ice advancing up there or melting seems to be the clue, glaciers being unholy sensitive as well). So Lake Warner will be back.

Meanwhile, the valley full of greasewood and sage and rabbitbrush goes on. When I have a choice I take the road that moves me north, or west, tacking toward the hardtop highway that I know is out there west of this. On the hills all around are strandlines, beaches, three of them one above the other. Three times this lake dropped, then found a new level, then dropped again. Then here's a delta where some river came.

Three antelope cross my bows, heads up and hindquarters pumping. Half a dozen sage grouse peck in the track ahead, then burst up and off with wings held level as the level ground.

Playas are the worst deserts that there are. Flat, some more alkaline than others, like oceans of baking chalk. The Black Rock and Smoke Creek and Forty Mile deserts of Nevada were, a century ago, strewn with bones of oxen and rusting rims of wagon wheels, books, Dutch ovens; they were part of the huge irregular playa of Lake Lohantan. Similar flotsam littered others, too: Great Salt Lake Desert. Fort Rock Valley. On and on.

The Spaniards navigated on the deserts with sextants and chronometers, they moved by the stars out here like mariners. I come to a fork in the track and stop, imaginary sails slatting in the stays. I fish a lukewarm Coke from the cooler and grab a bag of chips and turn windward toward the sun, there being no real choice, and any harbor anywhere out here a long way off.

Pronghorn

Pronghorns are curious about people and will come very close; they've been known to wander right into hunters' camps to find out what is going on. They range throughout the open arid brush country of all the deserts; they were once more numerous on this continent than the buffalo. They relied for survival on their fine long legs — they can outrun anything except a bullet, they've been clocked at over forty miles an hour. They now rely on game refuge borders and hunting laws, but their numbers are increasing again in many places. They seem more sculptural than animal, formed and colored by a Mondrian or a Picasso. When they're alarmed, their white rump patches flare like bristling fires.

30

Idaho Hotel

Silver City, Idaho

Silver City is a historic mining town that sits high in the mountains in the middle of Owyhee County, and Ed Jagels has owned the Idaho Hotel here and has lived in it for most of the last twenty years. All this time he has filled it with collections of historical impedimenta, with heyday material culture for the most part: sepia-colored photographs, tobacco ribbons, tea caddies, lamps, heaps of documents, furniture, medicine bottles, books, china and glassware, a player piano and two older pianos, three pump organs, antique nickel slot machines, mirrors, maps.

There have been times when, for six months on end, he has been unable to leave, the dirt roads to and from Silver City having become impassable with snow. It doesn't take much weather to do violence to dirt track, and there are twenty-five miles of that in either direction to the first paved roads. Meanwhile, he has cared for the near-ruin that this hotel was when he came. He has hired people or found volunteers to shore beams, patch roofs, triage the tunnels that run beneath the hotel, and he has refurnished some of the rooms upstairs. One can stay in these rooms as a guest, though you need your own sleeping bag, there being no laundry and no linen. Staying here is a kind of camping out. Ed says:

"Well. It could be likened to Miss Havisham's long-preserved bridal-feast-setup dining room in Dickens's *Great Expectations.*"

Ed is more than ready for guests. He has bought cases of kerosene lamps and chamber pots. He has made the dining-room bar inviting, with its windows facing the creek and its neat wooden tables and chairs. The 1874 bar fixture is stocked with twentieth-century beer and chips, but the brass bar rail shines with nineteenth-century glory.

"Glory?" Ed says. "More like the simple wear from thousands of boots and shoes."

Most of those boots and shoes came and went before he was born, but people do still come, in summer, to see this justly famous mining town: Silver City, after all. In winter some come to ski when there's snow on the hills. But there have not been quite enough people of either kind to make the hotel "work" in one sense of the word, though in another sense this is irrelevant.

Ed dreams of renovation, of putting it back. Of having his collections housed in the greatest collector's item of them all: a grand hotel in a nineteenth-century gold-and-silver boomtown. Outside, there are Douglas firs and aspens on the slopes of Florida and War Eagle peaks, eight-thousand-foot mountains that punctuate the bony scarps, hills of sage and mountain mahogany, pocked with pale spilled tailings of mines: Black Bart, Big Fish, Floreta, Eureka, Gentle Emma, Silver Cloud, Blazing Star, Trade Dollar, Dashaway, Sinker, Rose. Between 1863 and 1865 there were more than two hundred and fifty major mines out there. After that there were hundreds more; enough to keep more than sixty ore-processing mills running and more than two dozen towns, camps, and cities flourishing. Those mines were the lifeblood of the city, and the death of it when they emptied or the prices skewed.

Ed buys kerosene for the hotel in forty-five-gallon drums. Before the last red glow has faded from War Eagle Peak he lights the lamp on our table, adjusts the wick with a practiced flick of the wrist, then lights another two in brackets behind the bar and pours a propane-cooled beer into a tall glass, with a flourish; all this with the graceful fussiness of someone who is accustomed and at home, a hotelier of the old school, a host to his guests, something of a showman. As the night deepens he lowers, lights, and hoists ornate overhead lamps complete with brass curlicues and colored glass globes, until the great cluttered room of the old hotel is filled with a soft, golden, miraculous light.

One is not used to this kind of quiet, not indoors. The absence of machinery hum, of automobile noise, is a lovely thing. There is the sound of the creek rushing down the rocks outside, cool, among willows, in the desert-mountain night. In here in the gold light a huge bechromed potbellied stove ticks and sends out waves of welcome heat.

Ed is moustachioed and stout and polishes the bar with a towel. The son of German-Irish immigrants and educated in part by Lutherans and in greater part by himself, he has a gentleman's patrician dignity, a dignity honed through primitive lone adventuring of gold-camp wilds. This must once have been a common thing. It is not a wholly lost thing. The hotel is proof. So is Silver City, Idaho, once the county seat, rivaling Boise in size and sophistication, now nearly empty — but not quite.

On one side of the bar is a set of gold scales with the miniature weights one moves with the aid of tweezers, and an assayer's kit, and Ed knows how to use them. There is still placer gold in the creek where Michael Jordan's party panned up that first color in May 1863, when the creek was wild with snowmelt and the men hot and rough with apocryphal settlers' tales of nuggets so plentiful they'd hammered them out on their iron wheel rims to make sinkers for fishlines. The settlers had had Oregon in mind, not gold, and were a little vague about the location of those nuggets, having been half-starving at the time, potential trout being worth more to them than mother lodes.

"They call it Jerdin Crick, right?" Ed says now. Coulter and I nod. "A crick is what you get in your neck. *Jordan Creek!*" He chuckles, shakes his head, and he goes upstairs to light the stove in our room.

"Be right back, folks," he says. "You'll want it cozy when you go to bed."

He goes off in his brisk hostly way, efficient and somewhat in a rush, though we are the only folks here, the only guests tonight at the grand hotel that was established in the year of Michael Jordan's big discovery. Things moved fast in those days: first the tent camps then the assayer's office then the cemetery the freight wagons the saloon the drummers and prostitutes and the hotel keepers and their guests, many of them taking ship to Panama and crossing the Isthmus by railroad, then coming north by ship again on the Pacific side, then up through Paiute country on the same roads of alkali dust as run there now.

They came. Of course, there were setbacks. There was a deep slump in the bank panic of 1875, followed by a revival in the 1890s — the period of Silver City's greatest growth and strength — and a milder revival late in the 1930s (the briefest of booms, when gold prices rose and there was something to be had picking over tailing piles and picking up old claims). So people came. Now most of them have left.

Most. Not all. A few buildings have burned or have collapsed; much of Silver City was simply torn down, around World War II, and used for building materials elsewhere. Some buildings are boarded up in expectation of better times, of renovation and a tourist trade, perhaps.

Nowadays, Silver City has a population of six. That's not counting summer people. That is counting Ed.

"What did it look like then? In the nineties?" I ask, because it seems the thing to ask.

"Let's see here." Ed goes to a pile of papers, there are piles like this all around the room; on the piano, on tables, countertops. "Here it is." He pulls out a map, in miniature. "This is the Sanborn Map of 1903. It was drawn up for fire insurance purposes, I believe. See, here."

Again and again he does just this, whatever I ask he finds the answer, everything is to hand and he is at home in a scholar's disorderly order, no other kind being needed here.

Over the years there have been battles with the Bureau of Land Management over the hegemony of Silver City, he tells us, and he and the other few remaining townspeople have fought hard and long in these, denying Silver City's death and insisting eloquently on its rightful life — its existence, its city-hood — and on his residence and on that of others, present and future; on their right to live and keep the place alive. Although some people may be tempted to call this a ghost town, Ed is severe on this subject. When I was tempted to call this piece "Ghost Hotel," he was severe with me:

"Since there are no such things as ghosts, I therefore cannot accommodate ghosts! Another way to read that is to say that the hotel is a ghost; which is erroneous also. Another title would be appreciated."

I understand. I do. Meanwhile, I do not share his disbelief. Listening to and watching him, one knows: in any place it's the heyday spirits that are the most alive, though one is unsure sometimes where life and death leave off; this is the meaning, after all, of ghosts.

"Would you two like to borrow a book?" he will say, later, when we are gathering our things, moving toward bed. "I have quite a library back here. You're welcome to anything you like."

We will follow him through the kitchen with its woodstove into his own sanctum, a booklined study-library-office and next to that a bedroom with — among other things — an eight-foot-tall Renaissance Revival bed, covered with quilts. This is also a museum of Victoriana except that it is not a museum. Coult's eyes will be very big and will meet mine, spooked, in the high-ceilinged room with its rows of dark books, having lost the thread, as I have, of exactly when and where we are.

Ed will go unerringly to the end of a shelf and will pull out one slim volume that looks newish, and is; a children's book written by Alan E. Leisk, a Boise resident and the restorer of a house up on War Eagle Mountain. "It's a children's mystery novel," he will say, to Coult, seriously, in the way that bachelors have with children, not knowing how to treat them differently from anyone else. "The fictitious 'ghost' — all 'ghosts' are fictitious — turns out to be a cougar. Not scary stuff by any means. You might find it interesting."

Later we'll read a chapter or two. These first chapters will feature a "ghost" that screams from time to time on the stairs of a hotel, a hotel very much like this hotel with stairs very much like the stairs outside our bedroom door. It's supposed to be the ghost of a woman who fell down them to her death on her wedding night and continues to scream a century later, as well she might, suspecting as she fell that she might be denied all things. After reading this far we will be glued together rigid in our sleeping bags, eyes wide staring at each other, and I won't blow out the light till half an hour after Coult has gone, at last, uneasily, to sleep.

★   ★   ★

Already, early in the evening, there is no need for stories here to do the summoning; in the golden light of the hotel bar we have entered another time. Just down Jordan Street a red-light district features Big Dick's, Georgie's, Mother Mack's (some girls marry miners when their contracts expire; others, perhaps wisely, don't). In daylight there will be whistling of mill and hoist engines, the muffled crumps of powder blasts shattering quartz veins. Across the gulch: China-town with joss houses, laundries, groceries, New Year's night with dragons and firecrackers, opium dens. Silver City in her booming prime: four lawyers in town, two doctors, two hardware stores, a photo gallery, four restaurants, a brewery, a Catholic church, two Masonic temples, a soda-bottling works, an undertaking parlor, eight saloons. More than forty million dollars in silver and twenty million dollars' worth of gold will be picked out of the mountains via hundreds of miles of tunnel, via Cornish miner and Chinese water carrier, a quantity of precious metal only just topped by Nevada's Comstock Lode.

A photo taken ten years after the hotel's birth shows the elegant three-story structure with white balconies lined with thirty-nine folks standing one deep along the rails and porches, leaving room for forty more. A stage with four horses stands in front of women in long dresses, a nursemaid holding an infant and a man proudly holding another, men in vests and bowler hats, one sitting on a chair with that cock-legged, arms-and-legs-crossed posture that seems, now, to have vanished with the century, except that Ed Jagels does just that, when he quits his barroom bustling and sits down.

Nowadays the hotel itself is not much changed, except those balconies and porches and rooflines have developed sways and paint is sometimes nonexistent. Upstairs the floors tilt, all of them, in sixteen directions, and the paper is genuine turn-of-century made and placed, now waterstained and peeling, so one remembers that it came all the way from New York City by horse and boat, through states that were not yet states. The functioning bedrooms — twenty-two of the original forty — have their own kerosene lamps and their own chamberpots, and ten of the rooms have wood-burning stoves. There is no electricity, there are no toilets, no central heat.

There is, however, a telephone in the bar. The telephone is powered by a magneto and a flashlight lantern battery. You crank the magneto and put the horn to your ear and hug the mouthpiece to your chest and you can place a call to eleven other places, all of them in Silver City. It's one of the last magneto systems in the United States. There are twelve numbers on the single line and a two-page phonebook (one page white, one yellow, the cover blue, the whole held together with two staples) and there's a familiar picture of a bell on the cover, but the bell is strangely marred by a crack pasted over with a Band-Aid. A motto surrounds this insignia: "Mater Campana Potest Descendere Ad Infernum," which translates as Ma Bell Can Go to Hell.

Next morning, after breakfast and woodstove-brewed coffee, in the morning light, we set off down the track that borders Jordan Creek and that will take us, in the end, back down to the desert, across the Oregon line, south to Nevada. Ed Jagels in shirt and waistcoat stands on the porch to say good-bye, standing as men stood there in 1873, exactly.

After we'd been driving down the creek awhile:

"He was the ghost, really, wasn't he, Mom?"

"He isn't a *ghost,* honeybunch!"

"Mom!"

"Oh . . . I guess he was, in a way. He took wonderful care of us, though."

"A good ghost, you mean?"

"Yes."

And I think this: that if there are good spirits, independent spirits in the world, then Silver City is still home to them. For the place to be other than deserted, that is what it takes.

31

virgin camps

Santa Rosa Range, Nevada

I've learned to make squaw fires (meaning fires for cooking things, small no-nonsense do-it-every-day pragmatic fires) out of not much: papery slabs of sagebrush, spine-hard twigs of horsebush or shadscale, twists of dry grass. When I go through highlands I stop the car and gather a bagful of juniper bark. It makes a great flaring resinous fire-starter and is better than birchbark, even, which is what I was used to at home. Stone circles can be made of dolomite knobs, shards of sandstone, basalt hunks holey as meteorites, glittery quartzite, dry-wash pebbles heaped in a ring. In a new camp the first concerns are stones and dry fuel, stones and fuel being this: the commonplace of human habitation, matériel of fire and defense.

Somewhere back on the rutted track that Coulter and I have been on for hours now we crossed the Nevada line. It seemed to me that the sky got bigger there and that the mountains rose to take more of the landscape. The basins between them held no water-made canyons and no riverbeds, no sign even of the ghost waters of the glacial age. Then, suddenly, here over the rise of a naked mountain's shoulder are clumps of small round willows, and a dark streak of water meadow in a hollow of gray slope.

"Nevada is the biggest bunch of nothing you was ever in," Cobby told me before I left Idaho. "Watch yourself," he said, and what he meant was: watch your gas gauge, your waterbags, don't trust anyone, the bunch of nothing is between you out there and the next gas pump, water tap, any help, don't forget.

"And say 'Naavaada,' not 'Nivahdah,' or it's a dead giveaway you're from someplace else," he said, and we've been practicing. The broad central "a" as in "gasp" seemed foreign and already doesn't, it's closer to the Spanish, which means snowed or snowy, and Nevada is ribbed with mountains lined range on range. In winter, when the Spaniards must have seen it first, the whole place is snow after snow like toothy jawbones.

According to our maps we're in the Santa Rosa Range, at the lip of the Great Basin itself. Great Basin is a massive dent in the continental breast, a hollow stretching from Oregon and California clear into Utah and down nearly to the Arizona line; basin and range country, all of it, streaked with mountains but contained, rimmed all around by higher ground. In here, nothing drains to any sea. Not that there's much, nowadays, to drain. Ten thousand years ago, when there was more water here, it all went inward to the basin lakes. Nowadays Nevada is the driest state in the Union; rainfall statewide is from three to ten inches a year, and averages out at four. Most of that comes in as snow.

South of here, perennial rivers end. Ephemeral streams carry montane snowmelt in the spring, for a while, and here near the Santa Rosa's backbone we've come on one of these: a snowmelt creek with its clumps of willows as round as clipped topiary, and between them the water meadow of level green. "Camp," I say, and stop the car.

A single vulture circles in his thermal watchtower, barely visible, though we are clearly visible to him. Yellow warblers fly along the creekbed, bright as canaries.

Later, after this, and after the other virgin Nevada camps — meaning places where there's no evidence of anyone's having camped before — Coult will say:

"But Mom, you have to tell them, how beautiful it is. Like . . . Mom! Like you can't see anything like that around *houses!*" An un-eleven-year-old intensity. I blink.

"Tell them what, exactly?" I say, hoping he'll tell me.

"Mom!" he says, "*tell* them!"

So, can I tell anyone how clean the creek water is, like brown glass? The brown chuckling ripple. Like music. That's just what it's like. One gets funny out here about water.

What else? Only that all ideas of time seem as cleanly washed away as beach footprints after a smoothing wave. I put away my camera as if I'd been foolish to bring the thing. It is stupid here; no way can it hold the vast place in which we are. The scale of the world has overwhelmed its aperture.

We are happy, we are happier here than we can remember being anywhere.

The water meadow is full of birds: robins and red-winged blackbirds and song sparrows, nothing fancy, but all of them are more curious about us than they are shy: people are the rarities, here. We walk up the creek, the streak of their habitat to which we've gravitated, too. Among the green blades of rush that are thigh deep and thick as shag rug are patches of Rocky Mountain iris and blue common camas, and buttercup and larkspur and pennyroyal. Upstream there are fields of wild blue flax. A pair of black-crowned night herons has a nest there and they follow us as we walk, flying forward and perching with a threshing of willow twigs. Always one of them is watching us with a ruby eye. In the rushes we find a single softball-sized vertebra of an elk, dry as chalk. Then a single rib. The irises are nearly white where the light strikes through the petals. They glow like milk glass against the green. A bee rummages and the iris petal dips and then the whole flower tips as if it were listening.

Above the water meadow are dry slopes of scattered sagebrush, high caulkings of aspen forest, a brown peak with drifts and tags of snow. Big shadows of clouds are flowing over the land. To the east a terrifying roll of mountains drops away. We are high here, just under the pass, and I feel unsteady when I look east as if I were standing over the eaves of a roof; it's a rough body of range clothed in faded camouflage canvas: the texture of high desert spring. Bedrock juts like compound fractures. Far away there is low, pale distance.

Camp is simple: two-man tent with bedrolls unrolled inside, a full waterbag hung on a branch and next to the waterbag the striped towel, the bottle of liquid soap, the tin cup, the pocket mirror. We are good at this; it takes fifteen minutes to make bed and bath. Raingear and down vests and a change of underwear are at the feet of the bedrolls, along with the two drawstring bags that are all our defense against disaster.

Then we concern ourselves with stones. Up in the scattered sage I find white rocks and use my shirttail for a basket.

Should I tell how quickly life becomes simple? And how simple it is?

Later, at the virgin camp in the Toquima Range, near a red dust track in a waterless forest of single-leaf pinyon and Utah juniper — the juniper with its pale leaves pressed into coralline sprays and the fibrous bark that's so great for starting fires (or making sandals or rope or caulking logs in cabin walls) — among flat red stones like jumbled potsherds, I'll pick up one stone for the fire and there will be a rattlesnake coiled underneath. It will buzz and we will run. It will be greeny yellow with a banded tail, a western rattler, thick as braided rope.

Three times that night I will wake up gasping, eyes wide, neck stiff as a girder, with my fists clenched against that punch and jab that could have been into forefinger, wrist, the pad of muscle at the base of the thumb; feeling how my fingers could swell like potatoes and my arm like a gourd; feeling how glad I was I'd taught Coult to drive in case I couldn't, but how many hours would it be, him driving the dirt track in the dark with mother sagged shallow-breathing on the seat beside him to even the first paved road, and along that over the high passes in the dark to the town of Austin, Nevada, with only the one rowdy bar open at that hour, and could he do that? How can I tell?

How can I tell the way the heart lives in the throat?

"Weren't you scared, out there?" people will ask.

"Well, yes," I'll say; what else can I say?

But how can I tell them the way the fear is married to the joy? There are worse things than being scared. There is that despair which rides pillion with security, I want to say that. Take a measure of freedom, you take terror by the hand every time.

So we make our circle of stones and fill it with a sacrament of wood and touch a match to the saved tinder of crushed bark. We wash our hands. We open a can of chili and put it in the pot. The vulture draws his circle in the sky and the sun draws his over the rim of the world, throwing a veil of gold and rose over the range, a sundown veil embroidered with black shadow. We have those two small drawstring bags we pack in everywhere, we're never without them: the kit bag with thirty feet of fine nylon rope, two pocket knives, roll of duct tape, water treatment pellets, candles and candle lanterns, windproof waterproof matches, sewing kit, coil of fine wire, lightweight pack straps with fastex buckles, waterbag that folds like a handkerchief but can hold a gallon and a half; then the medicine bag with the first-aid kit, snakebite kit, injectable antihistamine, sunblock, insect repellent, analgesic tablets, codeine tablets, broadspectrum antibiotic, bandages . . .

The chili is good. Afterward, we lie by the fire and look at the sky.
    "Mom, do you know where we are?"
    "Not exactly."
    "Who owns this place?"
    "We do."
    "But I mean really."
    "I'm not sure there is an answer really."
    There is a sort-of answer. This is part of the Humboldt National Forest, here, even though there is no forest of trees to speak of; the largest sage or willow stem is the width of my wrist, but that's beside the point. More than 70 percent of Nevada is publicly owned (according to my maps), meaning that the National Forest Service (in the ranges) and the BLM (everywhere else) and Teddy Roosevelt's Wildlife Refuge System (here and there) and the National Park Service (one fragment of the Snake Range on the Utah border) and then the Washoe and Shoshone and Paiute Indian Nations (more fragments, scattered) and the U.S. Air Force (seventy-five square miles or so between the Cactus Range and the Pintwater) and the state and federal Fish and Wildlife Services (anything to do with wildlife anywhere) all deal out entry permits and grazing rights and mineral rights and timber rights and hunting and fishing rights.
    But we're not exercising any of these rights, tonight. So maybe

it is ours. Ours by virtue of our being in it with no one present to tell us no. Ours to take a few dry sticks from and move a few stones in. We'll scatter our stones, bury our ash. We'll leave the place with minimized signs of temporary tenure, something only Cobby could interpret. We'll move on, as people did, before divvying of ground became convenient, or mandatory, and the question of whose became a question one asked.

32

tree line

Wheeler Peak, Great Basin National Park, Nevada

We are ten thousand feet up on the Utah-Nevada border, at tree line, and here they are.

After we've stood awhile breathing, watching them, it occurs to me that we are waiting for them to move. To continue to move. They look caught in mid-gyre; reaching, clasping, flowing, splitting, leaping. They whirl, they clench, they point to the sky in liquid attenuations.

They are very big. Their colors are as vivid as costumes: ochre and russet, and brushed silver, and a green so bright it looks false. They are bristlecone pines. Some of them have not moved in thousands of years, since the seeds that carried their embryos rattled down between the stones.

Unless you count growth and death as movement. This one is more than three thousand years old and still growing, still reproducing, still dying. It is in motion in place, one frame of a time-lapse.

The bristlecones live in a desert of quartzite stones that have the glistening sterility of freshly dynamited marble. It is the moraine of a mountain glacier. Some of the stones are the size of automobiles, others the size of chairs. They look bulldozed and dumped, which is more or less the truth.

Even the small trees are old. A bristlecone the size of a Christmas tree (the firs that take a dozen years maybe to grow to harvest for the trade) will be older than the American Constitution. It has passed its bicentennial, and is young.

The mountain glacier is old, and is the godparent of the bristlecones, the founding father. It's still here; the only glacier left of the old swarm. It has shrunk to a lens of dirty white against the more than eighteen-hundred-foot headwall, in a quartzite amphitheater that was quarried again and again in colder, wetter times by larger, more unsettled rumps of ice. Glacial cirque: humongous sag in an armchair of stone. The bristlecones live on the lip of this chair.

We move on, up, into the amphitheater in the mountain peak. We climb over naked talus and drifts of old snow. A few limber pine and Englemann spruce grow here, pruned and broomsticked, with skirts of wind timber. The sun is hot and clean.

Alpine desert. Water here is snow or ice most of the time: in other words, not water at all. The sun has no mercy in the white stones. The wind shears leaves, branches, bark, blows what would make soil away, dries our snow-wet boots in minutes.

Here in the rock rubble there are patches of arctic-alpine tundra. A currant bush twines between stones where the wind can't go; it has long coppery thorns and furry leaves, defense against the light. There are swatches of mosslike foliage with full-sized flowers, true dwarfs: a purple milk vetch, a white phlox, a daisylike composite. Farther on there are more snowdrifts and a steep lip of stones, and we are on the glacier.

The ice here is under the stones, the stones are a kind of carapace. From the air this looks like a tongue of rubble; it's called a rock glacier. We hear meltwater underneath, running through holes. We've left the tundra behind. Here there are only lichens.

We lie down for a rest, pillowing our heads on packs, and around us the cirque is like a citadel of stacked metamorphic layers. The sun is like a blanket on our legs. Around us there are battlements, towers, ruined buttresses. Wheeler Peak is Cambrian quartzite, five hundred and fifty million years old, brittle, fractured by the uplift of the Snake Range, crazed with northeast–southwest-trending joints. It made easy meat for ice.

There are streaks of snow all down the cirque's flanks and

dust-wrinkled drifts, and under the headwall — facing northeast where it gets most shelter from midsummer sun — a bigger drift. In summer a crack appears between big drift and wall, a *bergschrund,* all of seventy-five feet deep. Looking down, we see the light in this crevasse is the jewel-like blue of years-compacted snow. Snowline — orographic snowline — is the size of a room, where more snow falls each year than melts. Unmelted snow stacks up there and the weight of it settles the whole a little, every year, like a person leaning back in a chair. All glacial movement is a species of settling, grinding rock forward under the rump.

Sixty-five million years ago during what's called the "Tahoe Glaciation" (mountain glaciers being a species different from that of continental ice-sheets, their seasons have different names) the Wheeler ice went down as low as eighty-three hundred feet, along Baker Creek, down to eighty-six hundred on Lehman Creek. That's as far as it ever went. Then it retreated. Between thirty-five and thirteen thousand years ago it went to the valleys again, out of its cirque and down the creekbeds, fattened by heavier snows and defended by deeper cold. It retreated again, leaving rubble and scars. Ten thousand years ago and again within the last five thousand, glitches in weather fattened the ice and sent the rock tongues moving down. Within the last century there's been a half-degree centigrade rise in mean annual temperature, and that's enough, the "glacieret" is dying from lack of food, the rock tongues are stilled, pitted with melt pools. Stilled long enough, a few centuries, a few thousand years, the alpine desert dwarfs will colonize the cracks between these stones, too.

Between this alpine desert above and the Great Basin desert below, there is forest. Mule deer live in the forest, and coyotes, squirrels, raccoons, the Clark's nutcrackers that gather bristlecone pine seed and bury it in clutches. Pinyon and juniper trees grow lowest of all, then ponderosas, then white fir and Douglas fir, drier slopes of mountain mahogany, cool patches of aspen, then Englemann spruce and limber pine, and highest and loneliest of all, at timberline, the Great Basin bristlecones.

They are some of the oldest living things in the world. They have been known to live for more than four thousand years. Below and out of sight where even the junipers fade down into coppery haze, the Great Basin desert lies between its ranges like a sea. Scattered brittle shrubs: sagebrush, winterfat, shadscale, horsebush, a few grasses, gravel and dust. We are glad to be out of that and into this. We've come to an island world, ice desert in desert air, filled with light and stone and the clean breath of snow, the kind of place where bristlecones can live.

Nevada Fleabane and Wheeler Peak

The tiny and the immense are what one sees; there is not much in between. Notice how distinct the tree line of Wheeler Peak is from this distance, and how the dark zone of evergreen forest lies between tundra above and desert below. Foothills wear a scattered forest of junipers and pinyons and sage. There are no rivers. On the summit where we stand there is only broken gravel and these little purple flowers.

33

on the edge

Caliente, Nevada

Coming south now into the funnel of Nevada, we're looking for creosote bush, five dollars on the table (the glovebox will do), creosote being the symptom of having crossed from cold high desert down into hot, from the Great Basin we've been in now for weeks, into the Mojave. So, this being Nevada, we've bet good money on who will see it first.

The sign says Caliente, Nevada; the Spanish word for hot and that's true. Bright dusty wide hot and no town in sight, pale hills pocked with bumps of shrubs, mostly saltbush, greasewood, sage still on northerly slopes, sage looking gap-toothed, blasted, crushed, pale shoots poking into bloom. Sage is of the Great Basin. With the creosote, the sage will cease. We'll pass from one desert to the other like changing partners at a dance. By what margins do they dance in this topography?

Creosote is evenly speckled over most of the Mojave and Chihuahuan and Sonoran deserts, too, through all the hot deserts, that is, taking the place of the sage that speckles over cooler Great Basin and Colorado Plateau. Some would say that sage — hovering as it does on the ten-inch-a-year rainfall mark — isn't really desert anymore. If it's not then it's the lace edge of it. I'll argue anyone into the ground on sage. Heat gives my temper an edge, my opinions durability, my thirst a passionate expanse, so the Mojave must be close. As dunes are of sea. The fringe of broiling inundation. We are close.

We've stopped three times when Coult called *Hey, there!* but it was cliff rose every time (very creosote-like in color and shape, though; he's getting too good) with leaves shrunk and in-curled and oily as the needles of pines; not creosote, but close. The entry to Mojave is also in the burnt colors of the hills.

Downtown Caliente, suddenly, and we stop at the café for lunch, mostly out of thirst, putting the moment of passage off.

The Brandin' Iron Restaurant, meanwhile. The red-checked curtains, with frills. The basket of saltines and the tabasco sauce, salt and pepper, slant-topped pot of sugar (with the metal flange that waggles as you pour), canning jars for drink glasses. Decor: Olde West, not so old really. A mirrored bar. High shelves around the room filled with branding irons and gold pans, enamel coffee pots, enamel spoons, a washboard, brass spittoon. Lunch comes with french fries whether you want 'em or not. Outside is a tangle of electric and phone wires and a train track: technology in raw snarl across pale sky and dust. There is a casino (shabby) and a mercantile store; hardware and car parts, mostly. Houses are all of a pattern, sided with horizontal boards, four posts holding each porch roof.

Creosote

The men in here wear jeans, belts with big buckles that grab for attention like a codpiece, suspenders, work or riding boots. Vehicles parked outside are trucks. On the bar is a giant jar of humongous peanut-butter cookies. There are, for once, no "wanted" posters circa 1880 anywhere. The impedimenta on that shelf, with the possible exception of the spittoon, are not anachronisms here. Mining, ranching. Gold, silver, cattle. Casino, and somewhere out there whorehouse, too, this being Nevada.

Afterward, just beyond Oak Springs Summit, right outside of town, Coult sees not cliff rose this time but creosote, and in bloom, still. Fair enough. The five bucks is his. Just east and north of the junction of 375 with 318 at the turn of 93, I write that down. We both get out of the car to double-check and, standing in the tarry smell of it and the blaze of light in the pale stones, the Mojave hills too scantily clad in just this lacy bush, we do know we're back.

34

bighorns

Lake Mead National Recreation Area, Nevada

4:58 A.M.: Vegas Boulevard, 79° F

It's still dark and this town never sleeps but at this time of day it does snooze a little. I sip from my thermos cup of iced coffee, glad of the relative emptiness of the boulevard with its zippy glitz, the adult fairy tale that lasts (they want you to think) forever; and glad too of the relative cool, which won't last long. I'm going to Lake Mead to look for desert bighorn sheep, and right now the heat is holding back for the power punch. I can tell.

Desert bighorn sheep are hard to find at the best of times, difficult to see; their country is hard to get to and once you're there the animals are the same color as it is. They stand motionless, giving you no clue. Or slide off uphill over impossible crags. This is what I know.

They need water in summertime, so mountains that have no summer water have no sheep in them. Otherwise, from Canada into Mexico and from Death Valley through Grand Canyon country, bighorns are to mountains as beavers are to watercourses: indivisible.

Bighorns are good to eat, and they are magnificent, and these are good reasons to hunt them; no one argues with the fact that bighorns have been hunted to near-extinction when they could be. They were hunted heavily by native people, and between that and the drying up of their landscape, the wild sheep were already gone from much of their ancestral range when the white man came with domestic flocks carrying diseases and parasites that could spread unchecked through the wild herds. Domestic sheep stayed in places until they wore out their welcome or the range or both. And the miners, ranchers, adventurers of the day had guns that could kill at a distance that an arrow or a spear never could. Hunting and domestic livestock acted like a one-two punch. Bighorns vanished from more ranges. The story is that, nowadays, hunters are putting them back.

There are people in the Nevada Department of Wildlife who work all year for the benefit of bighorns. They put catchments and dams in slickrock to make new watering places. They census the flocks and hand out hunting tags accordingly, so the sheep will not be harvested too much anywhere. They trap animals where they're numerous and move them to places where they're absent or scarce: a young nucleus herd to repopulate the range.

This year they will trap in the Black Mountains, an hour from here, in the southernmost tip of Nevada along Lake Mead. They aren't trapping today. Today they're laying out bait. The bait will be laid out daily until the sheep will come into the canyons, regularly, in numbers. When they do they can be trapped there: caught under nets, blindfolded, hobbled, carried in a boat and then a truck, and set loose somewhere else. Today the Department of Wildlife men are leaving the dock at Lake Mead at six A.M. in a boat, to bait the canyons and watch the sheep come in.

I have no trouble getting out of town. Once past Vegas the road cants uphill through a sprawl of fast-food joints and condos. The mountains rise flat and black; behind them the air is clear yellow with desert dawn. I stop at a buntinged fast-food box (it looks like a carton for a toy, red and white and thrown down upright in the dust), remembering the warning to down as much liquid as I can. The red quart-sized paper cup rattling with ice cubes seems as surreal as Vegas glitter. I sip fizzed sweetness like a medicine. The heat (they've warned me) will be deadly real. The only way to hack it is to drink and drink. Drink before you're ready to, long before you're thirsty. Once you're thirsty it's too late. You'll never catch up then, you're dehydrated to the danger point then, the human machinery of thirst was never designed for the Mojave in July.

6:04 A.M.: Lake Mead, 86° F

The boat has an open fiberglass hull, twenty-eight feet long and eight feet wide, powered by a 175-horsepower outboard. It was made for hauling sheep. It moves from the pier with skittery grace, with Craig Stevenson at the wheel and Adam and Scott and me sitting on our coolers in the middle.

Craig is a Fish and Wildlife biologist and he works all year with bighorns. This is his expedition. In the order of things at the department, Dan Delaney is the lead biologist; Craig is second in command. The bighorn transplant program was pioneered back in 1969, but when Dan came along in '82 he got things going in a big way.

Craig is mid-thirtyish, muscular, of middle height, and has the kind of face that slips into a smile without his really noticing. He has a farmer's head for apposite detail; he can scale a trophy ram by eye — scale number being the result of a complex equation built from horn diameter, breadth, and length. All day long he takes into account the shapes of slickrock, the state of forage plants, the whereabouts of a particular ewe, the presence of burro dung, and countless other things, all of which are important to the sheep and important to him.

Craig may be absorbed in his work but he does not take himself too seriously. This is a combination that has, in anyone, considerable charm. Somewhere late in the morning it'll come out that his wife is eight months and two weeks pregnant, a fact that makes him proud and embarrassed in equal measure; the boys will tease him gently, making him go pink. Months later he'll write me a long detailed description of the remainder of his sheep-trapping escapades in the Blacks "working with a lot of girls and babies up there" and as a postscript: "My wife had the ram lamb on July 13. His name is Matt."

Adam Truran and Scott Huber are biology grad students, Craig's summer workers. They are as athletic and close-groomed as cadets. They tease Craig all the time. Craig replies in kind.

"We teach 'em the difference between management and research," Craig shouts over the engine roar. "We teach them it's the difference between reality and dreamland."

Scott and Adam roll their eyes.

"No, really!" Craig says, grinning now. They're all three grinning. "These boys put in nine, ten-hour days!"

"Craig takes care of us. Buys us Frosties," Adam says, loud enough for Craig to overhear.

"They're cheap dates," Craig says, and laughs.

"God, you got to remember who's paying the bill!" he shouts. The engine is revved now and we're scooting over the dark water, holding our hats.

The Department of Fish and Wildlife is funded by hunters — by taxes on guns and ammo and by the sale of hunting permits. The hunting of bighorn sheep is an exclusive business. If one comes from out of state, it will cost eight hundred dollars for a bighorn tag, and one can wait decades for the chance. For in-state hunters tags are cheaper but are also handed out by lottery, and once you've had a tag you have to wait ten years before you can put your name in the lottery again. Two tags are auctioned off every year: the minimum bid for these is twenty thousand dollars, and bids have gone as high as sixty-five. All of this is returned to the sheep in the form of management and protection.

"The reality is, if there was no funding and no one to represent the interests of wildlife, the big threat would be loss of habitat to development *and* indiscriminate hunting. Poaching. That's the *reality!*"

Even so, there are folks opposed to hunting under any terms.

"A lot of the media people in Vegas are from somewhere else," Craig says, "and are just about as un-outdoor-oriented as Vegas is. Their attitude is, we're just putting sheep out there so we can shoot 'em."

Scott grins. "Politics!" he says.

"Politics are pretty simple," Craig says. "Hunters versus nonhunters. Pretty simple."

★   ★   ★

We wear shorts, T-shirts, sneakers, shades, and perch on our coolers or the gunwales with farmish slouches, as if this were the bed of an empty pickup. Not quite empty, though. There are the two hundred-pound bales of alfalfa hay wrapped in a blue tarp. There is a pair of pantyhose stretched over the engine air intake to prevent alfalfa from clogging the engine. There is a big aluminum rake.

6:40 A.M.: Finger Cove, 89°F

The lake is windless and dark, loopily patterned with the light of reflected sky. Dawn painted the mountains a molten orange and spilled fire into air and water, then the sun rose over the mountains a moment ago, as if a furnace door had opened in our faces.

We pull into the first shadowed cove with relief. The lake level has dropped, leaving a flat of fine-grained muck:

"Don't step in that. You'll be gone so fast we'll have to pull you out by the ponytail."

"Scott calls it *spooge*."

"Stinks to high heaven if you pardon my French."

The sediment is fine, dark, semifluid as potter's slip. The tracks of great blue herons and smaller birds are punched in it as if stamped there by metal.

The lake has been dropping for some time, Craig says, due to the drought in general and the Greater Las Vegas area draw-down in particular. It's fifteen to twenty feet below normal, forty feet below the spillway of the Hoover Dam. As it drops it leaves a pale crust on vertical rock and spooge on any horizontal place. Bits of spooge float on the water surface, too; this is called *gak*. Where spooge has lain exposed for weeks it has dried, cracked deeply, baking hard in rough pentagonal geometry, in the familiar playa way. Where the sediment is fresh there's a sewerish smell to it, nastier than low tide.

There are carp in the shallows, bluegills, bass. The fish flick off, obliquely, shadows the shape of a finger or a hand. We cut the engine and slide in. The men scan rock walls and horizon.

Adam takes a chunk of alfalfa hay and the rake and we leap the spooge line to solid stone and walk up-canyon. We come to the place where wisps of hay have been scattered and trampled, flecked with pellets of dung. The dung looks like that of domestic sheep or goat, or deer, except that each pellet has a kind of nipple at one end and older bits have crackled longitudinally; they look like miniature pecans. It's important to notice these things.

Adam rakes the wisps into a pile and the new hay is loosened and laid out.

Around this bait are the metal posts that will, someday, hold the net.

"The posts get so hot you have to wear gloves," Craig tells me.

"How hot does it get?"

"Not hot enough to bother the sheep." He laughs. "Whatever it gets in town, add five degrees. We're lower out here."

"We're generally out of here before the heat peaks out," Scott says, squinting upward at the rugged slope whitened by sun.

"Brought plenty water?"

"Yes."

He nods.

The net to catch the sheep, they tell me, will be hoisted like a circus tent with four corner winchposts, four side posts, and an eighteen-foot-high centerpost. Between each connection and each support will be yellow rope with blast caps twisted into the weave. Craig and the boys will sit seventy-five to one hundred yards away, watching with binoculars, waiting to see that the sheep are well in under there before they blast the net.

Down at the cove will be a boatload of volunteers to help subdue the animals and carry them to the boat, once the net is down. The faster they're processed then the better, they have less time to injure themselves. It takes a man per sheep at least to hold them upright so they won't aspirate cud and get pneumonia, to keep their heads down to stop them struggling, to put the blindfold on — a section of pants leg from a wornout pair, the soft cylinder of cloth pulled over the animal's face and held there by ties behind its horns. Then the sheep are hobbled with wide leather straps and carried to the boat.

"When they get the blindfold on they calm right down."

"Bunch of babies after that."

"They're a great animal to work with," Craig says. "Deer'll try to kill you. Elk'll try to kill you. Antelope are fragile. Sheep . . . sheep just want to get away."

Most of the volunteers will be members of the Fraternity of the Desert Bighorn, a group consisting almost entirely of hunters. The fraternity has given the transplant program hundreds of thousands of dollars and thousands of hours of free labor over the years, in spite of the fact that any one individual can only expect to get one bighorn tag in his entire life, and most of the fraternity has already had theirs. The transplant program couldn't work without them.

"Ever think you'd see an environmentalist out here? Doing something for the sheep?" Craig asks.

"Do they come, too?"

"Heck, no. They're busy over at the legislature, where they can keep cool."

As we walk back to the cove, Scott stops, points to the horizon, and looks at me, nods.

"Right," Craig says, his voice low. "Two rams. A four, five-year-old. And a two-year-old."

What I see in black silhouette is what I've seen pecked in rocks at desert springs in the Arizona Kofas, along the Snake River in Idaho, in the Coso Range of California: a dark double curve as if an anchor stood upside down on the horizon, tines spread.

"Breakfast time, boys," Craig says.

7:45 A.M.: Boulder Wash, 90° F

Desert bighorn ewes average one hundred and five pounds, the rams between one hundred and forty and two hundred — depending on age, the time of year, the state of forage. They are fattest just before the rut, in fall, but whatever their body size the dry weight of an average ram's horns is more than ten pounds. Think of carrying that on the back of your head, like a cast-iron jester's cap.

We've come through Black Canyon, sheer walls three and four hundred feet high around us like a fjord. In the cove of Boulder

Wash the water is a strong green bordered by dry, steep mountains. One slope is made of boulders; above this looms a cliff face of brown tortured rock, all colors of volcanic ash and massive breccia. Lying on a ledge no wider than my shoulders, a single two-year-old bighorn ram is chewing its cud.

Aside from the silver snarls of dried up bursage, nothing grows here but a khaki-colored dusting of creosote bush, widely scattered and almost leafless with the drought. In the wash are smatterings of a yellow nettle, glistening with stinging hairs. This has been christened "snotweed" by the crew and is to be avoided at all costs; the hairs will sting like bejesus and if you get them in your socks no amount of laundering will ever get them out.

"What do the sheep eat?" I ask.

"Everything you see, they eat," Craig answers.

A pause.

"Creosote?"

"Absolutely."

"Snotweed?"

"I dunno about snotweed."

Later he'll write me that Adam and Scott saw a two-year-old ram eating snotweed. Like much of what they know about the sheep, this is anecdotal knowledge; it comes from the intimacies of their work among the animals, not from Official Print, not from the data-backed documentations of Official Research.

Sheep eat according to season, availability, and rain. In the uplands there is sagebrush, grass, juniper berries, mountain mahogany. Downslope the rams butt Joshua trees to shake off fruits, they nip agave stems and eat the fallen buds. They chew dry tree bark, cactus spines, fibers of yucca. They eat the flowers of pentstemon, primrose, thistle. They paw up and munch the roots of wild parsley, desert poppy. Nowhere in any book or published study does it say that they eat creosote.

A ewe appears on the skyline twelve hundred feet up, then another beside her. There's a blurt of sheep talk as the second one appears.

Craig looks through binoculars.

"The first one's a one-horn ewe. Pretty old gal. The second one is her lamb."

He lowers the binoculars.

"Last year she'd come to meet the guys in the cove." He nods toward Scott and Adam. "We had to push them up the canyon to place the bait. The sheep would circle within fifteen feet. She — " he nods toward the ewe on the cliff top, still peering down at us, so distant she could be a stick — "she can get down here from up there in five minutes, when she wants."

"How old is she, then? How old do they get?"

"Don't know how old she is. Pretty far along."

He looks at her again, sweeps the horizon again:

"Oldest known wild sheep will be eighteen this year. Last year, that sheep raised a lamb. She's in the Last Chance Range. She was caught and tagged as a yearling in the Rivers. Later, she was transplanted up there. She's done well, that old gal."

"Why are you trapping in here?" I ask.

"According to the latest survey there are three hundred and fifty sheep in the Blacks, and this is a small range, and that's a lot of sheep."

He says that Dan Delaney wants thirty of them out of here this year. Of those they'll move twenty to the Gabbs Valley Range, northwest of Tonopah. The other ten they'll move to the Specter Range near Mercury.

"We've done four water developments in the Specters. There's not one sheep in there. This is a complete reintroduction."

"Where else are you trapping?"

"Boulder City."

"That's a *city!*"

"Yes, ma'am! We've had depredation complaints of sheep in Boulder City. That's a fast-growing community and it's great sheep country over there. People just moved into the bighorns' backyard and planted stuff that tasted great. What can I say? And one of these days some big ram'll lower his headgear and get some kid or old lady and then it'll be our fault."

He ups the binoculars again and does another sweep for horizon shapes, for flick of motion. We listen for echoes of dislodged stones, for the grating noise of bleats.

★   ★   ★

Craig baits five canyons in the Blacks. Like grazers and browsers anywhere, bighorns have daily rounds, amended but predictable, so that if you're predictable too — laying hay down each day in the same place at some same hour — the sheep will come.

Things go wrong. If it rains in the mountains the bighorns vanish. Summer rains are not the norm but there is no norm; so little rain ever falls in this part of the Mojave that the timing of its fall is not the slightest bit predictable. When it does rain, the natural stone hollows and tanks called tinajas fill up inland, and then the sheep stay up on their preferred "escape terrain" away from the lake. Last month a rain came and took the sheep off for more than a week. Now, right now, they're coming back.

When we're in the boat again and moving from the cove, we see a ewe, a yearling ram, and a lamb on the rocks, ten feet from the water's edge, aware of us but unafraid.

"Disney One." Craig laughs. He explains: "'Disney' means a ewe, a lamb, and a ram. Family style. That's what we say when we're doing the count. 'Disney Five' means it's a five-year-old ram. 'Disney Eight' means a ewe and a lamb with an eight-year-old ram, and so on."

A second ewe appears over the shoulder of brown rock. She takes a mouthful of creosote bush, and still chewing comes toward us over the stones. She stands staring at us as we leave.

8:45 A.M.: Little Gyps Cove, 94° F

At first I think it's a mountain of salt. It's gypsum; almost as soluble as salt, pale and dark in streaks and dissolved to holey laciness where it touches water.

It is strange in this heat to be floating into something that looks so much like rotting ice. As the boat slows, we get serious again about water. Each of the men drinks from a gallon-sized plastic milk jug. They tell me the trick is to fill the milk jug two-thirds with water and put it in the freezer overnight; in the morning you take it out and top it up with water. It thaws as fast as you can drink. They have two of these each.

The light is white in here and reflects more whitely from the gypsum of the cove. Cove, canyon — hard to say what this is. For millennia these were canyons that led to the Colorado River. Now they are coves along Lake Mead. The comings and goings of water seem beside the point. The water is clear enough here to look down and see the shadowed plunge of what was once a canyon's walls. It seems familiar, this notion of drowning in what was dry; I've seen the opposite so much; playas, sinks, beaches of vanished lakes. Desert water is not to be trusted. Looking down into the drowned canyons' plunge, I hold the gunwales of the boat as if I were in air.

"Weird, huh?" Adam says. He's seen me doing this.

I nod.

"When we swim at lunchtime, we always use one of those floatable pillows. Makes you feel like maybe you won't fall."

"Fall?"

"Yeah. Drown."

Uphill there are dust heaps of volcanic ash and cliffs of breccia — dark basaltic chunks embedded in tuff like raisins in bread. I have the old sense of tilt and tunneling, vertigo, in the evidence of stones and time: the gypsum was laid down in the bed of a saline lake as the lake dried to nil. Like dolomite and salt, gypsum is laid down in drying pans, but where and when or what lake it was that laid this silty mountain down as depth, not height, no one knows.

Gypsum is hydrated calcium sulfate. Fine-grained and massive, it's called alabaster; a fibrous silky form called satin spar is used for jewelry; it's called selenite as a mineral in soil. Calcined, gypsum becomes plaster, is used for plaster of Paris or wallboard. Here it's been topped by volcanics and is redissolving in Colorado River water, the warm green water of a man-made lake. Tilt, vertigo.

No sheep appear in Little Gyps. No one likes the whiteness of the sun. We lay out hay, drink more water, as much as we can hold, and go.

9:53 A.M.: Coyote Cove, 102° F

On the way here we hauled the boat aside into a hollow like the inside of a huge stone pipe, like a cathedral belfry polished smooth, carved over years by flash-floodwater plunging down. I don't know why we went except that the place delighted them, they had nothing to say about it; they looked up, and held the boat away from the rock with their hands. Against the creamy stone the water was the color of pine needles at dusk, an almost paintlike green. In the slick-rock overhead a canyon wren made its shady sweet desert noise: *chew chew chew chew*, a nasal descent of notes accompanied by coppery flicks of light through little wings. A lizard went up the rock in hurries and stops. That was all.

These summer months are the only months, Craig says, that big-horns need water every day. They need it now because of the parched forage and because of the heat. Their need for water limits the range they feed on and defines the places where predators can easily find them.

Resting, chewing their cud — most of the time — they like to lie up with backs to solid stone, where they can look out below and nothing can come at them from above.

Above Coyote Cove are two hollows in the rockface fifteen feet above the canyon floor, facing north, shady in midday with a view up the wash, old sheep beds that have been used for years. Now Craig and I are in one, the boys in another, perched in gravel and sheep pellets. Behind me is a packrat nest complete with eclectic collection: bobcat dung that looks like Tootsie Rolls, the leg bone of a lizard, two twist-off soda bottle tops, twigs of creosote. Below us, the heap of green alfalfa hay looks strange in the gravel and bleached rock. This is like the photographs I've seen of Mars: barrenness over-exposed.

A rattle of stones: it's just a chuckwalla foraging along the canyon wall, a fat foot-long lizard with a jowly tortoisy face, jerky in his movements like a bogus dinosaur in an old sci-fi flick, one of those black-and-whites now the exclusive territory of serious insomniacs . . . my mind must be going. More rattles of stones and then, as if the rock itself had poured into motion, seven sheep appear flowing down the cliff, sheep the color of the hot stone, taupe and cream and rust. Four ewes, three half-grown lambs, all their coats satiny and all of them fat. They touch down on the canyon gravels with the rump-high head-high trot of animals in high spirits and high health.

Later a ram comes down the wash. He's a three- or four-year-old, as square-bodied as a beef bull and with a set of horns so massive that he seems misshapen. Notice the grace with which he lifts his chin to scent the ewes, like a woman with a grand coiffure. He comes on with little rushes, stopping to lift his chin again and roll his eyes, making a grand entrance that the ewes and lambs ignore. They go on eating, butting one another off the hay, dragging wisps away, the lambs cocking their heads back and swinging their rumps, teasing each other, the ewes digging expertly to get the soft leaf meal; like cake to them, I imagine.

Another ram appears, more slowly, from the east. Craig nods and lowers his chin to his chest.

"Five-year-old," he says, in a whisper, having counted the growth lines without binoculars.

"Good God," I say, nothing else being appropriate to say. This ram looks as if he were wearing a pair of golden tires.

"You haven't seen a big one yet." Craig laughs under his breath.

The older ram comes down with no fuss to the ewes and smells their rumps one by one in a businesslike way. They squat and pee for him without for a moment stopping their attack on the hay. He throws his head back and lifts his lip, smelling their urine for the scent of estrus, with an assayer's exactitude; between each sniff and lip-lift there's a connoisseur's pause. It's not mating season, none of the ewes is in estrus now. That doesn't matter to him, he gives each one of them attention, he is a professional.

11:35 A.M.: Bearing Cove, 117° F

There is a western grebe on the water of the cove here; it looks like a rusty bathtub toy. Eight rams stand shoulder to shoulder up the wash as if they were penned: this summer bachelor group is typical of the sheep, Craig says, the ewes usually traveling together in a matriarchal herd, the rams in a separate bunch: a rule to which there are countless Disney exceptions.

We don't stay long, though there are plenty of sheep here. The mountains loom like charcoal, grayed over with ash, red-hot. My skin crisps as though I were standing in the middle of fires. The breeze from the peaks is like the air that rises from the oven when you lean to check the roast.

We rake the scattered wisps, place fresh bait, take a look at the ram bunch through binoculars. They stand in the full sun, without moving. I feel nauseated; I breathe and don't seem to take anything in. The men's faces look set. When we reach the lake again, I follow their example and wet my arms and legs but am dry before the engine starts up. Later I'll find out that today was the worst day of a record-breaking heatwave that has rolled across the Southwest, going high into the 120s in all these desert valleys, though at the time I think that this heat is nothing exceptional, that this is the way it always is.

In the rocks by the cove there are six more sheep: an older ewe with a lamb, a lone middle-aged ewe, and three yearlings — two ewes and a ram — grazing and picking among the stones. They look at us and we look back as if this were a barnyard, not the Black Mountains of the Mojave and the green silty water of the dammed Colorado, but as though this were the usual way of things.

But it is not usual. It is, in fact, revolutionary.

The archaeological records that I've read elsewhere say this: ten thousand years ago, in the Zagros Mountains of Iran and Iraq, people stopped being merely predators of wild sheep. They began to drive off other predators. They began to select their own prey: they harvested older rams instead of younger tastier ewes. They did this with a view to the future. The bones in their Neolithic caves say that this happened almost overnight: a revolution. A new symbiosis.

Here it is again: sheep and people with nothing wonderful about it, though everything about it is wonderful. In spite of the heat the men smile between attacks at the water bottles. They smile at each other and at me and at the bighorns, too.

Desert Bighorn Ram Drinking at a Spring

The ram is a seven-year-old. Notice the broken edge of his horns, cracked off in some mating battle. This was drawn from a photo taken by Craig Stevenson.

Table of Geologic Time

Era	Period (or Epoch)	Years before the present
CENOZOIC	Pleistocene Epoch	recent–2 million
	Tertiary Period	2–65 million
MESOZOIC	Cretaceous Period	65–136 million
	Jurassic Period	136–190 million
	Triassic Period	190–225 million
PALEOZOIC	Permian Period	225–280 million
	Carboniferous Period	280–345 million
	Devonian Period	345–395 million
	Silurian Period	395–430 million
	Ordovician Period	430–500 million
	Cambrian Period	500–570 million
PRECAMBRIAN		570 million–4.6 billion

35

moving mountains

West Central New Mexico

We are eating fajitas on top of twenty-two thousand feet of sediment washed into the Rio Grande rift. Down there, a massive wedge of basement rock is falling away like a keystone dropping down while some tectonic Samson pushes the arch apart. This rift runs all the way from the Mexican state of Chihuahua to Sawatch, Colorado, and is variable in width; from thirty miles wide near Albuquerque it thins to a couple of miles here, in Socorro.

The rift began to open some twenty-eight million years ago, when the Colorado Plateau to the west began to pull away from the craton — stolid basement rock — to the east. Both craton and plateau are moving west, mind you, but the crust of the continent here is extending, expanding, the plateau is moving faster, like a raft pulling ahead in a slow drift race.

"Over time the intensity of the extensional forces has varied," OJ says. "There's been no major volcanic activity here for the last million years. There's quiescence now. It's comfortable right now."

And there's a hint of a smile, but only a hint. Geologists work in a different time frame than other people do, so a million years may not be long, but he's right about the comfort. The fajitas are very good. The tortillas are soft and fresh, the salsa fragrant, the beer is cold, and the rocks will wait for us to finish up.

OJ is slim, athletic, grizzled, and his sense of humor is considerable but dry. He's a field man by trade, an outdoorsman, a pragmatist.

He's a geologist with the New Mexico Bureau of Mines and Mineral Resources in Socorro; it's one of the largest state bureaus of mines in the country. Right now he's in charge of remapping the entire geology of the state, putting onto one large multicolored sheet all the field research done by anyone before and after the last geologic map of New Mexico was done. Since I barged into his office eight months ago, on a whim, in a tizzy, a steady correspondence has led to this: to a Mexican dinner in the rift and a two-day journey, starting tomorrow at dawn, northwest into the Zuni Mountains and through the country where he has mapped the rocks, himself, for years.

We are starting in the rift: extended terrain. I picture it something like this: like a shelf of books between bookends. Pull the bookends apart — extend them — and the books will tilt, "faults" opening between volumes. Some volumes will flop nearly flat on their sides; these are low-angle faults. Some will stand nearly straight up: these are high-angle faults. Where the bindings have slid past each other, the spines coming out of plumb, you have strike-slip faults. If you look at your extended shelf from the side you will see the bedrock of basin and range in cross section: peak and valley, range and basin (you have to imagine those book-corner peaks weathering down and filling the V-shaped hollows nearly flush), and you realize you've seen this before, in fact you've seen it everywhere, in all these deserts (except on the Colorado Plateau; though it wraps the plateau on three sides).

In any case the plateau isn't considered desert at all by some folks — they call it semiarid brushland or grassland — though other folks agree it's a true subset of the Great Basin desert to the northwest. (Just to confuse the issue the names are almost the same, but the things they name are not. Great Basin desert is a biological unit. Basin and range physiographic province, the extended terrain, is a geological unit. Most of it does happen to be desert, though.)

This basin and range physiographic province runs from southern Idaho and Oregon through most of Nevada, through southern California, central Arizona, south through West Texas, and up here into central New Mexico, clear on past the Great Sand Dunes National Monument in Colorado, where this journey began.

"The eastern margin of the rift is the eastern margin of basin and range," OJ says. "The rift is part of it. It's an asymmetrical graben.

It lies like a ribbon, the down-warping greater on one side than the other. It's the grand expression of basin and range."

The bookshelf isn't lying on a solid surface anyway, but on something with the flexibility of a waterbed, a hot waterbed: seething rock, fluid magma. Where the books bob up past each other, these are thrust faults. The convection cells down there, the slow swirls of heated rock, push the basement rocks sideways as well as up and down, now this way, now that way. This is plate tectonics.

Before the terrain began to extend itself there was something else, the opposite: compression. From seventy to forty million years ago, compressive forces had the upper hand here, and that was the time of the Laramide Orogeny — orogeny meaning mountain-building time. It was during the Laramide that the Rockies rose into being.

"The Colorado Plateau? It has a thicker underlying crust. It's a microplate, in the parlance of the tectonics people. It's only four, five hundred miles across."

We order coffee. OJ goes on, softly:

"The plateau resisted that compressive deformation during the Laramide Orogeny. It also resisted the tensional forces which came with extended terrain, later on. There are a few little drape folds over thrust faults in the basement, drape folds in the overlying sediments. Those monoclines are the hallmark of the Colorado Plateau. But for the most part it has behaved as a coherent mass. Resisted breakup. There's less volcanism. Basin and range is shot through with volcanism."

Tomorrow we'll be climbing the west edge of the rift toward the plateau, onto the plateau, across the rim of the microplate, through a region of chaos. Mountains have been created there; massive fields of volcanoes. And mountains have moved. They have moved up and sideways and have since worn, partly, down, so that you can read the pages. Those mountains are The History of New Mexico going back hundreds of millions of years. This is where we're going.

The next morning just past sunrise Magdalena Peak is to our left, we've come up the rift, past the fields of little cinder cones and past the road to Water Canyon. The mountains are nearly pure volcanics, made of rhyolite and ash-flow tuff.

"Ash-flow tuffs are nasty rocks. No soil formation," OJ says.

Round the corner of the range is Magdalena, a dusty shabby near-ghost town now. Though people do live here most businesses have left.

"Magdalena here was a bustling community at the turn of the century. Great mining country. Ranch country. This old brick hotel? Used to be full, all the time. The boardinghouse, too. Railroad workers, cowboys in the wintertime, miners. Cowboys in the winter . . . they were bored, troublemakers, found moonshine, raised hell. Wasn't a fun life. Isn't it funny how ranching has been romanticized?"

To the south and west lies the immense Mogollon-Datil volcanic field that formed, or began to form, at the end of the Laramide Orogeny, forty million years ago, and went on forming for another fifteen million years or so, on and off, through the beginning of basin and range faulting; they mark the transition, so to speak. They're a subprovince unto themselves, a volcanic pile.

"There's nothing else exposed down there," he says, meaning no other rocks, the volcanoes have buried the lot. "It's a place of repeated and extensive volcanism. There's nothing else exposed."

The mountains here are the outliers of that Mogollon-Datil field, fringing the plateau. Tres Montosos is to the right: three peaks made of ash-flow tuffs.

"Ash-flow tuffs are nasty rocks," he says again. "When they came, they hugged the ground. They were a high-velocity base surge, shot out as a dense superheated fast-moving cloud. The expanding gasses and the sheer volume of material shot them out horizontally. We're talking extremely high temperatures and extremely violent events. It's not something you'd want to witness. Everything in their path was volatilized. These things go on for thirty, forty miles."

We come to the Plains of San Augustin, ringed by volcanic mountains, a huge, treeless, utterly flat space where the National Radio Astronomy Observatory has its Very Large Array, the largest radio telescope in the world. The VLA consists of twenty-seven antennas, each one eighty-two feet in diameter and weighing two hundred and ten tons, according to the sign. Spread on their railroad tracks in this vastness, they look like mushrooms.

"During the last pluvial there was a shallow glacial lake in here,"

OJ says. "Tall ponderosa pine and spruce surrounding a glistening mountain lake, crystal clear water . . ."

The heat is already burdensome, so is the dust. The lake was just a moment ago, ten thousand years, no more. We cross fingers of old dune sand, shorelines grown over by rabbitbrush.

"And all it would take is four, five inches of rainfall, and pretty soon the groundwater would intersect the surface, and that's all you need to form a lake. Then they'd have to put each of those VLA units on a canoe."

We're at Pie Town; a town that, like other towns out here, hardly exists. We turn north on a dirt road.

"This is what rural New Mexico is all about. Gravel roads. Pinyon and juniper. Abandoned homesteads. A few ranches, skunks, buzzards, coyotes."

We're on the Spears Formation now; water-laid volcanics worn and washed off the Datils to our east, laid down in a ragged tongue of debris as the volcanic mountains rose.

"These volcanic sediments cover the transition onto the Colorado Plateau. We're getting on it. We're on the feather edge of Spears. We'll be coming up on Cretaceous sediments. Older sediments. Seventy to ninety million years old."

We're going back in time. The rift, the volcanoes, the volcanoes wearing down, and now back to what they rifted and spewed onto and wore down over: the level-laid sediments of plateau. We're high here. Pie Town lies at nearly eight thousand feet.

"The entire sequence is upper Cretaceous, younger than one hundred million years. They're all associated with the presence of a shallow interior seaway."

Geologists call it the Western Interior Seaway. This was the coast then, traversed by rivers and swampy backwaters, sometimes flooded by the sea, then exposed again. The evidence is this: on the far side of the Zuni Mountains the Dakota Sandstone alternates — is interbedded — with Mancos Shale, a rich organic shale laid down in shallow seafloor.

"The seacoast came and went for twenty million years. It oscillated for two hundred and fifty miles. In the marine rocks we find marine organisms, ammonites and bivalves, molluscs. In the nonmarine and marginal rocks we find coal-bearing sequences, dune sandstones, tidal channel sandstones."

It's a picture I can visualize, something I can see. Shallow seafloor, wavelets of lagoon, swamps, estuaries: coast. Now over the wide sky of these North Plains a line of squalls approaches, dark flat clouds against the blue, a seam of convection cells. There is a dusty smell of rain.

The country is subdued, less harsh and angular. We're crossing a ridge: a small volcanic dike with shallow sills, outlier of eruption, the dike being molten basalt injected up into a slim fault, the sill being molten basalt injected sideways between seaway layers. There's the abandoned village of Hickman; collapsed and collapsing log cabins. There are a few Brangas cattle, a sprinkling of rain hard as pebbles, a smell of dust.

"Since seventy-five million years ago, the sea was in regression to the present ocean basins. The North American continent has not been inundated by ocean since."

After the Western Interior Seaway left, the Rockies rose.

To the west is a rough line of darkness: the North Plains lava flows and the low black peaks of the Zuni Bandera volcanic field. The cones are less than three million years old, some active as recently as a thousand years ago. They are the newest thing around. They lie in a southwest-northeast-trending line that ends, to the northeast, in volcanic Mount Taylor. The line of these volcanoes parallels a kind of "bone" embedded in the earth's crust. It's an ancient bone, and runs straight through the softer body of the plateau. It's part of what some people call the Jemez Lineament. It's made of basalt that is very dark and dense and rich in magnesium. It's five hundred million years old, or older.

Along the lineament, strike-slip faulting made a fracture zone, a deep crack.

"It was ultimately utilized as a magma conduit," OJ says.

In other words, it let volcanoes come on up.

It's past noon, nearly one P.M. There's a dark swarm ahead on the horizon. It's the edge of the malpais, the bad country, and it is that: a recent basalt flow from the Zuni Bandera field, two or three hundred thousand years old, forty miles across from east to west, one slim lobe flowing into Arizona. The newest malpais near here is the McCartys flow near Grants, just to the north, and that's less than a thousand years old. I remember the malpais of Carrizozo, months ago. The stuff is rugged, spiky, full of holes and edges, an annealed froth. Picture a torn loaf of bread forty miles across and made of iron.

"You'd shred a pair of Nikes in one day out there. Leather-soled stuff would be torn to shreds out there," he says.

No road crosses the malpais. Here, at The Narrows, the malpais has crowded close to the base of a cliff of pale sandstone: Cebolleta Mesa, a jut of pale rock visible for miles and miles, its walls made of pinky-cream sandstones typical of the plateau. The top of the mesa is brown Dakota Sandstone, the oldest of the Cretaceous layers, laid down when the Western Interior Seaway was first advancing. It's made of sands washed down by rivers onto sinking coastal plain. Below the Dakota lies something else. Older. A high streaky bulk, spectacular stripes of salmon and cream, the foundation and main body of the mesa, made of a rock sixty million years older than the sea: this is Zuni Sandstone. Jurassic rock.

When the Zuni Sandstone was deposited here, it was an immense field of dunes. You can see this. The Zuni is made of tiny interbedded layers; winds sifting sand over dune crests a hundred and sixty million years ago.

All across the Southwest the Jurassic is famous for its thick deposits of dune sandstone. This was drier, hotter, real indubitable desert, nothing growing anywhere. This was more equatorial then; the continent has since drifted northward. These were huge seas of dunes, their sands oxidized — rusted — by a dry continental climate.

The salmon-colored Navajo Sandstone of Zion, of Monument Valley, the Echo Cliffs, and so on, cropping up all across Navajo country? That's one of the greatest deposits of dune sand in the world. Jurassic dunes. And the peach-colored de Chelly Sandstone of the canyon of that name, immense cliffs pocked with Anasazi ruins? The cross-bedding made by Jurassic winds is so visible there it hurts. Sixty million years before the Western Interior Seaway came, this was like the core of North Africa, one sand sea after the next, and the seas of sand were pink and cream and red.

The sixty million years? They're gone. Worn away. Pages torn out. Here, Dakota Sandstone sits on top of Zuni Sandstone. This is known as an unconformity.

"Sixty million years is a big-time unconformity. All the upper Jurassic and lower Cretaceous is missing here."

To map the rocks you carry a Brunton compass to give direction and location, and an inclinometer to measure the dip angle of deposits. However they were laid down, formations rarely lie perfectly flat. You go from one bedrock outcrop to another. You put the contacts, where one formation ends and another begins, on a topographic map.

"You cover six, eight miles a day on foot. Doing little traverses. You can cover a lot of ground in six weeks."

What comes to light is structure. There are fold axes: an anticline, where a formation has domed up. A syncline, where the rocks have sagged. You find the crests and troughs. Where the formations have draped over a fault like blankets over the edge of a bed, that's a monocline, and then you look for the rollover, the steepest limb. You map faults: high- or low-angle, thrust, reverse thrust, strike-slip. You look for the blocks that fault patterns might encompass. You look for the evidence that the faults are basement involved, or not — basement being old deep crust of the continent itself. Did formations become detached and crumpled on top of basement rocks, scrunched like blankets on an unmade bed?

You have a ten-to-twelve-power hand lens so you can see the grain of the formation and measure it against the grain-size chart: fine, medium, coarse; angular or rounded. Angular sand grains are water-laid, more rounded ones have been bounced by wind. You have an acid bottle to test for chemistry, looking for the carbonate fizz.

Thick sediments with no volcanic rocks; those have fossil fuel potential. The volcanics — and native rock reheated and metamorphosed by volcanic heat — may have rare minerals associated with them; base or precious metals. Sulfide-bearing rocks often have metals complexed with the sulfides: zinc, lead, copper.

You need a pocketknife and a topo map.

"A topo map is a geologist's best friend," OJ says. "What you really need is your topo sheet, a four-wheel-drive vehicle, and a promise of a cold beer at the end of the day."

We come to Grants, Uranium Capital of the World — malpais keeping us company all the way. Then after less than ten westward highway miles we go south again on rural Route 53, along the far side of the malpais.

"No road crosses the malpais. And this, this road here, this is the ancient way. Coronado followed it from Zuni to Acoma in 1540."

We climb Bandera Crater to the continental divide — 7,882 feet here, the sign says — then turn up on forest roads to parallel the divide. To climb the Zuni Mountains. The roads are rough. These are rugged tracks and back ways. This is OJ's country. He names the outcrops without looking up from the track. A forest rises: pinyon, juniper, ponderosa. We pass abandoned cabins; so many I lose count.

An ancient complex of rocks underlies the works, here and just about everywhere else on the continent, and on all continents, and this is aptly known as basement. It was formed in the Precambrian era, more than five hundred and seventy million years ago. So many things have been built — layered, blown, washed over, spewed out — on top of it since, that this basement is easy to forget. It's a storehouse of fragments from a planet that, if you were to go there, you would never recognize. It had no life on it larger than microscopic single cells. The atmosphere would asphyxiate you with the first breath. There was no ozone shield in place, oxygen being scanty, so the earth was clawed by the naked ultraviolet rays of the sun. You wouldn't last there for a nanosecond. Mountains grew and were worn down, all the same. The basement complex is made of ancient rock that has since been reheated to taffy consistency and has stretched, compressed, warped, recrystallized, remelted, and rewarped. It is also made of granite domes, molten magma that surged up, stopped, crystallizing slowly in place, deep down. This is basement.

As the Zuni Mountains rose, the layers on top of their rising tilting basement wore away. Here the Dakota Sandstone is long gone. The Zuni dune Sandstone is gone. We're on the Chinle Formation, back

Mule Deer and Pinyons

Mule deer have black tail tips and oversized ears. At dawn and dusk they wander out to feed in little groups of fawns and does, and if you move quietly they will let you get close. They are most common in dry open forests of pinyon pines and junipers; canyons, foothills, the scattered woodlands of desert mountains are their habitats, with the bighorns on the scarps above and the pronghorns on the flats below, though of course there is some overlap. The pinyons themselves are low and rugged and their cones drop meaty nuts the size of beans, food for wildlife as well as for people. When you look out between the scattered trees of this dry forest, you can often see the desert below, the color of dust.

in a vast river system more than two hundred million years ago. There are mudstone floodplain deposits, sandy layers of grit, pebbles in what were stream channels. This was laid down by a huge west-by-northwest-trending river that drained all of what was West Texas, most of New Mexico, much of Arizona and southwestern Utah, emptying into the sea at what was then the West Coast: northwestern Nevada. The river ran here for ten to fifteen million years. The Chinle Formation that the river left here is soft, gray, greenish, flaky and granular, easily eroded. It is (before erosion) twelve to fifteen hundred feet thick.

We're still climbing, not steadily, up and down now through forest, and the Chinle vanishes, returns, vanishes, then it's gone. After it goes, the early Triassic is absent; more pages torn out (or maybe never written at all here), and we're in the Permian. The rock is suddenly pale pinkish gray, dense, and the surface has the peculiar "melted" look of karst terrain, full of holes. This is San Andres Limestone. This is shallow sea bottom. This was laid down, here, in deep quiet seawater when the Capitan Reef began abuilding in West Texas. There are about one hundred and eighty feet of it here, or were, before erosion. There are fossils in the San Andres. Fossil species are something OJ knows, species being clues, both definite and general clues, to time.

Then the limestone is gone, too, and we're further back in the Permian, at the edge of that sea, that Permian sea known to geologists as the Sundance Seaway. We're back before that sea covered all this up. There are thin layers of sandstones, redbeds so called because of their color. First the Glorieta Sandstone, then the Yeso Formation, and below it the Abo Formation. Marginal marine deposits. Old red dunes. We're at the edge of the Sundance Seaway. At the edge in place, and time.

The Sundance ran all the way across Oklahoma and, of course, Texas.

At 6:35 P.M. — I wrote this down — somehow a historical moment, though why should it be? Since I knew last night that this was where we were going; but it's not the same when someone *tells* you how the book ends as getting to the ending having read the pages — or at least the chapter headings and subtitles and having looked at some of the pictures — at least enough to be able to follow the gist of it, the story. Because we're back to the beginning. We're on Precambrian granite. Basement rock. It's the color of deep rust, and is decaying into square-edged gravel in the ponderosa needles. As if nothing were fantastic about it at all. Just granite decaying away calmly up here in the forest.

Right here, the ancient beam of the Jemez Lineament pushed a chunk of basement rock and all the rock on top of it, too, up thousands of feet into the air and, still pushing, swung it partly around like a pole pushing off-center on a massive crate. All the layers on top of this basement chunk — thousands of feet worth — wrinkled like a pile of rugs. Here at the mountaintop these layers have all worn away. They're gone. On the west side of the Zunis, the wrinkle still shows. Delta sands, floodplain muds, seabeds full of fossil shells, coastal sandstones left ripple-marked by ancient tides or cross-bedded by ancient winds, thin coal seams of backwater swamps; more than two thousand feet of sediments — hundreds of millions of years' worth of New Mexico history — stand straight up on end. This is known as the Nutria Monocline.

Of course this history-of-the-earth tale is the kind of story that you can see in other places, though it would never be the same in other places. And I've seen it all right, but in fuddled bits, not right the way through. In the granite gravel on top of the Zuni Mountains I stand around not knowing what to do with myself. Not even thirsty anymore. I'm back on a planet that I don't even recognize, and it's the same one I've lived on all along.

We go a little farther and make camp on San Andres Limestone, on the lip of the mountain where it drops away and becomes the Nutria Monocline. We'll go through the monocline tomorrow. We'll see the rocks all stood on end. We'll go on and visit the ranch of old Max Garcia, whose parents came from Cebolleta Mesa and home-steaded the place when his father was in his early twenties and his mother barely seventeen. When OJ was doing his field work up here, he spent months living in a trailer close to Max, using Max's spring for water. Max's parents cleared all the fields by hand. Max himself built the huge log barn. He's an old man now, alone up here, none of his children want the place. But he hates the trees coming into the pastures — he's down to thirty cattle, from two hundred, but the ranch is still full of peacocks. The peacocks have the same slim patrician somehow *Spanish* grace as Max.

We'll go through the Zuni village at the Upper Nutria River, the neat stone houses made of Gallup Sandstone; forward in time, now; the Gallup is Cretaceous, younger even than the Dakota.

We'll follow the Nutria River through its confluence with the Pescado, to the Zuni. Beyond Zuni Pueblo we'll be on the Chinle again.

"The Cretaceous sediments are way up, over our heads, thousands of feet," OJ will say.

"In the past."

"Yep."

We'll visit an oil rig that's just begun drilling on a miniature monocline, where the sedimentary Yeso may (don't know, yet) make a trap for oil or gas. The oil will be (if it's there) from marine organisms that once lived in the Sundance Seaway. We'll meet the oil men, meaning the money men (it costs fifty thousand dollars to drill a thousand feet), one from New Orleans and the other from Pecos, Texas, both wearing ten-gallon hats and cowpoke boots. We'll meet the mud logger in his trailer, with his Nikon microscope for inspecting the drill cuttings. We'll meet the drillers, they'll be naked from the waist up and will be wearing bandannas around their heads. The monocline was mapped by OJ so he'll have a proprietary interest and will ask a lot of questions, and he'll stand around for a long time grinning in the mud and ruckus.

It will become clear that OJ knows everyone in these parts, not that there are a lot of folks to know. When we stop at the Fence Lake Store (Fence Lake almost doesn't exist, either; whether it never did or doesn't anymore isn't clear, but it does exist just enough), Carl Quintana, who runs the place, will give us flyswatters and plastic mugs with "Fence Lake Store" written on them, and will chat with OJ for a long time while I forage for candy bars. The store has canned goods, watermelons and potatoes, pinto beans, wool plaid hats, Day-Glo work gloves.

When we leave, OJ will say:

"There are four cultures here. Mexicans, Indians, homesteaders, and Mormons. Mormons gravitate to productive farmland. So we've fallen back here to the old-line Hispanic families and good ol' boy rancher types. There's one ninety-some-year-old Anglo lives out here, sits on milk pails, burns wood, hangs out at the Fence Lake Store. Urban folks might have headed for an old folks home but rural folks are too cussed independent!"

We'll be on the Fence Lake Formation, then. Huge volcanic boulders the size of heads, the size of chairs. Round boulders. A huge deposit.

"Younger than the Spears. Laid down five to twenty-five million years ago. Guess by what."

"Water."

"Yep. Shed down off the Mogollon-Datil pile. Must have been way up there, then. High, high mountains. And water! These were *hellaceous* rivers."

And that will be the end, almost.

More gravel roads. Then we'll come to it, surrounded by mesas topped with basalt. In the belly of the volcanics, there it will be. A perfectly round hole in the country. A cinder cone, popped open with a single phenomenal blast twenty-five thousand years ago. No time ago at all. It will be a mile and a quarter across, the floor of it one hundred and seventy-five feet below the surface. Like a kindergarten volcano. In coming up from deep deep down, from below even the basement, it tapped into some saline plumbing. After it burst, the crater — the *maar* as these things are called — filled up with salty water: brine. The brine evaporated. Still does. The cone now holds anywhere from one hundred to seven hundred feet of pure salt, topped by a few feet of slushy brine. It's a sacred place to the Zunis. They own it now. Didn't always. Coronado's report of 1549 states: "The Cibola Indians have very good salt which they bring from a lake a day's distance away," and Oñate reported to Spain, not much later, that the salt was "the best that Christians have discovered," which says it all, or almost all. According to the Zunis, this salt lake is the place of origin of their people. This is where they came from. It is the home of the Salt Mother. It is the center of the world.

Where the salt comes from is a mystery, though. When OJ tells me about the cinder cone and the maar — Zuni Salt Lake, it's called —

up there in the evening at our camp on the mountain rim, I don't quite believe him. I believe the cold can of beer because I have it in my hand. I believe the basement granite, too, because there are pieces of its sharp-edged gravel wearing a hole in the pocket of my jeans.

As for the forces that swung the mountains of Zuni like a jibboom and wrinkled up two thousand feet of sedimentary rocks like so much tissue . . . the less said the better. Only that my conclusions are nothing new and are roughly this: we are tiny, we live a tiny time, our understanding of nature may span the breadth of a juniper needle; and for power all our megatonnage amounts to no more than the capacity to tweak the nose hairs of a minor deity, a godlet living out its days in some retirement pantheon in the salubrious climate of a celestial desert, perhaps.

I blink at the notion, presently so much on thoughtful people's minds, that we can, through our life-style, change climate. Perhaps we can, perhaps we have and we will, but it won't be much in the general scheme of things. We think too much of ourselves. If dried lakes and deserted cities aren't enough to convince us that climates change anyway; if ancient reefs heaved into the cores of continents aren't enough to tell us that they always have; then nothing would ever be enough to humble us into perspective.

These are campfire thoughts, mind you. A quilting bee of fragments falling into place. Because there's more, too. Because if the plentiful strewings of shit and bones left by grand beasts, beasts that we can never see, aren't enough to prove that extinctions are common, that lives are fragile, then we can never take lives seriously enough to save them. Not even our own. If the agonizing bankruptcies and deep harmonic strengths of Native cultures — and of our own rural land-based culture, too, which is our native lifeway and the roots of our survival — aren't enough to prove that citifying "civilizing" culture can be hypocritical at least, blind at best, then the cities will die. What difference will that make to the desert? Not much.

We look too much to our own creations as the source of curse or blessing. In cities, among people, it is too easy to look to ourselves. And to our gods, perhaps. Though if we do carry a godlike spirit in us, then maybe too many of us too much of the time have stopped listening to its balancing wisdom. Our sins against nature are sins against ourselves. This is certain. But other things are certain, too.

The grandeur of spaces stretched and dried to a felt of sand, or sage, or gyp-grama, opens the skull; the chaw of mountains layered to the horizon is beauty to stun dumb.

OJ says:

"Another beer?"

"Thanks."

And then:

"After you live out here for a month at a stretch, like I did back in eighty-one, and then you go back to Albuquerque . . . when you get there, you think: *my God!* People *live* in places like *this!*"

And we laugh, because I understand this, the first lesson the desert teaches anyone. Is: beware the leaving.

DATE	ISSUED TO

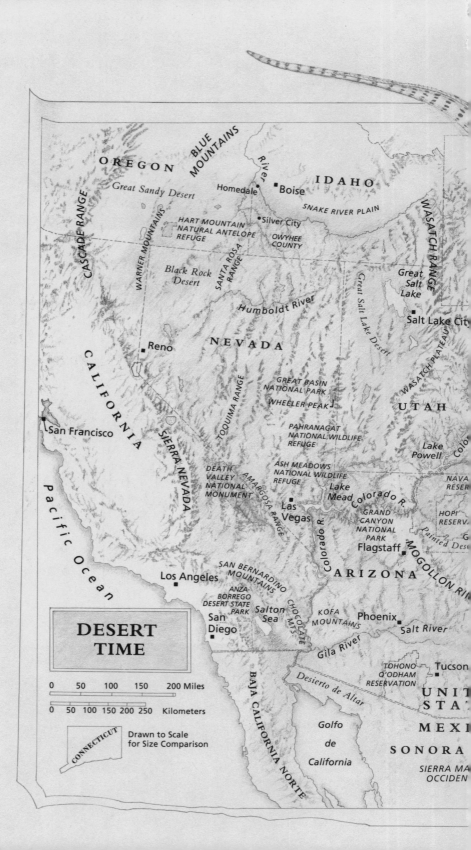

OREGON

BLUE MOUNTAINS

Great Sandy Desert

Homedale   ■ Boise

IDAHO

River

CASCADE RANGE

HART MOUNTAIN NATURAL ANTELOPE REFUGE

■ Silver City

OWYHEE COUNTY

SNAKE RIVER PLAIN

WASATCH RANGE

WARNER MOUNTAINS

Black Rock Desert

SANTA ROSA RANGE

Great Salt Lake Desert

Great Salt Lake

Humboldt River

■ Salt Lake City

CALIFORNIA

■ Reno

N E V A D A

Great Salt Lake Desert

WASATCH PLATEAU

SIERRA NEVADA

TOIQUIMA RANGE

GREAT BASIN NATIONAL PARK

WHEELER PEAK ⌐

U T A H

■ San Francisco

PAHRANAGAT NATIONAL WILDLIFE REFUGE

Lake Powell

Colo

ASH MEADOWS NATIONAL WILDLIFE REFUGE

DEATH VALLEY NATIONAL MONUMENT

AMARGOSA RANGE

Lake Mead

Colorado R.

NAVA RESER

HOPI RESERV

Pacific Ocean

■ Las Vegas

GRAND CANYON NATIONAL PARK

Painted Dese

G

■ Flagstaff

MOGOLLON RIM

SAN BERNARDINO MOUNTAINS

■ Los Angeles

A R I Z O N A

ANZA BORREGO DESERT STATE PARK

Colorado R.

CHOCOLATE MTS.

Salton Sea

KOFA MOUNTAINS

Phoenix ■

DESERT TIME

■ San Diego

Gila River

Salt River

0   50   100   150   200 Miles

0   50 100 150 200 250   Kilometers

TOHONO O'ODHAM RESERVATION

Tucson ■

BAJA CALIFORNIA NORTE

Desierto de Altar

UNIT STAT

CONNECTICUT

Drawn to Scale for Size Comparison

Golfo de California

MEXI

SONORA

SIERRA MA OCCIDEN